Palgrave Studies in the History of the Media

Series Editors
Bill Bell
Cardiff University
Cardiff, UK

Chandrika Kaul
University of St Andrews
Fife, UK

Alexander S. Wilkinson
University College Dublin
Dublin, Ireland

Palgrave Studies in the History of the Media publishes original, high quality research into the cultures of communication from the middle ages to the present day. The series explores the variety of subjects and disciplinary approaches that characterize this vibrant field of enquiry. The series will help shape current interpretations not only of the media, in all its forms, but also of the powerful relationship between the media and politics, society, and the economy.

Advisory Board
Professor Carlos Barrera (University of Navarra, Spain)
Professor Peter Burke (Emmanuel College, Cambridge)
Professor Nicholas Cull (Center on Public Diplomacy, University of Southern California)
Professor Bridget Griffen-Foley (Macquarie University, Australia)
Professor Tom O'Malley (Centre for Media History, University of Wales, Aberystwyth)
Professor Chester Pach (Ohio University)

More information about this series at
http://www.palgrave.com/gp/series/14578

Catherine Dewhirst • Richard Scully
Editors

The Transnational Voices of Australia's Migrant and Minority Press

palgrave
macmillan

Editors
Catherine Dewhirst
University of Southern Queensland
Toowoomba, QLD, Australia

Richard Scully
University of New England
Armidale, NSW, Australia

ISSN 2634-6575   ISSN 2634-6583   (electronic)
Palgrave Studies in the History of the Media
ISBN 978-3-030-43638-4   ISBN 978-3-030-43639-1   (eBook)
https://doi.org/10.1007/978-3-030-43639-1

This Palgrave Macmillan imprint is published by the registered company Springer Nature Switzerland AG.
The registered company address is: Gewerbestrasse 11, 6330 Cham, Switzerland

PREFACE

This book is the result of an interdisciplinary conference held at the University of Southern Queensland, Toowoomba, in 2017: "Voices of the Australian Migrant and Minority Press: Intercultural, Transnational and Diasporic Contexts". The conference marked the fiftieth anniversary of the publication of Miriam Gilson and Jerzy Zubrzycki's 1967 seminal study, *The Foreign-Language Press in Australia, 1848–1964*. Their work has inspired scholars and students alike to engage with migrant and minority newspapers as a central source for examining questions about community-building, inter-communal relations, transnational connections, and the national ideal. Gilson and Zubrzycki not only charted extant migrant and other minority community newspapers from the late 1840s to the early 1960s for the first time, but also established an understanding of the breadth and scope that this field holds for deepening our knowledge about Australia's multicultural, social, and political heritage, in ways that are relevant to today's world. Indeed, the existence of the printed presses which they identified, as well as the subsequent discovery and emergence of missing newspapers and other types of periodicals, suggest the understated yet great significance that Australia's minority groups have had in asserting a presence, and making contributions, against the backdrop of supposed Anglo-Celtic colonial, national, and cultural homogeneity.

Since Gilson and Zubrzycki's work, the study of the Australian migrant and minority press has developed more fully as a means of exploring Australia's history and global relations. Such research has nevertheless tended to be encompassed within studies of minority communities or is isolated across diverse disciplinary publications. The aim of this book (and a companion volume) is to present a concerted picture of the dynamism of minority community newspapers and other news periodicals from a historical perspective. We bring together the latest scholarship focused on how such print enterprises have contributed to shaping communities of the past and informing the present. While the purpose and services of such presses would have been clear enough for contemporary readers, they emerged from globally constructed communities and complex relationships with colony, empire, and/or nation. What do the business initiatives of these presses—initiated by individuals largely on the periphery of mainstream society—tell us about the influence of imperial and transnational connections, inter-cultural relations, and the national narrative? Using the lens of 'voices' as our analytical frame, the chapters in this collection explore the experiences and stories of Australia's minority groups, largely obscured from histories to date.

Whether long in duration, short-lived, or now missing from the archive, the complexity of the migrant and minority community press punctuates the landscape of Australia's nation-building processes, in ways that have been at once unsettling for the dominant British-Australian population as evocative of the nature of Australia's diversity. For a British colony and later Federated nation, it is important to note that the local experiences and narratives of smaller communities—many of non-English-speaking backgrounds—have always been forged and negotiated within the context of globalising forces. In many respects, minority groups belonged to at least three layers of community: the homeland, whether village, region, or nation; the new society; and the local community. Such communities, largely from non-British origins—and including those of Aboriginal and Torres Strait Islander Australians—were frequently disparaged within and ostracised from the mainstream. A fear of the influence of anything foreign (*viz.* Edward Said's *Orientalism*) meant that ethnic, cultural, and racial discrimination was never far from the surface, and indeed was often openly countenanced.

The authors in this edited collection, some of whom participated in the conference, bring multi-disciplinary approaches and linguistic skills to their areas of the specialised field of print culture—newspapers, journals, magazines, official bulletins—to engage with questions about diversity and the wider ramifications of these histories. Exploring the enterprises and concerns, sometimes crises, and reflections on the world around them through this evidence and other sources, offers insights into the convergence between local, national, and global experiences.

This book would not have been possible without the support of our respective universities, the School of Humanities and Communication at the University of Southern Queensland, and the former School of Humanities at the University of New England (now within the Faculty of Humanities, Arts, Social Sciences, and Education). We would like to thank the Ian Potter Foundation for a grant funding the conference, and the University of Southern Queensland's Office of Research for further funding. We also wish to thank the National Archives of Australia for the use of several images; conference co-convenors Dr Jayne Persian and Dr Mark Emmerson; and John Zubryzcki for sharing his and his family's memories of his father's vision, research, and achievements over Australia's multicultural era at the conference opening.

Toowoomba, QLD, Australia   Catherine Dewhirst
Armidale, NSW, Australia   Richard Scully
January 2020

CONTENTS

NOTES ON CONTRIBUTORS

Karen Agutter is an immigration historian at the University of Adelaide, with a specific interest in migrant identity and the relationship between new arrivals and receiving populations, 1890–2010. Karen has published widely on many aspects of Australia immigration and is researching the migrants who served in the Australian Imperial Force during the First World War.

Simone Battiston is Senior Lecturer in Italian Studies and History at Swinburne University of Technology, Australia. His research interests include Italian migration history, transnational politics, and labour and artisan history. He is a member of the Australian Historical Association (AHA) and of the Australian Society for the Study of Labour History (ASSLH).

Hilary Berthon has, over her library career, maintained a strong interest in nurturing collaborative approaches to the digitisation and preservation of library materials. At the National Library of Australia, she has fostered the National Library's emerging digitisation contributor programme and works in Trove Collaborative Services.

Mary Besemeres is an Honorary Lecturer in the School of Literature, Languages and Linguistics at The Australian National University. She is the author of *Translating One's Self: Language and Selfhood in Cross-Cultural Autobiography* (2002), articles on translingual memoir and travel writing, and co-editor with Anna Wierzbicka of *Translating Lives: Living* *with Two Languages and Cultures* (2007). She was founding co-editor of the Routledge journal *Life Writing.*

Catherine Dewhirst is Senior Lecturer in History at the University of Southern Queensland. Her research focuses on the transnational connections of Italian migrant families and communities between the 1870s and 1945. She has published on the Italian migrant press in the *Journal of Imperial and Commonwealth History, Studi Emigrazione, Journal of Australian Studies,* and C. T. Callisen's edited *From Bruni to Windschuttle* (2014). A recent joint article on Second World War internment memories appears in *Australian Journal of Politics and History.*

Michael Jacklin is an Honorary Fellow at the University of Wollongong. His research focuses on multilingual Australian literatures, with recent chapters in *Mapping South-South Connections: Australia and Latin America* (2019); *Migrant Nation: Australian Culture, Society and Identity* (2018); and *Bearing Across: Translating Literary Narratives of Migration* (2016); as well as refereed articles in *Antipodes, Australian Literary Studies, Journal of the Association for the Study of Australian Literature, Kunapipi,* and *Southerly.*

Clare Johansson is an academic at Swinburne University of Technology, Melbourne. Her research is focused on cross-cultural collaborations, particularly between Aboriginal and non-Aboriginal organisations in Australia and the ethnic press in Australia. Having studied a double degree in Business and Arts in her undergraduate years, she received first-class honours for her research on Italian ethnic print media in Australia.

Max Kaiser recently completed his PhD at the University of Melbourne, Australia. His writings on memory, fascism, migration, and borders have appeared in Overland magazine. He is one of the hosts of the New Books in Jewish Studies podcast, a channel of the New Books Network. His latest research has appeared in the *Journal of Modern Jewish Studies.* He is writing a book on Jewish antifascism and settler colonialism

Katarzyna Kwapisz Williams is Deputy Director and Jean Monnet Research Fellow at the Centre for European Studies, The Australian National University. Her research focuses on life writing and memory narratives, the issues of migration, displacement, and mediation of memory. She is the author of articles and book chapters on transcultural and migration experience, and a book on changes in literary production and reception (*Deforming Shakespeare: Investigations in Textuality and Digital Media*, 2009). Recently, she has worked on a series of publications on European memories in Australia.

Marianna Piantavigna is a graduate of the State University of Milan and a PhD candidate at the University of Western Australia. She is researching Australian Italian-language newspapers, focusing on the correlations between the context of their agency, their function as mediators, and their role in defining the Italian communities through an (ideological) representation of cultural, imagined communities.

Richard Scully is Associate Professor in Modern History at the University of New England. He is the author of *Eminent Victorian Cartoonists* (2018) and *British Images of Germany: Admiration, Antagonism & Ambivalence, 1860–1914* (2012); and the co-editor of *Comic Empires: Imperialism in Cartoons, Caricature, and Satirical Art* (2020) and *Drawing the Line: Using Cartoons as Historical Evidence* (2009).

Kevin Windle is Emeritus Professor at The Australian National University. His publications include *Undesirable: Captain Zuzenko and the Workers of Australia and the World* (2012), *The Oxford Handbook of Translation Studies* (editor, with Kirsten Malmkjær, 2011), *A New Rival State? Australia in Tsarist Diplomatic Communications* (editor, with Alexander Massov and Marina Pollard, 2018), and numerous articles on the history of the Russian community in Australia. His translations from various languages have received international awards, including the Fédération Internationale des Traducteurs (FIT) Aurora Borealis Prize for the translation of non-fiction.

LIST OF ABBREVIATIONS

AJO	*The Australian Jewish Outlook*
ANPlan	Australian Newspapers Plan
APIs	Application Programming Interfaces
CAFHOV	The Chinese Australian Family Historians of Victoria
DP	Displaced Persons
GRW	"Group of Russian Workers"
IRO	International Refugee Organisation
JCCFAS	Jewish Council to Combat Fascism and Anti-Semitism
JP	Justice of the Peace
LOTE	Languages Other Than English
NAA	National Archives of Australia
OCR	Optical Character Recognition
PRL	People's Republic of Poland
SCCFAS	Sydney Council to Combat Fascism and Anti-Semitism
UNRRA	United Nations Relief and Rehabilitation Administration
URE	Union of Russian Emigrants
URW	Union of Russian Workers
WPA	War Precautions Act

LIST OF FIGURES

Australia's Minority Community Printed Press History in Global Context: An Introduction

Catherine Dewhirst and Richard Scully

The processes of colonisation and the global networks they established engendered unprecedented change in the way people conceived of themselves, the societies and countries to which they belonged, and the wider world. The printed press was one of the many commodities transported through exploration/invasion and settlement in Australia and elsewhere. Beyond material culture, however, it also facilitated an ongoing sense of connection under circumstances of separation, which must have felt surreal to those who had never travelled beyond their village, town, or city before. The newspaper (which itself emerged in the seventeenth century

C. Dewhirst (✉)
University of Southern Queensland, Toowoomba, QLD, Australia
e-mail: catherine.dewhirst@usq.edu.au

R. Scully
University of New England, Armidale, NSW, Australia
e-mail: rscully@une.edu.au

© The Author(s) 2020
C. Dewhirst, R. Scully (eds.), *The Transnational Voices of Australia's Migrant and Minority Press*, Palgrave Studies in the History of the Media,
https://doi.org/10.1007/978-3-030-43639-1_1

in Britain and Europe from earlier forms of pamphlets, corantos, diurnalls, and newsbooks) was created initially "not within a small local compass but as an instrument for describing events across immense geographical areas".[1] This convergence between a local initiative and a broader, if not global, orientation can be illustrated by a story from the familiar history of the humble beginnings of print culture in Australia.

The first antipodean newspaper went to print on 5 March 1803 in the colony of New South Wales, produced by the government printer, George Howe (1765–1821). On the front of this modest four-page weekly, Howe advised his readers that *The Sydney Gazette, And New South Wales Advertiser* would provide:

> a source of solid information which will, we hope, be universally felt and acknowledged... [and that] Information is our only Purpose [...] our duty, in an exertion to merit the Approbation of the PUBLIC, and to secure a liberal Patronage to the SYDNEY GAZETTE.[2]

Howe was well-versed in his craft. A creole of Irish heritage from Saint Kitts in the West Indies, where he had completed an apprenticeship as a printer under the government printer—his father—and claimed a classical education, Howe found himself in difficulty for having "discussed the politics of George III so unfavourably" as to make emigrating to England the only option in order "to escape being embroiled in the American Independence question".[3] However, as a participant in the transoceanic migrations, his life became even more complicated after settling in Britain.

In London, Howe began work at *The Times* and other print houses, married, and had an infant boy, only to be charged for shoplifting in 1799 while in the Midlands. Yet he managed to escape the death penalty pronounced at the Warwick Assizes when his sentence was commuted to transportation to the colony of New South Wales in 1800. Once in Sydney Town, financial troubles followed in the wake of his taking on the job as government printer. In addition to the colony's fluctuating supply and variable quality of paper, his readers tended not to pay their subscriptions (something that worsened his cash-flow, especially after his convict salary stopped in 1806, when he was granted emancipation). He frequently addressed his readers about both issues in the newspaper.

The Sydney Gazette, however, reflects more than mere "information". In fact, Howe also explained to his readers that it would include a section on morality and religion, as the first issue reveals:

An English Paper informs us that a practice equally disgraceful and immoral had been prevented in the Town of Manchester since the ratification of the Treaty of Paris: Wives had been quickly exhibited for sale; good ones, being scarce, brought a great price – but the market being overstocked with those of a contrary description, they sold for little or nothing. Much to the credit of the Magistrates, they supressed the growing evil, and restored the Fair Sex to their ORIGINAL value.[4]

In this example of a popular cultural tradition, used to instruct the reading public on behaviour that was unacceptable, Howe was also articulating his vision of *The Sydney Gazette*'s role. He positioned the newspaper as a guardian over the civic and moral standards of this new society in the making, including respectful gender relations (based on the Bible's teachings). This guardianship suggests three features which the migrant and minority press would, in time, share: the importance of drawing from the homeland's political, social, cultural, and sometimes religious news for instructional purposes; the space created by such news for engaging in conversation or debate, and securing ongoing business (elsewhere Howe invited readers to contribute their own "Articles of Information"); and the authoritative presence of the editor through the personal "voice".

If the history of the printed press in Australia commences in 1803, then the historiography arguably begins with the late nineteenth century publication of James Bonwick's *Early Struggles of the Australian Press*, in which he chronicles and describes 77 major and minor print periodicals, including one extant copy of *Die Deutsche Post* (1848) and both *Melbourne Punch* (1855–1925) and *Queensland Punch* (1878–1885, 1890–1901).[5] One other study in the late 1930s and two in the 1960s updated the state of this history considerably, in line with twentieth-century developments: W. Macmahon Ball's edited *Radio Press and World Affairs: Australia's Outlook*; W. S. Holden's *Australia Goes to Press*; and Henry Mayer's *The Press in Australia*.[6] But these were definitely histories of the Anglophone mainstream. Although the foreign-language and minority presses date back to colonial times—some of the earliest being *The Aboriginal or Flinders Island Chronicle* (1836–1837), *Deutsche Zeitung fuer Sudaustralischen* (1848–1851), *Yang-Tang Zhaoti* (English-Chinese Advertiser) (1856–1858), *Sydney Punch* (1856, 1857, 1864–1888), *L'Italo-Australiano* (1885), *Le Courrier Australien* (1892–2011), *Australian Worker* (Sydney) (1893), and *Norden* (1896–1940)—there was virtually no scholarly interest until Miriam Gilson and Jerzy Zubrzycki's

The Foreign-language Press in Australia, 1848–1964. Three exceptions can be noted all the same, again in the 1930s and 1960s, with Rudolf Lowenthal's *The Chinese Press in Australia* appearing first and, in light of the American post-war interest in ethnic group studies, a similar focus appeared in works by Derek van Abbé on the German press in South Australia, and Desmond O'Grady on Italian-migrant newspapers.[7]

There is no doubt that Gilson and Zubrzycki's work stands out as a seminal study, which was published at a time when academic and wider political and societal attention was shifting from beliefs in assimilation to a recognition of the value of minority group cultural identity cultural identity and diversity.[8] Against a backdrop of developments in mass media technologies, the mass migrations of post-war refugees (Displaced Persons), the government's Colombo Plan of 1951, the Indigenous Australian land and civil rights movements in the 1960s, and the "boat people" asylum seekers of the 1970s, as well as bi-partisan support for a multicultural policy, acted as powerful contributors to change. Gilson and Zubrzycki's largely sociological approach linked the appearance and disappearance of foreign-language newspapers to migrant settlement patterns, pointing out the more dramatic change after 1945 when the mass circulation press resulted from an unprecedented volume of new settlers.[9] They remark on the "tremendous degree of enterprise and industry" displayed within such newspapers over Australian history and the characteristic "free opinion" that defined the first German-language and other early newspapers of the nineteenth century.[10] Their enquiry engaged with questions, first about whether the maintenance of cultural or ethnic identities was a central concern of these newspapers and, second, whether the aims of these newspapers went beyond providing news to communicating "Australian" societal values and customs. What became apparent was the tendency of the foreign-language press to advise readers on avoiding polemicising national politics and trade unionism, to encourage integration within mainstream society, and to condemn racial discrimination.[11] While acknowledging the great range of diversity of these presses, they also note how post-war editors tended "to exhort, criticize, and give praise", acting "as an agency of social control" over migrant behaviour.[12] What is interesting here, however—as they suggest—is the fact that this was not for the sake of reinforcing ethnic identification, but to direct the core business of the sale of news.

Gilson and Zubrzycki's study largely examined the migrant press but included other print ventures from religious, trade-union, and political groups, and government departments; which are best defined as the "minority" press. In essence, all ethnic journalism is part of a minority category when considered in comparison with the larger daily circulations of colonial and national mainstream broadsheets, as it mostly serves a distinct readership of non-English-speaking origins. Although the migrant press should also be understood as "transnational" because of an interchange of influence and print journalism with the homeland and diasporic communities, there is no separation. Conceptualising migrant newspapers and other periodicals as both migrant initiatives *and* minority enterprises provides a much more realistic appreciation of how their editors, writers, and readers understood them to be, and lifts them from the stereotype of "foreign" or "other" within the frame of Australia's media history. In fact, Australia's migrant and minority community newspapers have always resonated in character with the provincial press, in contrast with the metropolitan mainstream newspapers, most evident from their localised readership. According to Rod Kirkpatrick in his analysis of the Queensland provincial press, such newspapers exhibit "a personality, and the smaller the paper is the more that personality can be shaped by the editor".[13] In a similar vein, Gilson and Zubrzycki remark on another important distinction between foreign-language newspapers and the mainstream popular and tabloid presses:

> A spirit of intimacy exists between the editors and the readers in immigrant newspapers which may be contrasted with the essentially impersonal manner in which a large national or metropolitan newspaper conducts its business.[14]

This is reinforced by Simon Potter in his analysis of the British imperial press system, where he remarks that people across the empire gained news from the world more from reading their local or provincial newspapers, "which often encouraged complex identities [more than did national newspapers] and helped sustain some surprising senses of community".[15]

The challenge in writing histories of the printed press periodicals is not to lose sight of a close reading of the particular—not only of text but also of the unseen influences and layers of connection. Research today locates histories of the printed press within wider studies of empire, media, transnationalism and mobility, and the history of the book.[16] Over the past two decades, scholarship on the global circuits and communication systems of the British Empire has carved out challenging perspectives for understanding the complex interactions that occurred within the imperial-colonial relationship. With a focus on the imperial press system, for instance, Potter re-evaluates historical approaches that interpret the relationship between Britain and the settler societies/Dominions through a lens of "nationalist historical narratives" and agendas. He argues instead that a sense of national and imperial identities co-existed remarkably compatibly, providing colonial private press enterprises with commercial benefits at the same time as imported British printed matter also found a market (often the same readers).[17] An example comes from Peter Putnis's exploration of how Australia's troops were dispatched for Sudan in 1885 on the back of communications through the imperial cable (in addition to Reuters news agency, electricity, and steamships). Ultimately, the decision to send backup for Britain's war had "very little value" militarily, but it demonstrated instrumental and symbolic effect; the telegraph virtually revolutionised Australia's connection to such world events and to Britain, which created "renewed impetus to long-standing ideals of solidarity within the British Empire".[18] Much the same is evident from Richard Scully's study of the worldwide profusion of *Punch*-like satirical magazines, which reinforced a sense of Britishness in (e.g.) Australasia, but enabled more independent thinking in the Indian subcontinent.[19] Chandrika Kaul uses the term, "an imperial village", to describe the globalising effects on India through Britain's telegraphic network and Reuters news agency, where she identifies how the outcome was more unexpected. From the early profusion of the Indian press and the nationalising processes that colonisation had triggered, Kaul argues that the Indian newspapers and communication networks, "far from being unchallenged mediators and conduits of cultural imperialism, became an influential weapon of anticolonial opposition".[20] Such studies highlight how contesting assumptions of the past may emerge from a close interpretation of the sources from within wider fields of empire and media histories.

Three significant Australian works on historical evidence relevant to studies of the minority press make comment on the intricate nature of sources, and the necessity to interpret them in historical context. In her history of J. F. Archibald's *Bulletin* (1880–2008), Sylvia Lawson argues for the importance of a close reading of this magazine in order to avoid slipping into superficial interpretations of its "legend". From a view of Archibald's reality, she states that the *Bulletin* merits more than restrictive analysis in search of literary or political themes in order to grasp its fuller significance:

The Archibald paradox is simply the paradox of being colonial. Metropolis, the centre of language, of the dominant culture and its judgements, lies away in the great Elsewhere; but the task of living, communicating, teaching, acting-out and changing the culture must be carried on not Elsewhere but Here. To know enough of the metropolitan world, colonials must, in limited ways at least, move and think internationally; to resist it strongly enough for the colony to cease to be colonial and become its own place, they must become nationalists. [...] The *Bulletin*'s republicanism and nationalism flowered out of the paradox.[21]

Tony Hughes-D'Areth's history of the *Picturesque Atlas of Australasia* (1886–1888) suggests a similar approach:

What I have tried to do [...] is to get away from this separation of the architecture of 'history' from the imagined bedrock of its 'sources'. [...] the need to examine in detail how a text functions, its complexities, and the instabilities of its regime of signification. It is not sufficient to view a text simply as a document or a shard of evidence that can then be adduced unproblematically to support a historical proposition. The same caveat [...] also applies to images. In other words I have tried to allow the critical process of historical interpretation to flow in both directions: not only to source history, but also to historicise its sources. [...] One shines the light of history on the *Picturesque Atlas of Australasia* only to find that it already possesses its own shifting incandescense.[22]

Richard Scully and Marian Quartly get to the heart of the problem in *Drawing the Line: Using Cartoons as Historical Evidence,* when they explain:

despite the long-felt belief that cartoons are among 'the great sources' for students of the past, the history of their use in historical writing has been a chequered one. The meaning of a cartoon image, like a photograph, often seems to be immediately accessible to the reader, and herein lies the cause of much misuse of cartoons. In its mildest form the cartoon is introduced as a kind of decoration, to break up the text and give an impression of historicity, rather than adding to the historian's argument. Perhaps the most pernicious usage is the casual deployment of a single cartoon as supporting evidence, without any reading of the artistic and cultural conventions shaping its content. Modern historians have learnt to read written documents as complex texts whose meaning is rarely self-evident, but cartoons and other visual sources still escape critical analysis.[23]

The same kind of casual and unproblematic deployment is evident in countless analyses that mention the migrant and minority press, also. But minority community newspapers and other forms of print material are not unproblematic. They cannot be reduced to what appears on their pages. In fact, they require a greater familiarity with the culture of the group, and often language skills for understanding the nuances of communication. Implicit here is the importance of alternate sources for reconstructing the dynamics of the communities of the printed press of the past and for informing our present day of their relevance. Indeed, it has been said that "the history of newspapers has to be written from archives".[24] Archival records, specialised studies, oral histories, and memories, each offer a means for making theses presses more widely accessible.

This volume aims to combat casual and unproblematic histories by interrogating particular newspapers, journals, and magazines, in-depth. The contributions of the authors thereby approach a number of case studies through the lens of "voices" in the sense of postcolonial meanings of recovering what is hidden, overlooked, or obscured from view in conventional society. The authors' discussions are arranged in chronological order and speak to two overarching themes of "*defiant* voices" and "*narrating* voices". Although we gave no brief to the contributors in this book to align their research with a particular theme, when reading whose "voices" emerge from the research presented in this book, each chapter appears to converge around the key ideas of "defiance" and/or "narration". The discussions in five chapters reflect the concept of "defiance" quite clearly by amplifying how a particular genre or approach—irreverent, radical, propagandistic, or reactionary—was cleverly constructed through the medium of the press. "Defiant voices" as a theme exemplifies resistance against some form of pressure, which may be defined as cultural, social, or political. A further five chapters appear to marshal around the concept of "narration", demonstrated through a focus on several minority community histories which explore the dimensions of certain micro-histories embedded within their print ventures. "Narrating voices" encompasses discourses of conflicting ideologies, literary writings, life stories, the "voice" through letters and archival records, and the story-telling potential of a digital repository.

The authors we see as contributing to the theme of "defiant voices"—Richard Scully, Kevin Windle, Max Kaiser, Michael Jacklin, and Clare Johansson and Simone Battiston—analyse cases that span the colonial era from 1855 up to the fledgling decades of multiculturalism (see Fig. 1.1).

Fig. 1.1 "Immigration—Migrants in the community—Seventy ethnic newspapers printed in Australia, 1974", National Archives of Australia. NAA: A12111, 1/1974/13/4. Courtesy of the National Archives of Australia

Their chapters identify a strong degree of attachment to the homeland and to class, ideology, or ethnic group, some emerging from significant upheavals. They present analysis on five distinct migrant communities: the community-building enterprise of humorous satire, pioneered in Australia by the Anglo-Celtic British migrants of *Punch* and its varieties in Melbourne and Sydney, and more regionally characterised versions in Tasmania, Ballarat, Adelaide, Queensland, and Ipswich; the battle for free expression against the Australian government's censorship and surveillance, taken up by key personalities of seven early radical Russian newspapers; the inter-ethnic conflict in the cultural and political debate about the State of Israel amongst three Jewish magazines; the effects of a Latin American press tradition, the *crónicas*, for negotiating the identities of Spanish-language

Australians within *El Expreso* during the early multicultural years; and the reactionary negationism adopted by *Il Globo* for defending Italian communities from the mainstream press' racially-motivated sensationalism over organised crime and the 'Ndrangheta stereotype. These six authors of these chapters engage with provocative and politicised episodes of Australia's migrant history, covered in the minority community newspapers and magazines, whose editors or writers articulated strong views about mainstream Australian society.

The authors whose chapters we feel reflect "narrating voices"—Marianna Piantavigna, Catherine Dewhirst, Katarzyna Kwapisz Williams and Mary Besemeres, Karen Agutter, and Hilary Berthon—cover the late colonial era from 1885 up to the major technological initiatives of our current day. Analysed in detail are: the ideological discourses shaping an embryonic "Italian" community within the first and short-lived Italian-language newspaper; the economic and ideological pressures impacting on, and compromising, the integrity of an interwar Italian newspaper and its editors through their negotiation of the influence of Fascism; the abundance of literary works printed in the Polish-language press, articulating the existence of a strong cultural identity through a variety of literary genres, including that of satirical *felieton* style; the original letters of Displaced Persons sent into a government bulletin, expressing raw first-hand experiences of loss and resettlement; and the discovery of a myriad of intercultural stories from digitised newspapers and their potential for exploring little-known episodes of Australia's multicultural communities of the past and present (see Fig. 1.2). Each of the ten chapters within this edited collection shares a cross-over between the two themes of migrant stories and resistant approaches. However, the questions explored by these six authors bring a sense of the editors' or writers' narration into focus through the process of producing the printed press and/or navigating change within Australia's mainstream society.

The book thus begins in the colonial era of the mid-nineteenth century with Richard Scully's focus on the neglected history of the appearance of *Punch* magazine in Melbourne from the perspective of its emigrant nature (Chap. 2). He shows that Melbourne *Punch* must be understood within the context of the continuity of its British ancestor's satirical tradition. An argument can be made, Scully states, for understanding the ensuing flourishing of Australian *Punches* as "essential nodes" intersecting across a community at once emigrant as imperial. By 1885 another emigrant community had begun to emerge, which Marianna Piantavigna explores

Fig. 1.2 "Industry—La Fiamma, Italian newspaper published in Australia, 1975", National Archives of Australia: NAA: A6180, 24/10/75/72. Courtesy of the National Archives of Australia

through the first Italian-language newspaper, *L'Italo-Australiano* (The Italian Australian), from a transnational perspective of "cross-border inter-relations and connections" (Chap. 3). She focuses on the complex ideological discourse driven by the newspaper's editor, Francesco Sceusa, which created a narrative for Italian migrants around belonging. This narrative, Piantavigna demonstrates, hinged on *italianità* (a sense of "Italianness") but also reflected the contradictions inherent in the imagined and the real, the myths of Italy's national greatness and the realities of living in a colonial society, as well as the effects of association and exclusion within such a society.

In the early part of the twentieth century, Russian migrants began arriving in Brisbane, a small cohort of whom, Kevin Windle reveals, quickly became marked as "felons" but who were largely instrumental in infusing the fledgling Russian-language press with their radical political convictions (Chap. 4). He traces the activities of six of these men across the pages (and in the archives) of seven Russian migrant newspapers between 1912 and 1919, a period that witnessed unprecedented upheavals in Russia. In the context of Australia's early nationalism, Windle discusses how the increasing militancy of these newspapers and their editors caught the attention of the Australian censors, which reflects on important questions about free speech and censorship at this time in history. Similar concerns emerged during the interwar period for the Italian migrant press, which experienced severe political and public scrutiny although largely from the Australian government and local Fascist authorities, which Catherine Dewhirst explores in the history of *L'Italiano* (The Italian) (Chap. 5). She examines the life stories and voices of this newspaper's two consecutive editors as they navigated both the local and transnational economic and ideological pressures afoot. Dewhirst argues that the context of nation-building (Australian and Italian), ethnicity, and race contributed to the construction of Italian migrants as "disloyal" to which many appeared blind because of their need for respectability.

The era before the Second World War also saw the appearance of two other communities dedicated to the printed press and continuing into the post-war era. Max Kaiser focuses on the intensity of debate instigated from the foundation of the state of Israel, by analysing the cultural and political approaches of three Jewish magazines, *Unity*, *The Zionist*, and *Australian Jewish Outlook* (Chap. 6). Framing his analysis around the concept of "ethnicisation", he argues that the international situation complicated the already contested nature of a "Jewish community", evident in such magazines, which can only be read by encompassing the transnational context. The respective anti-fascist, anti-assimilationist, and assimilationist debates of the 1940s, Kaiser shows, shifted over the 1950s to a "consolidation of just one hegemonic political orientation" of Australia's Jewish community. Taking a longitudinal approach is Katarzyna Kwapisz Williams and Mary Besemeres's chapter on the "cultural and literary" character of Polish-language newspapers with a particular focus on *Wiadomości Polskie* (Polish News) (Chap. 7). Unlike other kinds of migrant newspapers, they show that the Polish-language press took up a specific role in this migrant community for a "dislocated diasporic intelligentsia" by facilitating their "literary ambitions" and producing an abundance of "intellectual and literary content". While the press tended to attract a small percentage of readership, Kwapisz Williams and Besemeres argue that Polish writers looked to their printed community newspapers as an outlet for expressing Polish culture and identity, establishing a unique literary tradition in support of the émigré culture.

While the immediate post-war era resulted in great hope for Jewish, Polish, and other European refugees and migrants, research into other migrant cases reflects isolation, trauma, anger, and the inherent fractures in community building at this time. Karen Agutter turns the focus to a neglected area of research relating to Australia's acceptance of more than 170,000 Displaced Persons (DPs) from war-torn Europe, in her analysis of the Department of Immigration's *The New Australian* newspaper (Chap. 8). This monthly bulletin was set up to assist with the process of assimilation, but as Agutter shows from her analysis of a selection of DP "voices" in their original letter form—sent into the "Write to us" column—it reveals a much wider range of concerns than the government clearly anticipated. Far from being homogenous, she also highlights how careful analysis of these letters not only reveals the heavyweight of trauma DPs had experienced, but also an overall picture of how they negotiated their new circumstances within Australia. Moving ahead to the shifts inaugurated by multiculturalism from 1973 under the Whitlam government, two further chapters use newspaper evidence to explore the continuities of fractured relations between minority communities and mainstream society. The first is Michael Jacklin's chapter which illustrates interpretations from the Spanish-language press, analysing the Latin American literary tradition of the *crónica* in *El Expreso* in 1979 (Chap. 9). He describes this genre as producing largely "fragile, ephemeral texts whose narratives, humour and critique were produced for the consumption of the day" and whose writers (the *cronistas*) often reflected wittily on the incongruities of life in Australia. With a particular focus on Chilean Luis Abarca—affectionately known as "Blady Woggie"—Jacklin makes a case for recognising the *crónicas* as part of Australia's literary and cultural history.

Another approach the migrant press took in Australia's early multicultural years was to "talk back" to derogatory depictions of the ethnic community within the mainstream press, which Clare Johansson and Simone Battiston engage with in their analysis of *Il Globo* (Chap. 10). They pay particular attention to the editorship of Antonino ("Nino") Randazzo between 1979 and 1989 in order to explore the racial stereotyping of Italian migrants from sensationalist reports about 'Ndrangheta cells, violence, and murder. As they argue, Nino adopted a counter-narrative of "negationism" in *Il Globo*'s drive to dismantle the logic behind claims that the ethnic community harboured organised crime, which reflected a wider societal reaction against multiculturalism. Our book ends with Hilary Berthon's discussion of Trove, the National Library of Australia's newspaper digitisation programme, to highlight the significant dimensions now available for the public to engage with the migrant and minority press (Chap. 11). Through the concept of the "historical curb", Berthon argues that Trove enables the "surfacing of 'hidden' intercultural stories" and facilitates "conversations around their documentary content". Noting statistics on the immense diversity of the migrant press in Trove's digital holdings, she offers a brief insight into the depth and scope of its text-searchable capacity to suggest the potential for conversations and collaborative projects.

In 1961 Sir Richard Boyer (member of the Australian government's Immigration Advisory Council and Chairman of the Australian Broadcasting Commission) spoke in defence of the decision to include representation of the foreign-language press on the Immigration Advisory Council, as a means for demolishing "the last vestige of suspicion" around ethnic groups across wider Australian society:

> the foreign-language press can take on a new significance. In our view it is not only a bridge between the country of origin of many of our migrants and this country, but it is also the means whereby the multilingual culture, which we have never had before, might be encouraged in this country.[25]

Australia's cultural landscape has transformed significantly from the colonial era to the present day, as analysis of the printed press of migrant and minority communities can reveal. Yet "suspicion" continues to divide Australia on the outdated mode of inclusion/exclusion, based on ethnic, racial, religious, cultural, and sexual differences, which fuel a legacy of fear reaching back into the history of colonisation instead of encouraging conversations. In our drawing together a number of themes from analysis of the foreign-language and minority community presses, the authors in this volume offer a variety of approaches germane to the historical analysis necessary for exploring such tensions and for revealing a number of commonalities around global, transnational, and/or inter-communal influences. By interrogating "communities" from the lens of the postcolonial "voice" through their print enterprises or contributions to them, this book may be read as an invitation for further enquiry into the cultural heritage implicit in the diversity of Australia's multiple and multi-layered communities.

NOTES

1. Anthony Smith, *The Newspaper: An International History* (London: Thames and Hudson, 1979), 13. See also Joad Raymond, *The Invention of the Newspaper: English Newsbooks, 1641–49* (Oxford: Clarendon Press, 1996), 7–9.
2. *The Sydney Gazette, And New South Wales Advertiser*, March 5, 1803, p. 1.
3. "Pioneer Australian Journalist", *Advertiser*, May 23, 1932, p. 12. Other sources drawn from are: R. B. Walker, *Newspaper Press of New South Wales, 1803–1920* (Sydney: Sydney University Press, 1976), 1–5; J. V. Byrnes, "Howe, George (1769–1821)", *Australian Dictionary of Biography*, National Centre of Biography, Australian National University, http://adb. anu.edu.au/biography/howe-george-1600/text2851, published first in hardcopy 1966 [Accessed January 7, 2020]; W. A. Thomas Fullerton, "Trials of George Howe- Pioneer of Australian Printing", *Western Argus*, November 8, 1932, p. 9; "George Howe: Australia's First Newspaper", *Sydney Morning Herald*, April 11, 1935, p. 10.
4. *The Sydney Gazette, And New South Wales Advertiser*, March 5, 1803, p. 4.
5. James Bonwick, *Early Struggles of the Australian Press* (London: Gotch & Gordon, 1890), 70, 77, 79.
6. W. Macmahon Ball ed., *Radio Press and World Affairs: Australia's Outlook* (Melbourne: Melbourne University Press, 1938); W. S. Holden *Australia Goes to Press* (Detroit; Wayne State University, 1961); and Henry Mayer, *The Press in Australia* (Melbourne: Lansdowne Press, 1964). For the most comprehensive publication guide, see: John Russel, Rod Kirkpatrick and Victor Isaac, *Australian Newspaper History: A Bibliography* (2nd edn, Andergrove, Qld: Australian Newspaper History Group, 2009).
7. Rudolf Lowenthal, *The Chinese Press in Australia* (Peking: [s.n.], 1937); Derek van Abbé, "The Interests of the South Australian German Language Press in the Nineteenth Century", *Journal of the Historical Society of Australia and New Zealand*, 8.31 (November, 1958): 319–321; Desmond O'Grady, "The Italian Press in Australia—Italy's Three Faces", *Observer*, May 28, 1960, pp. 10–11.

8. Compare, for instance, the different approaches by W. D. Borrie and Charles A. Price: W. D. Borrie, *Italians and Germans in Australia: A Study of Assimilation* (Melbourne, F. W. Cheshire, 1954); Charles A. Price, *Southern Europeans in Australia* (Melbourne, Oxford University Press, 1963).

9. Gilson and Zubrzycki, *The Foreign-Language Press,* 21–22, 24, 41.

10. Gilson and Zubrzycki, *The Foreign-Language Press,* 23.

11. Gilson and Zubrzycki, *The Foreign-Language Press,* 45, 112.

12. Gilson and Zubrzycki, *The Foreign-Language Press,* 128, 164. For an update of the migrant press, see: Abe (I.) Wade Ata and Colin Ryan, ed., *The Ethnic Press in Australia* (Melbourne: Academia Press and Footprint Publications, 1989).

13. Rod Kirkpatrick, *Sworn to No Master: A History of the Provincial Press in Queensland to 1930* (Toowoomba: Darling Downs Institute Press, 1984), 273.

14. Miriam Gilson and Jerzy Zubrzycki, *The Foreign-Language Press in Australia* (Canberra: Australian National University Press, 1967), 157.

15. Simon J. Potter, *News and the British World: The Emergence of an Imperial Press System, 1876–1922* (Oxford: Oxford University Press, 2003), 215.

16. Christiane Harzig and Dirk Hoeder, "Transnationalism and the Age of Mass Migration, 1882–1920", in *Transnational Identities and Practices in Canada*, ed. Vic Satewich and Lloyd Wond (Vancouver & Toronto, UBC Press, 2006), 51; Tony Ballantyne, "Mobility, empire, colonization", *History Australia*, 11.2 (2014): 26–27; Antoinette Burton and Isabel Hofmeyr, "Introduction: The Spine of Empire? Books and the Making of an Imperial Common", in *Creating an Imperial Commons: Ten Books That Shaped the British Empire*, ed. Antoinette Burton and Isabel Hofmeyr (Durham, NC: Duke University Press, 2014), 1–28; Martin Lyons and John J. Arnold, ed., *A History of the Book in Australia 1891–1945: A National Culture in a Colonised Market* (St Lucia, Qld: The University of Queensland Press, 2001).

17. Potter, *News and the British World,* 13, 212, 216.

18. Peter Putnis, "Telegraphy, Mass Media, and Mobilization: Australians in Sudan, 1885", in Peter Putnis, Chandrika Kaul, and Jürgen Wilke, ed., *International Communication and Global News Networks: Historical Perspectives* (New York: Hampton Press, 2011), 122, 137.

19. Richard Scully, "A Comic Empire: The Global Expansion of *Punch* as a Model Publication, 1841–1936", *International Journal of Comic Art* 15, no. 2 (2013), 6–35.

20. Chandrika Kaul, "An imperial village: communications, media, and globalization in India", in *International Communication and Global News*

Networks: Historical Perspectives, ed. Peter Putnis, Chandrika Kaul, and Jürgen Wilke (New York: Hampton Press, 2011), 93.

21. Sylvia Lawson, *The Archibald Paradox: A Strange Case of Authorship* (Melbourne: Allen Lane, 1983), ix, x.

22. Tony Hughes-D'Areth, *Paper Nation: The Story of the Picturesque Atlas of Australasia, 1886–1888* (Melbourne: Melbourne University Press, 2001), 5.

23. Richard Scully and Marian Quartly, ed., *Drawing the Line: Using Cartoons as Historical Evidence* (Melbourne: Monash University ePress, 2009), 01.1. The forthcoming 27th volume of the Equipe interdisciplinaire de recherche sur l'image satirique's journal, *Ridiculosa*, focusing on migration cartoons, further highlights the need for closer scrutiny of sources within their historical context.

24. Joad Raymond, "Introduction: Newspapers, Forgeries, and Histories", in *News, Newspapers, and Society in Early Modern Britain*, ed. Joad Raymond (London & Portland, OR: Franck Cass, 2002), 8.

25. Sir Richard Boyer, cited in Gilson and Zubrzycki, *The Foreign-language Press*, 168–169.

CHAPTER 2

The Satirical Press of Colonial Australia: A Migrant and Minority Enterprise

Richard Scully

In 1855, at the height of the Gold Rush, the Colony of Victoria welcomed a very special arrival indeed. Apparently, *The Times* reported that "Melbourne Punch, Esq., son of the celebrated Mr. Punch of Fleet-street", had been cheered upon his departure from Gravesend by the Prince Consort, the Prime Minister and the Home Secretary, the Colonial Secretary, and a host of other notables; and it was rumoured that he had been offered the governorship of the colony in succession to Sir Charles Hotham.[1] By the time his ship—*Marco Polo*—arrived off the Port Philip Heads, the telegraph was able to flash the news of his impending arrival in time for the elite of the colony to assemble at the docks at Sandridge; *The Argus* reporting that "the illustrious stranger" was greeted not only by Governor and Lady Hotham but also by all the "principal Members of the Executive and Legislative Council" (including William Nicholson, the leading statesman and effective Leader of the Opposition).[2] Stepping through a triumphal arch, festooned with flags and emblems, to the sound

R. Scully (✉)
University of New England, Armidale, NSW, Australia
e-mail: rscully@une.edu.au

© The Author(s) 2020
C. Dewhirst, R. Scully (eds.), *The Transnational Voices of Australia's Migrant and Minority Press*, Palgrave Studies in the History of the Media,
https://doi.org/10.1007/978-3-030-43639-1_2

of a band playing "See the Conquering Hero Comes", Mr Punch was saluted by the recently formed Victoria Volunteer Rifles (under the command of the former Mayor of Melbourne, "Major" John Hodgson). A special train of the Melbourne and Hobson's Bay Railway Company was on hand to take him the short distance to "the metropolis of the Southern hemisphere", where he issued no fewer than three prefatory addresses to his fellow colonists (and then promptly fell asleep, exhausted).[3]

These momentous events, of course, never took place. The reports from *The Times* and the *Argus* were spoofs, which mimicked the actual articles that would announce the arrival of "noteworthy emigrants".[4] "Mr. Punch, Junior" was a fictitious character, the embodiment of the staff of the new magazine *Melbourne Punch*, who kept the same company as his "Father" in London: allegorical figures such as the British Lion, the goddess Britannia, and caricatured versions of kings, queens, emperors, and statesmen (hence all the references to the great and the good attending his departure and arrival). What is striking, though, about the supposed account of Punch's arrival in colonial Melbourne is the cultural detail of the migrant experience, however deliberately overblown in its presentation. The fond farewells from "home"; the sense of the energetic potential of the younger son in the new land; the transplanted music and customs of the metropole out in the colony—all these are the imagined fantasies of countless male, middle-class migrants in the period when the British Empire continued its great, Victorian-era development.

While scholars have explored the pages of *Melbourne Punch* for a variety of reasons (for instance, seeking-out colonial attitudes to Europe, to Britain itself, and the growing Australian sense of self), the essentially migrant nature of the magazine has been less of an emphasis than historically seems appropriate.[5] The bulk of scholarly interest in *Melbourne Punch*—and the other *Punches* of Australia—belongs to the period of the late 1960s through the early 1980s, when Marguerite Mahood, Vane Lindesay, Jonathan King, and Suzane Fabian sought the origins of an Australian affinity for cartooning and caricature, or the evolution of a supposedly unique national sense of humour and character.[6] Only very recently have scholars like Mary L. Shannon exposed the importance of the Melbourne and Sydney *Punches* as nodes in a world-spanning colonial periodical marketplace, with links to Fleet Street (and thus confirming the pedigree of Punch Junior).[7] For her, it was essential to recall how "the emigrant's body carried the print culture of the imperial metropolis with it".[8] Going further, Shu-Chuan Yan has noted how Punch Junior's imagined experience is a reflection of "broader patterns of emigration"; emphasises the migrant nature of its "editors, writers, artists, and engravers"; and also makes explicit the essential nature of *Melbourne Punch*'s intended "white immigrant audience, the self-paid passengers who sought their fortune in the Antipodes".[9] A periodical such as *Melbourne Punch* was an essential part of the toolkit of the emigrant to Australia, argues Yan, citing Margaret Beetham: "Each article, each periodical number, was and is part of a complex process in which writers, editors, publishers and readers engaged in trying to... make their world meaningful".[10] As Shannon has alluded: "the strangeness of Melbourne" (or Sydney, or Adelaide, or Hobart), and the "hardships to be faced by the unwary middle-class emigrant", might be soothed by reference to the humour of the local *Punch*, and a sense of shared community built through regular recourse to its pages.[11]

Building on Shannon and Yan's foci, this chapter seeks to highlight the emigrant nature of the satirical press of colonial Australia. Migrant papers, the provincial *Punch*es and colonial *Charivari*s of Australia, were staffed by migrants, directed at a migrant readership, and filled their pages with migration-themed jokes, cartoons, and pieces of doggerel. In keeping with the theme of this book (and the conference which inspired it), such magazines can also be said to be a "minority" press, in the sense that— although they catered to the Anglo-Celtic British immigrants who made up the vast majority of the population—there were far fewer of them in terms of number of titles and circulation, than the serious newspapers that dominated the print cultures of the Australian colonies. In amongst the "close to 200 literary or partly-literary periodicals" produced in nineteenth-century Melbourne, there were only around three satirical magazines at any one time, and there was only ever one *Punch*.[12] The magazine's offices were themselves "surrounded on Collins Street" by those of the major daily newspapers: the *Argus*, the *Age*, and the *Herald*; and the weeklies the *Australasian* and the *Leader* (published by the *Argus* and *Age*, respectively).[13] Although circulation is difficult to gauge, Mahood put *Melbourne Punch* at merely 2000 in the 1850s, and "thousands" more by the mid-1880s.[14] By contrast, although the *Age* was initially selling around the same number of copies (2000 in 1859), this rose dramatically by the end of the 1860s (15,000) and further by the 1880s (38,000 in 1879, and 81,000 in 1889); the *Argus* was selling 12,000–13,000 copies daily by 1855 (dropping to 9000 in the 1860s before rising to 20,000 in the 1880s); and the *Herald* was selling 30,000 by 1880.[15] These catered for a population that skyrocketed from just 23,000 in about 1851 to 126,000 a decade later, and kept growing at a remarkable rate (281,000 in 1880, to 500,000 by 1890), before a period of stagnation in the depression years of the 1890s.[16]

This minority status is only underscored when one considers how rarely scholars have looked at the non-Melbourne *Punches*, and how difficult it has been for scholars to take these comics and their contents *seriously*.[17] Even the scholars most invested in studying the papers have not always paid close enough attention to the details of their rise and fall. Although Suzane Fabian dated Punch Junior's "perilous sea voyage" to 1856, as noted above, he had in fact been in the colony for at least a year prior.[18] The *Melbourne Punch* went undated until 7 February 1856 but—working backwards—we know that its first number appeared in time for 2 August 1855. Although this was a Thursday, it is important to remember that it would have taken almost a week to develop the issue—from an original editorial meeting or two, through to the drafting of the content, the engraving of the wood printing blocks, the actual printing, and then the distribution. Melbournians would therefore have been able to lay hands on a copy of their own *Punch* from sometime late in July, as indeed was advertised by the proprietors in the *Argus* earlier that same month.[19]

IMPERIAL AND INTER-COLONIAL CONNECTEDNESS

Melbourne Punch was, therefore, not fresh off the boat. And if we imagine that Punch Junior was in part meant to epitomise the character and experience of his editors, then it had been at least two-and-a-half years since they had alighted from their voyage out to the colonies. Two of *Melbourne Punch's* earliest contributors, R. H. Horne and William Howitt, had arrived in the ship *Kent* in September of 1852, something that was reported in both the Melbourne and the Sydney press.[20] It is easy to see in these kinds of articles, the basis for the "spoof report" of Punch Junior's arrival detailed at the beginning of this chapter, as Horne and Howitt did their best to give a sense of verisimilitude to the emigration of Punch Junior. Looking to make his arrival more recent than their own, however, they placed him on a different ship from their own: the celebrated *Marco Polo*. A "prince of clippers", the real *Marco Polo* was something of a wonder of the age, and her "dashing commanders" were feted by Melbourne society.[21] By the time *Melbourne Punch* appeared, the clipper had made the passage from Liverpool (not Gravesend) to Hobson's Bay and back five times, bringing immense wealth in gold to Britain's coffers from the gold-fields of Victoria.[22] She also carried that most precious of commodities: the mail, including newspapers and journals of all sorts, from which hungry eyes could discern the latest happenings in London and farther afield (including news of the Crimean War).[23]

It is tempting to imagine that amongst those papers and journals was at least one copy of *Punch; or, the London Charivari*. Despite having founded a local version, for Melbournians, the original was a constant means of reconnecting with home, even if it did arrive three months or so late.[24] *Punch* could be referenced for everything from bird life to house prices (a perennial concern for Melbournians), and the ludicrous, *Punch*-like over-pricing of land was something *Melbourne Punch* co-editor Howitt made particular note of in his first major Antipodean memoir.[25] Access to the original was a mark of being an informed gentleman and a true Briton, as in E. W. Hornung's *Stingaree* short stories; and it was not unknown for the cartoonists of the colonial versions to trace and then modify the original cartoons of Tenniel or Linley Sambourne in order to generate "the kind of intertextual knowledge beloved of the educated middle class".[26]

What more perfect way was there of binding the migrant to the home-land, at the same time as grounding him in the new land? *Punch*es helped to establish and maintain the "complex webs of contact and communication that bound the British Empire... together".[27] As the late Joan Kerr noted in 1999:

> Circulating in every part of the English-speaking world, *Punch* reassured colonists that the common thread of empire was not only blood but also the peculiar British sense of humour. Every town with any pretence to culture had to have its own version.[28]

This is also reflected in the sources themselves: in a mock letter to the *Sydney Punch* in 1864, the pseudonymous "Brown Jones Robinson" (writing from the comfort of a London-style New South Wales Club) went so far as to call a *Punch* "a world-known accepted social blessing and necessity".[29]

As well as a desire for connection with the Mother Country and its culture, it was in part a sense of inter-colonial rivalry—within this community of shared culture and interest—that led to the profusion of *Punch*es and *Punch*-like papers across Australia. While Melbourne was the most vibrant, fastest-growing, and economically significant city of the 1850s, its *Melbourne Punch* (1855-1925) was very soon aped by a *Sydney Punch* (1856, 1857, 1864–1888) and—not more than sixty miles to the north-west of Melbourne, also a *Ballarat Punch* (1857, 1867–1870). The 1860s saw a further set of magazines founded, with *Tasmanian Punch* (1866 & 1869–1870, 1877–1879) and *Hobart Town Punch* (1867–1868, 1878) catering for a colony then entering a period of economic crisis and in need of a dose of sardonic humour. *Adelaide Punch* (1868, 1878–1884) appeared to the west and, ten years later, there was also a counterpart in the *Queensland Punch* (1878–1885 and 1890–1901; it merged to form *Queensland Figaro and Punch*, 1885–1890 and 1901–1936). There was also—briefly—an *Ipswich Punch* (1871–1872) farther down the Brisbane/Bremer rivers, which was a pretty crude affair: "mostly hand-written, mechanically copied text with accompanying autotype cartoons".[30] To these can be added all those other *Punch*-like papers, which took different names, or aped the domestic rivals of the *London Charivari*—London's *Fun* (1861–1901) and *Tomahawk* (1867–1870) had their imitators in *Fun; or, the Tasmanian Charivari* (1867), and a Victorian-based *Tomahawk* (1880).[31] *Humbug* and *Touchstone* (both 1869–1870) acted briefly as foils to *Melbourne Punch*; as did the short-lived *Sam Slick in Victoria* (1879) and *Boomerang* (1877) even more briefly alongside Sydney's *Punch*.[32]

While it is easy to dismiss this phenomenon of "short-lived magazines all copying one another", the effusion of satirical magazines in the mid-to-late nineteenth century points to a situation of great vibrancy and creativity.[33] And while the London original may have provided the template, and was the gold standard to which all the provincial *Punch*es and colonial *Charivari*s aspired, as Marguerite Mahood noted very astutely, it was really the *Melbourne Punch* that was the "prototype" for the Australian versions.[34]

Indeed, the establishment of Sydney *Punch* on a firm footing from 1864 was an example of that other form of migration that characterised the Australian colonies: inter-colonial migration. It was Edgar Ray—co-founder with Frederick Sinnett of the *Melbourne Punch*—who created the new magazine. Ray had moved north from Victoria sometime in the early 1860s. The imagined arrival of Sydney's *Punch* was rather less grand than that of his Melbourne cousin, and far more deliberately tongue-in-cheek. Arriving on "the shores of this Southern Italy" ("without the ruins, and poverty, and brigands in steeple-crowned hats"), the main theme is the blazing weather and its impact on someone having experienced "prolonged sea-sickness".[35] In contrast to his counterpart to the south, the Sydney Punch found himself "quite alone, and addressed some feeling and suitable remarks to himself", before heading to a local pub for a drink (also alone)—something far more realistic than the pomp and ceremony that attended Punch Junior at Sandridge in 1855. True, he is presented to the Governor (at this time, Sir John Young), but that is the extent of the festivity. Again in contrast to his southern rival, rather than launch into a manifesto of grand journalistic intent, the Mr Punch of New South Wales waxes lyrical about "The Coves of Sydney", and observes the parading of the local volunteer force.[36]

What made Sydney *Punch*'s arrival all the more relevant to the migrant experience was that he had appeared—and failed—before. In fact, there had been two attempts to make a go of a *Punch* in Sydney before Ray's successful iteration.[37] The brief existence of a prior *Sydney Punch* was actually noted, and dismissed, in "Brown Jones Robinson's" mock letter-to-the-editor in the first edition of the new version. The writer claimed how that earlier Punch had been "a melancholy caricature" of the real thing, and his family (wife Judy and dog Toby) had undergone a "rake's progress" of sorts, down the social and geographical ladder of Sydney (first in George Street, then in Sussex, then Wooloomooloo, and then "perhaps Queensland").[38] The "miserable prototype" lived a debased life, subsisting on "colonial ale" and showing signs of "bronchitis", and exhibiting a quite un-British sense of humour (based on "lawless violence and matrimonial infelicity"). The arrival of the new Punch was a breath of fresh air, as Sydney was now home to a scion of the "real stock" of the "British Punch family".

STAFFING MIGRANT MAGAZINES

Edgar Ray was not the only inter-colonial migrant who helped sustain the culture of *Punch* in Australia. Within a year or two of the foundation of the Sydney magazine, the London-born cartoonist Eugene Montagu "Monty" Scott moved from *Melbourne Punch* to *Sydney Punch* (where he stayed for twenty years), while one of *Sydney Punch*'s key cartoonists—the Jerseyman Oswald Rose Campbell—went the other way in 1864.[39] Interestingly, financial stresses played a role in this exchange of talent: Scott was chasing a reliable source of income (not entirely successfully—he declared bankruptcy in 1870); Campbell had applied for a certificate of insolvency in April 1862.[40] Mary Shannon has identified a number of other key instances of inter-colonial (and inter-*Punch*) migration: Alfred Clint going from Melbourne, to Adelaide, to Sydney in the course of the 1860s; Garnet Walsh moving from *Sydney Punch* to Melbourne in the 1870s; and Henry Kendall moving from Sydney to join the *Melbourne Punch* circle.[41] The physical production of some *Punches* was also characterised by emigration in a sense: the engraver's signature on the title page of *Sydney Punch* (significantly, just called *Punch*) is that of the Prussian-born Frederick Grosse, the same engraver who worked on the Melbourne magazine.[42] It would appear that either the printed pages, or possibly even the engraved wood-blocks that were used to print the Sydney magazine, migrated north from Grosse's base in Melbourne.[43]

Whether from the neighbouring colonies or from the Old Country, there was a near-constant infusion of new blood to maintain the vibrancy of these satirical magazines: when Frederick Sinnett moved-on as editor of *Melbourne Punch* in 1857, he was replaced by the Kentish-born James Smith, and then he in turn by the Londoner William Jardine Smith.[44] While Archibald Rose Campbell was still in harness as *Melbourne Punch*'s chief cartoonist, he was joined in 1866 by Francis Thomas Dean Carrington (called "Tom"), who had been a student at the South Kensington School of Art, and had come out from London to prospect for gold earlier in the decade.[45] Carrington's twenty-year tenure as chief cartoonist (and one-time owner of the *Melbourne Punch*, together with James and Alexander McKinley) gave *Melbourne Punch* an artist of stature, almost approaching the skill and respectability of John Tenniel at the London *Punch*. Carrington deliberately cultivated his style to match that of Tenniel, and even adopted a "TC" monogram that resembled the famous "JT" of the master cartoonist.[46]

It is important to note also that, although in the main the staff and readership of the Australian *Punches* was British (whether British-born or first-generation "independent Australian Britons"), important non-British migrants were also critical to the development of the satirical press. One of the more interesting (but little-known) was Edward Castildine Martin, the publisher of two of *Melbourne Punch*'s only rivals (*Sam Slick in Victoria* and *Tomahawk*), who came out from Canada.[47] He employed a number of migrants, including the Englishman George Rossi Ashton, who drew the cover illustration and several cartoons for *Sam Slick*.[48] At *Melbourne Punch* itself, Frederick Sinnett came from Hamburg (where his London-born father had been working).[49] His paper's first great cartoonist—Nicholas Chevalier—was born in St Petersburg to a Swiss notable.[50] He was quite peripatetic, exploring the colony of Victoria, visiting New Zealand and Tasmania, and eventually sailing to London in HMS *Galatea* (in the company of Prince Alfred, Duke of Edinburgh).[51] Also from a Swiss background (and also involved, inter-colonially, with more than one *Punch*) was Grosse's successor as engraver on the Melbourne magazine, Rudolph Jenny.[52] Jenny did engraving work not only for *Melbourne Punch*, but also for the earliest pages of William Roberts and William Fawcett's *Adelaide Punch* (1868), as well as the cover design and several of Carrington's cartoons for the *Tasmanian Punch*.[53] Other *Punch*ites came from farther afield, the most notable being perhaps Carrington's successor on the *Melbourne Punch*: Luther Bradley. Bradley had come from New Haven, Connecticut (albeit via Chicago and London), and worked on the magazine from the late 1880s until his return to the United States in 1893.[54] Anti-socialist but suspicious of capitalism, and with more than a little independence of mind, he changed the way Australia's relationship with Britain was imagined in the pages of *Melbourne Punch*. His British lions were not the noble beasts depicted by his predecessors, but predators hungry to prey on the colonies; and his feminised colonial goddesses were more grown-up and equal in stature to their mother, Britannia.[55]

Addressing Emigrant Concerns

Along with the emigrant experience came an appreciation of politics on a global scale, and it is not surprising to see so much in the way of reference to overseas events in the pages of the provincial *Punch*es. Concern with the affairs of Europe can be seen in playful imaginings of Napoleon III, Emperor of the French, in *Sydney Punch* during the course of the Franco-Prussian War; and *Tasmanian Punch*'s loyal, congratulatory cartoon upon Benjamin Disraeli's successful negotiations at the Congress of Berlin (1878); through to "Queensland Patsy and Bridget" waving to the distant Charles Parnell in Ireland on the front page of the *Queensland Punch and Figaro*.[56] That British premiers like Lord Palmerston, Lord John Russell, and William Ewart Gladstone would appear in the same pages as their colonial counterparts speaks to the migrant's continued engagement with the affairs of home, even as local politics became more and more of a preoccupation.[57] The genuine article of the British parliament was itself often used as a means of criticising the petty squabbles of the colonial assemblies.

As illustrated by the disembarkation scenes of Melbourne and Sydney Punch (see above), there was plenty of commentary on the foibles of new arrivals by cartoonists and comic commentators who were themselves not long off the boat. Back in London, it was this aspect of the *Melbourne Punch* that Sidney Blanchard (writing for Charles Dickens's *All the Year Round* magazine) found particularly amusing, noting a catalogue of sardonic comments on the way "new chums" were inclined to "give [themselves] airs" and dress inappropriately.[58] Despite such a consciousness, the key underpinning of such commentary and humour was to reinforce the essentially unchanged nature of the Briton aboard, who managed to maintain the same standards and respectability (or even to improve upon) as his metropolitan counterparts. More work needs to be done in this space to identify—for instance—the dialect humour being employed for the various different kinds of British and non-British migrants. Differences in gender-based humour, or the differing motivations of migrants (imagined and real) are also in significant need of a scholarly analysis. Interestingly, the touchstone of *involuntary* emigration—convictism—was a constant point of reference. While the system and its supporters were damned (such as in the case of the 1864 announcement by the Duke of Newcastle that further shiploads of convicts would be sent out to Western Australia), the convicts themselves could be imagined as really "Jolly Good Fellows".[59] The depiction of the convict in Australian cartooning and humour is yet another fertile field just waiting for harvesting, and this is not lost on the scholarly literature, where greater attention to the "social cuts" of the *Punch*es has recently been called-for.[60]

If fun was poked at those who were trying their best to make the best of recent arrival, then a fair amount of ire was directed at those who, having come out to help build the new society, treated it as only a phase before their inevitable return to the homeland. In particular, the apparent lack of concern for his charges by the colonial governor—especially Sir Charles Hotham—was given regular comment. Chevalier's cartoon of 16 August 1855 shows the governor camped at the docks, leaning on his luggage, while "Fireman Punch" rushes to prevent "Victoria House" going up in flames (the smoke illuminating a scene from the still-recent Eureka Rebellion in Ballarat).[61] What does he care, Hotham muses, when he is "only a lodger". The same was true for the other officials who treated the colonies as a stepping-stone to greater things. George Thomas of the *Tasmanian Punch* attacked the outgoing Chief Justice, Sir Valentine Fleming, in 1869, on his retirement with a pension of £1000 a year.[62] Fly-by-nights, such as the Liberal statesman, Sir Charles Wentworth Dilke, also came in for their fair share of criticism. Dilke's otherwise celebrated work, *Greater Britain*, was not well-received by the *Sydney Punch*, who offered a review in the form of a rhyme:

> O worthy Mr. Wentworth Dilke!
> Whoever you may be,
> In the name of all Australia,
> Punch thanks you heartily,
> Because you've given the folks at home
> So truthful an idea,
> Of how we wretched exiles
> Make shift to live out here.
> [...]
> You came out on a flying trip,
> And took a hasty look,
> And, having drained your scanty purse,
> Went back—and wrote a book,
> You seem to think we're one half knaves,
> And t'other convict-born;
> Our institutions yield you mirth,
> Our ways excite your scorn.
> [...]
> To those who wish us well, we feel,
> Your book can be no bar—
> Can have no weight with those who care
> To know us as we are.
> We're strong enough to laugh at you,
> So, Mr. Dilke, farewell!
> Your book will answer all your hopes,
> It cannot fail to *sell*.[63]

Being so heavily suffused with the migrant experience—real and ideal—it is scarcely surprising that the Australian *Punch*es themselves became effective propaganda for emigration to the colonies. As Yan has noted, the *Melbourne Punch* in particular was keen to contrast the lifestyle to be had in a crowded England with that in a breezy, sparkling, golden land such as Victoria.[64] To that end, Chevalier produced a double-page "Summary for Europe" of the differences between Victoria and England, "respectfully dedicated to the old folks at home".[65] And in a purported letter to Queen Victoria herself, *Melbourne Punch* insisted that: "The time has therefore arrived… when the energies and industry of the British population might be beneficially transferred to a new country and a virgin soil".[66] Although the prime readership for this kind of propagandising would have been those already in the colonies, knowledge of the Melbourne and other Australian *Punch*es was not entirely lacking in Britain itself. As early as 1862, Clara Aspinall's memoir praised the portrait likenesses of *Melbourne Punch*'s cartoons; in 1863, Dickens's *All the Year Round* had focused on "Punch in Australia" (having received "a packet of recent numbers"); and by the 1890s, Marion Spielmann could add mention of the Melbourne version to his *History of "Punch"*.[67]

A continued—and increased—influx of migrants from Britain was of great import for the readers of the Australian *Punch*es. In catering for the humour and interests of the "three hundred thousand" Europeans in Victoria, *Melbourne Punch* in particular was always ready to point out that there were other migrants who sought to make the country their own, and who were the constant butt of cartoons and other racialised humour of the day.[68] Carrington "disliked Catholics in general and the Irish in particular", and aped his London counterpart, Tenniel, in depicting the Irish in as unflattering a light as possible.[69] But they were preferable to Jews, and infinitely more so than the most visible non-British migrants: the Chinese.

"Paranoid fantasies of a Chinese takeover" accompanied the rapid rise in their population (from only 2000 in 1854 to possibly 35,000 in 1857) and the satirical press felt the need to calm the fears of its readers in the only way possible: to put the Chinese in their place through constant ridicule, scaremongering, and infantilisation.[70] The desire to restrict, or reverse, Chinese emigration is epitomised by Chevalier's 6 August 1857 cartoon "Showing Him the Door"; which depicts the then-colonial premier, William Clark Haines, as a footman to "Mr Kangaroo Bull" (the supposed embodiment of the British-Australian nation, *à la* John Bull).[71] The stereotypical Mandarin character being pushed out of frame is told that "We've had too many of your sort here already", and that he cannot keep on "blocking up the place any longer". Other contributions by Chevalier imagined "Celestials" with ridiculous parodies of Chinese names requesting cat to eat; or "Civilized Celestials" dressed in western clothes laughing and poking fun at their newly arrived countryman.[72] It was even possible to joke that Indigenous Australians—dispossessed and disenfranchised as they were—took umbrage at being treated like "Chinaman".[73] Such attitudes continued throughout the decades, even as numbers declined by the 1870s, and gold-mining was replaced by market-gardening as the chief occupation of the colonies' Chinese population.[74] By then, the *Sydney Punch* could actually express a sneaking regard for the Chinese, faced with the continued attacks of "larrikins".[75] The editor wondered aloud how well these larrikins would fare if the situation were reversed, and they found themselves transplanted to China, and surrounded by an alien culture many hundreds of thousands strong.

CONCLUSION

The answer to *Sydney Punch*'s query may very well be found by some enterprising scholar of the future, and perhaps in the pages of the *China Punch*, which was launched in Hong Kong in 1867 and lasted on-and-off for almost a decade (1867–1868 and 1872–1876).[76] Although Chris Rea has recently given that publication some much-needed attention, in many ways the Australian *Punch*es are being left behind, as the Chinese, Japanese, and Indian (as well as Egyptian and Ottoman) *Punch*es are gaining a profile thanks to the collective efforts of a number of international scholars. As noted above, Mary L. Shannon and Shu-chuan Yan are at the forefront of correcting this situation, and returning to the subject-matter that so fascinated Maguerite Mahood and Clifford Craig many years ago (and Joan Kerr, more recently). This chapter has gone some way further to re-visiting the *Punch*es of Australia, and by reinforcing the view of them for what they were: essential nodes in the worldwide emigrant and imperial community that was the British Empire. Created and staffed by migrants, directed towards a migrant readership, and dealing with the concerns most important to migrants in a new land. They were an essential means by which those migrants maintained their connections to the motherland, while at the same time attempting to make sense of an entirely new situation, and doing so with more than a whiff of humour.

NOTES

1. "Departure of Mr. Punch from Gravesend." *Melbourne Punch* 1 (n.d.) [August 2, 1855]: 1.
2. "Arrival of Mr. Punch in Australia." *Melbourne Punch* 1 (n.d.) [August 2, 1855]: 1.
3. "Mr. Punch, Jun. ... ." *Melbourne Punch* 1 (n.d.) [August 2, 1855]: 2–3.
4. Mary L. Shannon, "Colonial Networks and the Periodical Marketplace," in *Journalism and the Periodical Press in Nineteenth-Century Britain*, ed. Joanne Shattock (Cambridge: Cambridge University Press, 2017), 208.

5. Elizabeth Webby, "Images of Europe in Two Nineteenth-Century Australian Illustrated Magazines," *Victorian Periodicals Review* 37, no. 4 (2004): 10–24; Richard Scully, "Britain in the *Melbourne Punch*," *Visual Culture in Britain* 20, no. 2 (2019): 152–171; Simon Sleight, "'Wavering between Virtue and Vice': Constructions of Youth in Australian Cartoons of the Late-Victorian Era," in *Drawing the Line: Using Cartoons as Historical Evidence*, eds. Richard Scully & Marian Quartly (Clayton: Monash University ePress, 2009), 05.1–05.26.
6. Marguerite Mahood, "Melbourne *Punch* and its Early Artists," *The La Trobe Journal* 4 (October, 1969): 65–81; Vane Lindesay, *The Inked-In Image: A Survey of Australian Comic Art* (Melbourne: Heinemann, 1970), 3–5; Marguerite Mahood, *The Loaded Line: Australian Political Caricature, 1788-1901* (Melbourne: Melbourne University Press, 1973); Jonathan King, *'Stop Laughing, This is Serious!' A Social history of Australia in Cartoons* (North Ryde: Cassell, 1980), esp. 29; Suzane Fabian, ed., *Mr. Punch Down Under: A Social History of the Colony from 1856 to 1900 via Cartoons and Extracts from* Melbourne Punch (Richmond & Drouin: Greenhouse & Landmark, 1982); Vane Lindesay, *The Way We Were: Australian Popular Magazines, 1856–1969* (Melbourne: Oxford University Press, 1983), 10–17.
7. Mary L. Shannon, *Dickens, Reynolds, and Mayhew on Wellington Street: The Print Culture of a Victorian Street* (Farnham: Surrey, 2016), esp. 165–199; Shannon, "Colonial Networks," 203–223. Also see: Richard Scully, "A Comic Empire: The Global Expansion of *Punch* as a Model Publication, 1841–1936," *International Journal of Comic Art* 15, no. 2 (2013): 6–35.
8. Miriam Magdalena Schneider, *The 'Sailor Prince' in the Age of Empire: Creating a Monarchical Brand in Nineteenth-Century Europe* (Basingstoke, Hampshire: Palgrave Macmillan, 2017), 239; Shannon, "Colonial Networks," 210.
9. Shu-chuan Yan, "'Kangaroo Politics, Kangaroo Ideas, and Kangaroo Society': The Early Years of *Melbourne Punch* in Colonial Australia," *Victorian Periodicals Review* 52, no. 1 (2019): 81, 83, 87.
10. Yan, "Kangaroo Politics," 85; Margaret Beetham, "Towards a Theory of the Periodical as a Publishing Genre," in *Investigating Victorian Journalism*, eds Laurel Brake, Aled Jones, and Lionel Madden (Basingstoke, Hampshire: Palgrave Macmillan, 1990), 20.
11. Shannon, "Colonial Networks," 213.
12. Lurline Stuart, "*Melbourne Punch*," in *The Encyclopedia of Melbourne*, ed., Andrew Brown-May and Shurlee Swain (Port Melbourne: Cambridge University Press, 2005), 468; Lurline Stuart, *James Smith: The Making of a Colonial Culture* (Sydney: Allen and Unwin, 1989), 83–84.
13. Shannon, "Colonial Networks," 207.

14. Mahood, "Melbourne *Punch* and its Early Artists," *La Trobe Journal*, 80.
15. Elizabeth Morrison, *Engines of Influence: Newspapers of Country Victoria, 1840–1890* (Carlton: Melbourne University Press, 2005), 73, 135, 261; Tom D. C. Roberts, "Herald and Weekly Times", in *A Companion to the Australian Media*, ed. Bridget Griffen-Foley (North Melbourne: Australian Scholarly Publishing, 2014), 203.
16. Asa Briggs, *Victorian Cities* (Berkeley: University of California Press, 1993), 278, 280, 287; Tristram Hunt, *Ten Cities that Made an Empire* (London: Penguin, 2015), 308, 322.
17. Here, I paraphrase: Brian Maidment, *Comedy, Caricature, and the Social Order, 1820-50* (Manchester: Manchester University Press, 2013), 16.
18. Fabian, ed., *Mr. Punch Down Under*, 1.
19. "Miscellaneous," *The Argus*, July 9, 1855, p. 7.
20. "Domestic Intelligence," *The Argus*, September 11, 1852, p. 5; "Our First Literary Arrivals," *Empire* 8 (October, 1852), 1490.
21. "Shipping Intelligence," *The Argus*, March 9, 1855, p. 4.
22. Basil Lubbock, *The Colonial Clippers* (Glasgow: J. Brown & Son, 1921), 32–40.
23. "Arrival of the Marco Polo," *Geelong Advertiser and Intelligencer*, February 27, 1856, p. 2.
24. Scully, "Britain in the *Melbourne Punch*," *Visual Culture in Britain*, 152.
25. William Howitt, *Land, Labour, and Gold; or, Two Years in Victoria*, Volume I, London: Brown, Green, and Longmans, 1855, pp. 26, 58, 103.
26. Scully, "A Comic Empire," *International Journal of Comic Art*, 21.
27. Scully, "A Comic Empire," 10.
28. Joan Kerr, *Artists and Cartoonists in Black and White—the Most Public Art* (Sydney: S. H. Irvin, 1999), 30.
29. "Brown Jones Robinson," "Correspondence," *Sydney Punch* (May 27, 1864): 7.
30. Kerr, *Artists and Cartoonists*, 30; Clifford Craig, *Mr Punch in Tasmania: Colonial Politics in Cartoons, 1866–1879* (Hobart: Blubber Head Press, 1980), 15.
31. Craig, *Mr Punch in Tasmania*, 129; Mahood, *Loaded Line*, 126.
32. Mahood, *Loaded Line*, 93-99, 126; Kerr, *Artists and Cartoonists*, 32.
33. Kerr, *Artists and Cartoonists*, 32.
34. Mahood, *Loaded Line*, 80.
35. *Sydney Punch* (May 27, 1864): 1.
36. *Sydney Punch* (May 27, 1864): 2.
37. Mahood, *Loaded Line*, 80.
38. "Robinson," "Correspondence", *Sydney Punch*, 7.
39. Shannon, "Colonial Networks," 221–222; Mahood, *Loaded Line*, 84; Ann E. Galbally, "Campbell, Oswald Rose (1820–1887)," *Australian*

Dictionary of Biography, Canberra: National Centre of Biography, Australian National University, 1969, http://adb.anu.edu.au/biography/campbell-oswald-rose-3157/text4717 (accessed December 13, 2019).

40. Suzanne Edgar, "Scott, Eugene Montagu (Monty) (1835–1909)", *Australian Dictionary of Biography*, Canberra: National Centre of Biography, Australian National University, 1976, http://adb.anu.edu.au/biography/scott-eugene-montagu-monty-4547/text7453 (accessed December 13, 2019); "Private Advertisements," *New South Wales Government Gazette* 55 (March 14, 1862): 586.

41. Shannon, "Colonial Networks," 222.

42. *Sydney Punch* 4, no. 87 (January 20, 1866), title page.

43. Grosse's work in the colonial print market expanded quite dramatically in the same period. See: Peter A. Dowling, "Grosse, Frederick (1828–1894)," *Australian Dictionary of Biography*, Canberra: National Centre of Biography, Australian National University, 2005, http://adb.anu.edu.au/biography/grosse-frederick-12955/text23415 (accessed December 13, 2019).

44. Scully, "Britain in the *Melbourne Punch*," *Visual Culture in Britain*, 154.

45. Scully, "Britain in the *Melbourne Punch*," *Visual Culture in Britain*, 155, 157; Marguerite Mahood, "Carrington, Francis Thomas Dean (Tom) (1843–1918)," *Australian Dictionary of Biography*, Canberra: National Centre of Biography, Australian National University, 1969, http://adb.anu.edu.au/biography/carrington-francis-thomas-dean-tom-3170/text4725 (accessed December 13, 2019).

46. Scully, "Britain in the *Melbourne Punch*," *Visual Culture in Britain*, 157; Scully, "A Comic Empire", *International Journal of Comic Art*, 19–21; Richard Scully, *Eminent Victorian Cartoonists—Volume I: The Founders* (London: The Political Cartoon Society, 2018), 28, 133–134.

47. Mahood, *Loaded Line*, 126. "Sam Slick" was a Canadian invention of the 1830s. See: Richard A. Davies, *Inventing Sam Slick: A Biography of Thomas Chandler Haliburton* (Toronto: University of Toronto Press, 2005).

48. I am inclined to support the identification of Ashton with the artist "GRA", as per the entry: "GRA," *Design and Art Australia Online* (19 October 2011), https://www.daao.org.au/bio/g-r-a/ (accessed December 18, 2019). On Ashton, see: Katherine Harper, "Ashton, George Rossi (1857–?)," *Australian Dictionary of Biography*, Canberra: National Centre of Biography, Australian National University (1979), http://adb.anu.edu.au/biography/ashton-george-rossi-5654/text8461 (accessed December 18, 2019); "George Rossi Ashton b.1857," *Design and Art Australia Online* (October 19, 2011), https://www.daao.org.au/bio/george-rossi-ashton/ (accessed December 18, 2019).

49. Dowling, "Grosse".

50. Marjorie J. Tipping, "Chevalier, Nicholas (1828–1902)," *Australian Dictionary of Biography*, Canberra: National Centre of Biography, Australian National University (1969), http://adb.anu.edu.au/biography/chevalier-nicholas-3200/text4807 (accessed December 13, 2019).

51. Science and Art Department of the Committee of Council on Education, *The Cruise of His Royal Highness the Duke of Edinburgh – Catalogue* (London: George E. Eyre & William Spottiswoode, 1872), 4 ff.

52. "Rudolph Jenny," *Design and Art Australia Online* (October 19, 2011), https://www.daao.org.au/bio/rudolph-jenny/ (accessed December 13, 2019).

53. Mahood, *Loaded Line*, 90; Craig, *Mr Punch in Tasmania*, 184-185; *Tasmanian Punch* 1, no. 4 (August 25, 1877), cover page.

54. Marguerite Mahood, "Bradley, Luther (1853–1917)," *Australian Dictionary of Biography*, Canberra: National Centre of Biography, Australian National University (1979), http://adb.anu.edu.au/biography/bradley-luther-5333/text9015 (accessed December 13, 2019).

55. Scully, "Britain in the *Melbourne Punch*", *Visual Culture in Britain*, 159, 161.

56. Unknown cartoonist, "Latest War Telegrams," *Sydney Punch* (October 1, 1870): 164; Unknown cartoonist, "Tasmania's Congratulations to Earl Beaconsfield," *Tasmanian Punch* (September 7, 1878): n.p.; Unknown cartoonist, "Brethren Across the Ocean," *Queensland Punch and Figaro* (March 16, 1899), 1.

57. Scully, "Britain in the *Melbourne Punch*", *Visual Culture in Britain*, 159.

58. [Sidney Blanchard], "Punch in Australia," *All the Year Round* 9 (August 22, 1863): 613. I am very grateful to Jeremy Parrott for his identification of Blanchard's contribution to *All the Year Round*. Having already written a piece on "Punch in India", in 1870 Blanchard wrote the first history of the *London Charivari* (which is commonly mis-attributed to Mark Lemon): *Mr Punch: His Origin and Career* (London: Jas. Wade, 1870). On Blanchard's authorship, see: James Kennedy, W. A. Smith & A. F. Johnson, *Dictionary of Anonymous and Pseudonymous English Literature*, New and Enlarged Edition, Volume Four (Edinburgh & London: Oliver and Boyd, 1928), 128. On the attribution to Lemon, see for instance: Ritu Gairola Khanduri, "*Punch* in India: Another History of Colonial Politics?" in *Asian Punches: A Transcultural Affair*, ed. Hans Harder and Barbara Mittler (Berlin & Heidelberg: Springer, 2013), 169.

59. Scully, "Britain in the *Melbourne Punch*," *Visual Culture in Britain*, 161; Unknown cartoonist, "Jolly Good Fellows," *Sydney Punch* (October 1, 1870): 170.

60. Scully, "Britain in the *Melbourne Punch*," *Visual Culture in Britain*, 164.

61. Nicholas Chevalier, "Let It Burn, I'm Only a Lodger," *Melbourne Punch* (August 16, 1855): 22.
62. G. H. T. "Welcome the Coming, Speed the Parting Guest," *Tasmanian Punch* (December 18, 1869): n.p.
63. "Mr. Punch to the Author of 'Greater Britain'," *Sydney Punch* (June 19, 1869): 35.
64. Yan, "Kangaroo Politics", 90–91.
65. Nicholas Chevalier, "Punch's Summary for Europe," *Melbourne Punch* (April 25, 1861): 52–53
66. "Melbourne Punch to Queen Victoria," *Melbourne Punch* (September 8, 1859): 55.
67. Clara Aspinall, *Three Years in Melbourne* (London: L. Booth, 1862), 83–84; [Blanchard], "Punch in Australia," *All the Year Round*, 610–616; M. H. Spielmann, *The History of "Punch"* (London: Cassell & Co., 1895), 393.
68. "A Reward of One Thousand Pounds," *Melbourne Punch* (August 2, 1855): 2–3.
69. Gordon Morrison and Anne Rowland, eds. *In Your Face! Cartoons about Politics and Society, 1760–2010* (Ballarat: Art Gallery of Ballarat, 2010), 39; Dianne Hall, "'Now him White Man': Images of the Irish in Colonial Australia," *History Australia* 11, no. 2 (2014): 179.
70. Fabian, ed. *Mr. Punch Down Under*, 77.
71. Nicholas Chevalier, "Showing Him the Door," *Melbourne Punch* (August 6, 1857): 12. On Kangaroo Bull, see: Scully, "Britain in the *Melbourne Punch*," *Visual Culture in Britain*, 158.
72. Nicholas Chevalier, "A Celestial Delicacy," *Melbourne Punch* (September 27, 1855): 70; "Should Auld Acquaintance Be Forgot," *Melbourne Punch* (August 20, 1857): 31.
73. [Blanchard], "Punch in Australia," *All the Year Round*, 614.
74. Tom Carrington, "The Agricultural Labourer of the Future," *Melbourne Punch* (January 11, 1872): 9; Unknown cartoonist, "Return from Brandy Creek," *Tasmanian Punch* (August 24, 1878): n.p.
75. "The Larrikino-Chinese War," *Sydney Punch* (July 26, 1879): 19; "The Chinese Puzzle," *Sydney Punch* (January 28, 1882): 29.
76. Scully, "A Comic Empire," *International Journal of Comic Art*, 25; Christopher G. Rea, "'He'll Roast All Subjects That May Need the Roasting': Puck and Mr Punch in Nineteenth-Century China," in *Asian Punches*, ed. Harder and Mittler, 389.

CHAPTER 3

"Cement, Guide and Representative for the Exile and the Emigrant": Ideological Discourse and *italianità* in *L'Italo-Australiano*

Marianna Piantavigna

L'Italo-Australiano was the first Italian-language newspaper published in Australia, and the only one to be published pre-Federation (1901). Gianfranco Cresciani identifies this newspaper as the first socialist paper in Australia.[1] Although the radical and socialist stand of its editor and his collaborators is clear—as is the implicit aim of the newspaper to organise Italian workers towards mechanisms of mutual aid and unionism—the newspaper was presented to its readership as interpreting and representing the interests of all Italians in Australia, and as such it addressed its readers not as a socialist newspaper but as a guide, "inspired by democratic principles", for all Italian compatriots.[2]

M. Piantavigna (✉)
The University of Western Australia, Perth, WA, Australia
e-mail: marianna.piantavigna@research.uwa.edu.au

© The Author(s) 2020
C. Dewhirst, R. Scully (eds.), *The Transnational Voices of Australia's Migrant and Minority Press*, Palgrave Studies in the History of the Media,
https://doi.org/10.1007/978-3-030-43639-1_3

Even though it had a short life (it lasted only for six issues), *L'Italo-Australiano* is particularly significant for two main reasons: the role and the person of its editor, Francesco Sceusa, and the historical context of the newspaper's production. The project of the newspaper was initiated in 1885 within the context of the Italian Democratic Club, where, since 1881, the elite of Sydney's Italian community had gathered. Hence, its story is strictly correlated with the vicissitudes of its editor in the first place, as well as with the experiences of the Italian community it aimed to address.

Like many ethnic-language newspapers, *L'Italo-Australiano* acted as a connection between "home" and "here", bridging and mediating between two physical and cultural places of belonging, and hence contributing to the creation of a transnational social field in which people were able to forge cross-border identities. Furthermore, as media text, it must be understood as a product of cultural stances which contributed to the reproduction and creation of new cultural attitudes: newspapers impact on social identity through their role of mediation, through which they produce relationships between parties, based on shared social identity and cultural values. Newspapers link social institutions and organisations, their discourses, the events surrounding them, and the audiences who read, view, and listen to media texts. Finally, like any cultural object, ethnic-newspaper content is never neutral: it conveys meanings and it offers a representation of reality, becoming part of a broader ideological discourse.[3]

L'Italo-Australiano may be considered as part of a historically and culturally specific "discursive formation", according to Michel Foucault's approach to discourse as a system of representation that delineates and produces the objects of knowledge related to a certain historical context.[4] When analysing the representation of individuals and groups of individuals in this newspaper, it is important to bear in mind some elements that derive from the socio-cultural context of its agency. Concepts like "civilisation" opposed to "barbarianism", together with an interpretation of humanity organised on the basis of a hierarchy of races, from both of which the idea of white supremacy is drawn, are interpretative filters through which this periodical represented relationships between social groups, societies, and nations. A second factor that needs to be considered is the power relationships that developed between editorship and readership, within Italian communities, and between components of Australian society.

A transnational and multidisciplinary approach to the study of ethnic-language newspapers considers the roles they assume, through their news discourse, within the "imagined communities"[5] they address and represent: the elements that, in these discourses, determine and represent such communities; the way in which they may shape and influence the real communities in which these newspapers are active. The transnational perspective makes it possible to analyse these elements within the context of cross-border social and symbolic interconnections.

The ideological discourse of *L'Italo-Australiano* played a role in the processes of "geographical sense-making" related to the Italian presence in Australia. It was, in fact, part of the cluster of "discursive and extra-discursive practices involving the formulation, naming, classification and management of collective identities".[6] The chapter will discuss some aspects related to the character of *italianità* (a word that can be translated with 'Italianness') as elements that often identify certain markers of an Italian collective identity. It considers how *L'Italo-Australiano* built its ideological discourse around such character, contributing to the development of a cultural and political myth. The first section of the chapter concerns the historical and cultural context of its production, whereas the second and the third, respectively, present the newspaper's project and some structures and mechanisms of representation in the discourse of this, the first Italian-language newspaper in Australia.

BETWEEN ITALY AND SYDNEY: THE SOCIO-CULTURAL AND POLITICAL CONTEXT OF MIGRATION

People arriving from the Italian peninsula were generally perceived as "Italians" in the host country, even when, before 1861, an Italian nation did not exist, nor Italian people. The matter of Italian nationality is strictly connected with the process of building and developing a sense of belonging among the Italian migrating masses, which contributed to the creation of the concept of an Italian nation. As many scholars have underlined, the process of "making Italy abroad" has always been present in the Italian diaspora, and has played a part in the changing and shaping of Italy itself. Concepts such as *italianità*, *civiltà italiana* (Italian civilisation), and "Italian nation" appear in all stages of Italian migration, and their meaning changes progressively according to the era and the place of migration, in a continuous exchange between Italian communities within and outside Italy.[7]

Considering the wider context of the Australian colonies, the newspaper was published in a period—between 1870 and 1890—that presents some long-term effects of the process of demographic dislocation set in motion by the 1850s goldrush; the rapid growth of cities, the availability of new infrastructures that facilitated exchanges and communication, and the consequent increased movement of population and goods between the colonies are factors that stimulated people's new search for economic opportunity and security, as well as for identity. In this context, a debate grew around Australian nationhood and the issue of independence from Britain, and different attitudes consolidated in the Australian public sphere, with regard to race, politics, religion, and education. At the same time, the 1880s were characterised by a new stimulus to trade union activity, as a consequence of an increased pressure on resources and job opportunities.[8]

Furthermore, *L'Italo-Australiano* occurred within a significant period in the history of the Italian nation, both from a political and a cultural perspective: in the 24 years since unification, Italian governments and cultural and political movements had just begun to deal with the problem of national identity and the process of building a 'national sentiment'—which included defining the role of the Italian nation on an international level, as this was the moment in which Italy entered the land-grabbing competition between colonial powers, taking (a belated) part in the "scramble for Africa". On the other hand, as a consequence of the deep inequalities within the country, Italy was the scene of great internal social conflict between social groups, and between the Italian North and South.[9]

Overall, within this historical context, nationhood and the social question are two important aspects that characterise the discourse of this newspaper, both from the Italian and the Australian perspectives; in fact, because of the time of its publication, its viewpoint on these issues differs from that of all subsequent Italian-language newspapers published in Australia. The following parts of this section consider some aspects related to Italian settlement in Australia that define the context in which *L'Italo-Australiano* was conceived and published, foregrounding the role that Sceusa progressively carved for himself amongst different public spheres.

The history of Italian migration to Australia begins with the first gold rush that occurred in Victoria during the 1850s. It took place in a context of colonisation, in which practices and policies of dispossession, exclusion, and exploitation had been rationalised and justified on the basis of principles that indicated whiteness as the foundation of cultural and socio-political life in the Australian colonies. According to the social-Darwinist hierarchical interpretation of societies and of races—which positioned the European (possibly Anglo-European) at the top—the idea of a white and homogeneous society was seen as the precondition for maintaining the character of these colonies, as well as for preventing the contamination and degradation of the white (British) race. Immigration control, which determined who could enter the colonies (basically excluding the "inferior races"), together with the expected "natural" extinction of First Nations people were at the heart of the idea of a white Australia. Implications of this institutionalised racialism are seen in the relationship between Europeans and both First Nations people and non-Europeans, as well as between northern (British especially) and southern Europeans.[10]

Before the gold rush, immigration support schemes had been established in the Australian colonies to encourage the arrival of free immigrant workers, who entered the territory in significant numbers for the first time. The need for a new, skilled workforce had grown with the rapid disappearance of convict labourers, and as colonial capitalists started to push for a more diversified economy. The discovery of gold deposits and the new pattern of economic activity that developed in subsequent years attracted many new European migrants to Australian shores, resulting in the first period of real migration from continental Europe to Australia. Moreover, in this phase, the first substantial flow of people arrived from the Italian peninsula—many of them were from the alpine valleys of Lombardy, the Eolian Islands, and Sicily, as well as from Piedmont, Veneto, and Tuscany. It is not possible to assess the exact number of people arriving from Italy, but it is certain that Italians had settled in every mining centre of Victoria and New South Wales, employed as stonemasons, mineworkers, or even establishing small commercial enterprises.[11]

The coexistence of different work typologies—free, indentured, and forced labour—created tensions and rivalry among workers. Free immigration allowed greater ethnic differentiation, even though the British and northern Europeans were favoured in immigration schemes. On the other hand, indentured labour was used as a means of opposing the power of an emerging working-class, which had started to organise politically. As a consequence, the issue of cheap labour was fought by labour movements on a racist basis: the idea of indentured workers serving colonial-capital interests, and their non-European origins (hence, corruptive of a progressive society) became two sides of the same coin.[12] The fact that Italians were not categorised as homogeneously white meant that they were considered close to races that were regarded as inferior; consequently, they were judged untrustworthy and became to be perceived as unfair competitors in the job market. This in-between position of Italian migrants "is central to any understanding not only of the discrimination they endured, but also of their strategic attempts to contrast and mitigate such discrimination".[13]

During the 1880s and 1890s a small but steady flow of Italians arrived, mainly through processes of chain migration: the 1881 Colonial census attested the presence of 1880 Italians throughout Australia, including 521 in New South Wales.[14] Those who arrived in Sydney were agricultural workers, fishermen, street musicians, stonemasons, and figurine makers. They found employment in restaurants, or as fruit and vegetable growers and vendors, as fishermen, or by importing and selling goods from Italy. Others would earn their living as street musicians and organ grinders.[15] Because of their increased numbers, and because of (controversial) bilateral agreements between Italian governments and some Australian colonies, the 1880s are years in which Italians progressively became "visible" to the rest of the Australian society.[16]

An article in the 8 December 1887 issue of the *Australian Star*, a Sydney penny newspaper, well illustrates the prejudiced representation of Italian migrants in Australia. Italians are defined as "the Chinese of Europe", and the article draws a parallel between the undesirable presence of "the Chinese" and "the Italians" in Australia, in Sydney in particular. Referring to the Italians, the article reads:

> Of recent years, however, another [other than the Chinese] race equally enervating to vigorous nationhood, equally formidable to deal with as the law stands, and fully as non-contributing a factor to the wealth of the nation as the wall-eyed celestial, has forced itself on public attention.[17]

This identification is significant for two reasons. In the first place, it shows how, for at least a part of the Australian press and public opinion (which included Italians), the word "Chinese" had semantically become a carrier of negative stereotypes ascribed to non-Caucasian migrants, and how this ethnic group tended to be taken as the prototype of the "inferior", not-wanted migrant: in this article, stereotypical habits and attitudes ascribed to "the Chinese" are described as "vicious", corrupt, and corruptive, with the aim of presenting them as a danger for the integrity of the "white race". Secondly, the epithet "Chinese of Europe" shows that Italians had begun to be perceived and represented as a group other than the more desirable European one: a group of people who could barely speak English, and whose religion, mores, and culture were different from the majority of Australian society.

The attitude towards Chinese migrants, that at this point was also applied to Italians, shows the extent to which the strategy of racial denigration—and persecution—had been embedded in the struggle between opposing poles of Australian society.[18] Labour unions and politicians close to the workers' cause "feared for working conditions and wages if inferior races used to inferior conditions were able to dominate the labour market".[19] Hence, while undesired immigrant labour was lobbied against on an institutional level, the Australian public sphere would debate the presence of these "alien subjects" on Australian soil, frequently raising the issue of their racial inferiority.[20]

The polemic on Italians in the *Australian Star* is relevant here, because it represents one of the cases in which Francesco Sceusa directly intervened in the debate, as an Italian spokesperson within the Sydney public sphere, as well as within the Australian socialist and unionist movements. Indeed, in the 16 December 1887 issue, he replied to the article with a letter to the editor, in which the concept of "Chinese of Europe" is semantically re-connoted to define a "race" of:

> organ-grinders, harp-players, fruit-sellers, which are no better than the almond-eyed Mongolians, and as enervating and demoralising as the latter.[21]

Sceusa aimed to prevent the Italian community from being associated with the category "Chinese", distancing *his* Italian community, the "Italian *colonists* [italics in the original]", from this group of people. In his view, "these disguised beggars" were from many parts of the Mediterranean region, and hence it was a mistake to sustain that "these *white* [italics in the original] Chinese are all Italians, and that Italian residents are so". Moreover, while Sceusa's discourse insists on the lack of nationalism and sense of identity among these Italians as an indication of their not being part of the group of "Italian residents", it also challenges the assertion that Italians were "an enervating race", enlisting the qualities that brought them to create a united nation that "in a quarter of a century present [*sic*] herself to the world as a Great Power".[22]

Francesco Sceusa had arrived in Sydney in 1877, at the age of 26. He was one of the many anarchists, socialists, and labour-movement militants who had fled repression and prosecution in Italy after the uprisings of 1874 and the subsequent period of social tension.[23] Sceusa would continue his political activism in the country of immigration, taking part in the network of people, ideas, and political strategies that had progressively been established between Italy and the many countries of Italian migration. Apart from the years he spent in Orange (1885–1890), his initiatives took place within the context of a group of anarchists and socialists who, between 1880 and the end of the century, started to organise a system of mutual aid and support between Melbourne and Sydney that operated on different scales: at a broader level, it was active within the network of the Second International, supporting and celebrating the workers' fight on a global scale; the members would collect money for the victims of clashes with police and for the diffusion of socialist propaganda in Italy.

This group of Italians also kept up regular correspondence with newspapers in Italy, wanting to represent the Italian presence in Australia to their readership—often enraging the moderate and conservative component of Sydney's Italian elite. At least since 1897, Sceusa (alternating with other immigrated socialists like Pietro Munari, Giuseppe Prampolini, Quinto Ercole, and T. Talamini) started to send periodical "Lettere dall'Australia" (letters from Australia) from the Australian colonies to the Italian socialist newspaper *Avanti!*. The articles by Sceusa express admiration for the successes gained by Australian workers' organisations and for the Australian way to socialism.[24] Salvatore Costanza argues that these accounts may have nourished the development of the myth of *Australia felix* within the Italian public sphere—that is, the image of a country where the workers' life was generally better and culturally advanced, in which social conflict was less exacerbated and greater social and economic rights had been gained through unions' contractual power.[25] Between the end of the century and the first decade of the twentieth century, Sceusa's collaboration with *Avanti!* was also aimed at discouraging Italian migration to Australia through indentured labour programmes in which Italians would have been used as "cheap labour", as this would compromise the mechanisms of social reforms activated by Australian socialist organisations.

On the other hand, in Australia, the mutual aid network aimed to provide migrants with aid and assistance, conscious that the Italian workers found themselves in a position between the Australian workers' fight for the improvement of working conditions and the employers' attempt to nullify such a fight.[26] Hence, this organisation had the task of protecting these workers from underpaid and exploited work, from the racist attitude of sectors of the Australian press, and from that of labour militants who lacked "Internationalist class consciousness" and were carrying on racist campaigns against non- and southern-European migrants.[27]

L'Italo-Australiano was certainly conceived as one means to reach the goal of involving Italian workers in a more politicised and organised structure of mutual aid and assistance, insisting on the nationalistic leverage of common ethnic origin. However, it came early in the process, still an expression of the cooperation between the radical and the moderate components of the Sydney Italian elite.

L'ITALO-AUSTRALIANO: PRODUCERS, PROJECT, AND PROGRAMMATIC IDEAS

The newspaper was published monthly in 1885, between January and September, in Sydney. The first issue, handwritten and hand-drawn by Sceusa himself, was lithographed, while the others were typeset. It was produced and printed by Cesare Carpena, and distributed in Sydney, Melbourne and Brisbane by Gordon & Gotch, as well as in Italy by the publishing house Sonzogno of Milan. Sceusa is a central figure in the venture, not simply as the editor of the new paper, but also because his initiative appears to have been the main driver for the project – the newspaper was entirely curated by him, and he is also the author of many of the articles published; on the other hand, the project quickly faded and came to an end once Sceusa was transferred to Orange by the Department of Lands.

Each issue consists of eight pages organised in three columns, with the last page entirely dedicated to advertisements. Many of the commercial activities advertised were connected with members of the Italian Democratic Club, which counted for a substantial part of the Italian elite of Sydney. The Club seems to be a constant reference as well as one of the privileged interlocutors of the newspaper.

Notwithstanding its short life, *L'Italo-Australiano* presents a relatively defined structure, as content is organised in sections and columns. The front page usually featured Sceusa's editorial and sometimes the beginning of the column "Note del Mese" (Notes of the Month)—featuring three to five news items from different parts of the world, with regard to politics, foreign affairs, and social events relevant to the debate on the Social

Question. Moreover, from the May issue, this section included the column "I Figli del Popolo" (the Sons of the People), which brought out the
prominent anti-aristocratic, socialist stance of the newspaper, as the column was conceived to:

> demonstrate that 80 out of a hundred great inventors, artists, legislators,
> commanders, or, in a word, civilisation founders and benefactors to the
> humankind have been humble workmen.[28]

The section related to Italian news always opened at page four, with the
column "Notizie Italiane" (Italian News), which offered short news items
on the latest events related to the political and the workers movements'
spheres. This section covered news on the evolving situation of the Italian
invasion of Eritrea. The May and June issues also presented a column
titled "Italiani all'Estero" (Italians Abroad) which offered accounts of
Italian migrant communities in other countries (Tunisia, California) and
other cities (Paris, Marseilles, London).

The following pages were dedicated to news from the British colonies
in Oceania, and to Australia in particular. The column "Notizie Oceaniche"
(Oceania News) provided updates on wool-market trends, and on issues
from the labour market, with particular attention paid to strikes and to
matters related to the Social Question. Moreover, it reported vivid episodes from "bush life"—usually tragic or sensational news presented in a
dramatic tone. News relating to colonies other than Australia and New
Zealand often presented references to the process of colonisation in the
Indo-Pacific area, focusing in particular on the tensions between Britain
and Germany. The column "Cose Locali" (Local Issues) reported news of
interest to the Italian readership in New South Wales and Sydney.

"Il Perché" (The Whys and Wherefores) is the inaugural editorial of
L'Italo-Australiano. It presents features that characterise the newspaper
agency—in relation to its community of readers, as well as to the public
sphere of the Italian communities in Australia. Both editor and producers
expected the readership to consist of Italians in Australia, as well as in
Italy.[29]

Programmatic ideas are preceded by a preamble through which Sceusa,
as editor, prepares the ground for the newspaper project, describing the
context of its inception, and identifying the void that the newspaper aims to
fill. The preamble provides the space for positioning the experience of the
newspaper within an ideological narrative. The socio-political framework of

the project is then followed by explanation of the purposes and motives of the initiative. Furthermore, the editorial provides an overview of the characteristics and principles of the newspaper, and it implicitly calls for compatriots' support. Sceusa writes about a newspaper that is going to be "cement and guide for the exiled and the migrant", aiming at creating a space within which to represent Australian reality—and, somewhat paternalistically, to explain how to behave (and how not to) in such an environment—to an implied reader who has just landed in Australia, or lives in a corner of such a vast territory, while at the same time reporting on Italian news. Compatriot support, both moral and financial, is also emphasised in an inaugural article by Carpena in the same issue, which insists on the importance of the project receiving a positive response from Italians in Australia, as a guarantee of success in the creation of a social and communicative network, the centre of which was meant to be occupied by the newspaper.[30]

The connection with the home country is a significant aspect in defining the motives at the foundation of *L'Italo-Australiano*, alongside its aims to create a network amongst Italians in Australia and to mediate between the Italian migrants in Australia and British-Australian society. Such a connection is developed in (at least) two directions. In fact, the inaugural editorial claims the newspaper is a resource at the service of Italians and Italy in its commitment to help migrants in maintaining a relationship with the home country, and to offer an understanding of the Australian dimension (and of the Italian community they represent) to Italian compatriots in Italy. In certain passages, such a transnational connection presents a more accentuated business-minded perspective, which is oriented to promoting Australia as a place of work or business for the Italian working, middle, and industrialist classes:

> It is our sacred duty to point out this semi-unknown Australia, miles and miles away, to the Italian worker, to the speculator and to the industrialist. And this duty cannot be fulfilled except through the press.[31]

IMAGINING AN ITALIAN COMMUNITY: IDEOLOGICAL DISCOURSE AND *ITALIANITÀ*

The element of *italianità* in the ideological discourse of *L'Italo-Australiano* will concern here three main nuclei of representation: Australia, Italians and Australians, and Italy. Within this context, *italianità* is also defined through a double process of association and opposition, according to what

Joseph Pugliese identifies as "an internal system of othering". A system, adopted by the minority, that embraces the dynamics of hierarchical organisation of society imposed by the dominant Anglo culture, and that conceives "Anglo as other to migrant as other to Indigenous".[32]

Representations of Australia here concern the socio-political dimension in which Italians had to operate. The second nucleus—Italians and Australians—is developed by exploring the narratives constructed from depictions of Italian migrants, in Australia and in other destinations of migration, and of (British) Australians. The third includes representations of Italy, which were related to building a sentiment of belonging and to developing an Italian nationalism to oppose and juxtapose to the Australian one.

In representing the Australian socio-political dimension contemporary to its publication, the discourse of *L'Italo-Australiano* is conditioned by the fact that, in 1885, Australia was not a united body. Besides, the primary reason for covering news related to politics and society in colonial Australia comes from the intention to mediate and offer an interpretation of such matters to a small, scattered, and inexperienced (at least, to the editor's eyes) Italian community, as Italians are:

> disseminated throughout the Oceanic lands, without an address, without a cement, without a voice; unaware of what happens in their native country, forgetful of its aspirations and traditions, about to be absorbed by an alien race, if virtuous, to be rejected if dishonest.[33]

This brief excerpt is another example of how Sceusa's rhetorical devices aimed to overturn a discursive pattern, in order to re-connote it—in this case with regard to the use of the term *alien race*, with reference to the British: Sceusa uses against 'them' the same judgemental society-organising categories that the main social group was using when referring to non-British subjects. This is not to say that he does not embrace the same logic of hierarchical division of society imposed by the dominant Anglo culture; on the contrary, he—like other Italian-language newspaper editors—aims at having the Italian community acknowledged by the dominant culture as being part of the white, civilised society.[34] However, the fact that Sceusa refers to British Australians with such a term is indicative of (his, at least) conflicting feelings towards this portion of the society, as well as of his aim to somewhat underline the distinction between Italian nationality and British Australian.

It is clear, especially in the editorial articles, that the newspaper reflects Sceusa's position on Australian political issues, such as independence from the United Kingdom, federalism and republicanism, and upon matters related to the organisation of a future white Australian society. The discourse of *L'Italo-Australiano* promotes a republican and federalist Australia, using similar arguments to those employed in mainstream debate. The views embraced by the newspaper were very close to those of Australian radicals (who were lobbying for a federated republic, independent from the British Empire), to the extent that the periodical becomes a supporter within the Italian community of an Australian nationhood built on elements like anti-imperialism, a need of self-defence from external menaces, and egalitarianism—with regard to white (male) Australian society.[35] The editorial from the second issue (3 March 1885) is a good example of Sceusa's positive view of the progress the Australian colonies had made in the 97 years since first settlement—"how many phases had she to endure before she could boast suburbs and cities?"[36] He draws a parallel between the independent United States and the not-yet-independent Australia:

> A century ago, the United States of America formed an independent republic. Will these [Australian] Colonies find a common ground for once, overcoming regional jealousies and tariff differences, and proclaim an Australian federal Republic, or will they be an integral part of the federated British Empire?[37]

Here, Sceusa is referring to the political debate between republicans and the Anglo-Australian loyalists, who were led by the Imperial Federation League. From his comparison between the Australian colonies and the federated United States, it is clear where he stands.

Moreover, the editorial praises the "progress" towards civilisation that Australia has made in less than a century: it has gone from being "the pandemonium of cannibalism" to "being now a nation of more than three million febrile spirits, for whom […] the future is a golden dream". Furthermore, whiteness is indicated as a substantial component of this civilising process, given that colonised Australia is bluntly presented as the inevitable domination of the superior "white civilisation" over "inferior races":

> Indian [Native American] tribes [were] flushed from the Rocky Mountains, [their] last refuge; down here, our Aborigines and Maori in New Zealand are vanishing […]; on the other side of Bass Strait, the Tasmanian race is extinct! And on the soil of red and black races, dying and dead, new populations grow flourishing – the American, the Australian.[38]

L'Italo-Australiano describes Australia as a nation in the process of gaining its independence and of determining a new state organisation. It does so by observing the "vanishing" of Aboriginal peoples and their cultures, as a necessary step to become a white, "civilised" country. In this regard, the discourse of this first Italian-language newspaper is framed within the preponderant discursive formation which claimed Australia for the white man, on the basis that First Nations were "doomed to extinction"—a consequence of the "inevitable" process put in place by the impersonal force of "evolution", rather than because of the violence and dispossession perpetrated by the European settlers.[39]

The narratives that develop in *L'Italo-Australiano* from depictions of Italian migrants, in Australia and in other destinations of migration, present some notable features: firstly, Italian migrants tend to be mainly depicted as workers and as Australia's guests and co-colonisers; secondly, they are represented both as individuals and collectively, either as members of a social class or all together as a community; and thirdly, in all these cases, it is the male component of the community that is largely represented. This is particularly evident if we consider that news about Italians either concerns community events in which only male participation is enhanced or depicts men's jobs as representative of Italians' working life in Australia. These narratives are clearly a product and expression of the context of their production, both from a historical and from a cultural perspective, in that they are part of a history of Italian migration characterised by a "strongly gendered" process of migration and settlement.[40]

Moreover, in identifying those members of the community who are worth being named and celebrated in their individuality, individual representations highlight the newspaper's perspective on the dynamics within the Italian community in Sydney, and, in some way, they help to define and reinforce a social hierarchy that conceives the Italian economic and cultural elite as the thinking and debating fulcrum within this particular public sphere: even though Sceusa is often at odds with the moderate and conservative component of this group, his and the voices of these individuals are the ones that most frequently appear directly in the discourse.

On the other hand, though, outside of the specific dynamics of the Sydney community, Italian working-class migrants are presented as resilient and strong workers: in *L'Italo-Australiano*, the discourse develops narratives related to the workers' struggle and to the Social Question, juxtaposing the Australian context with the Italian one, and with that of other destinations of Italian migration. The newspaper reports on strikes, denounces situations of injustice, and campaigns for social reform and for the intervention of politics to tackle social problems. In such narratives, parallel representations of Italian and Australian workers celebrate their fight for the improvement of their working conditions: these workers are represented as the expression of the international struggle of workers' movements for recognition of their rights.

The deep involvement of the newspaper (and of Sceusa) in the workers' struggle, on the one hand, and the fact that the newspaper represents a point of reference for Italians in Australia, on the other, put the newspaper in the particular position of encouraging Italian workers to join Australian unions in order to organise the fight more efficiently and to increase their leverage. With this purpose, the newspaper assumes an educative role, in explaining to its readers what they need to do in order to be accepted by mainstream "Anglo" society.

The educative role of the paper is particularly evident in its promotion of a code of work ethics that is meant to teach Italians which work types and attitudes are appropriate, so that Italians "would not humiliate themselves and their native fatherland".[41] Quoting from the newspaper:

> Never put off until tomorrow what you can do today [...]. Without work, the land produces nothing but bramble and thorns: Work! – Everything is movement and work in nature; the indolent is a loathsome being to himself, his neighbour and nature: Work! – Nations are made of work. In your work is the greatness of your Fatherland: Work! It is better to suffer wrongs, than to inflict them.[42]

It could be said that the newspaper promotes a lifestyle in which work is the most fulfilling aspect, and condemns any kind of attitude that is seen as not respecting this Italian-Australian way of life. Divergences and discriminations within the Italian community become apparent in relation to specific groups that are seen as constituting a threat to the integrity of the community—*L'Italo-Australiano* is worried about the image the community projects to the rest of society. Hence, any kind of social behaviour that deviates from the norm needs to be addressed and tackled. In this sense, important social issues such as begging, vagrancy, and the problem of child labour exploitation are perceived as major problems that are dealt with within the framework of *italianità*: people presenting borderline behaviour or attitudes labelled as not socially acceptable are not recognised as belonging to the same "imagined Italian community", and are rejected, especially in their being Italian. *L'Italo-Australiano* aims to solve these problems by promoting a campaign against "buskers, and similar riffraff, calling for the collaboration of all honest Italians and for the help of laws against vagrancy".[43]

On a different level, the matter of the relationship with the British part of Australian society is connected, first of all, with the campaigning for Italians to be recognised as a people who are representative of a great civilisation, and thus who rightfully belong to the white European group. Secondly, such recognition, together with the fact that Italians are good workers, should provide sufficient justification for the claimed right of Italians to settle in Australia. The discourse of *L'Italo-Australiano* is intended to reinforce such an approach amongst Italians, as well as to identify and indicate those sectors, within mainstream society, to which Italians may relate. In this regard Anglo Australians appear in the discourse to be the privileged element of interaction. In particular, workers and their representatives are meant to be the main interlocutors, since *L'Italo-Australiano* aspires for the Italian workers to be united and equal to their Australian counterpart.

In moving now to consider the third nucleus of representation, images of Italy that emerge from *L'Italo-Australiano* are defined by choices related to news selection, to the use of symbols and a lexicon of sacredness relating to the *patria*, and to the editor's leanings with regard to central issues in Italian politics—such as the polemical relationship with the aristocracy, the monarchy, and the Church; irredentism; and Sceusa's ambiguous position towards Italian colonialism. Italian foreign affairs are often part of the narrative on the Italian nation, in terms of its relationships with other European countries, as well as in relation to the beginning of an Italian expansionist policy. Moreover, Italian and Australian interests in foreign affairs represent the privileged perspective from which the newspaper looks at the rest of the world.

Representations of *patria* appear, first of all, in relation to the myth of the Risorgimento and to republicanism. These two elements are, in turn, strongly connected with, and through, the mythical (and manly) character of Giuseppe Garibaldi, who is celebrated as Italy's hero and most important founding father. His character incarnates the ideals of freedom, equality, and republicanism that, in *L'Italo-Australiano*, are strongly considered as substantial in defining *italianità*.[44]

In this light, *L'Italo-Australiano* is conceived as a medium through which the Italian community gathers and celebrates the myth of the

Risorgimento and its heroes, as the fundamental factors upon which the idea of *patria* and nationhood is built. The Risorgimento is enhanced as the fulcrum that brings together nationhood, freedom, and civilisation, and as such provides the basis for the gradual building of the political myth of a Greater Italy.[45] This celebration of *italianità* appears to be opposed to, and juxtaposed with, the Australian nationalism.

The representation of the *patria* reflects a specific interpretation of the myth of the nation, which, in the view of Sceusa and his collaborators, is meant to be profoundly secularist. In *L'Italo-Australiano*, nationhood appears to be the only religion of the state, celebrated through rituals such as the commemorations of Garibaldi's death and the breach of Porta Pia: a religion with its saints, the most important of whom is Garibaldi, presented as "our Redeemer" and whose story is depicted in the June issue.[46]

Secularism goes hand in hand with republicanism. In *L'Italo-Australiano*, loathing for the Italian monarchy is perceivable in articles with titles like "Quanto costano le monarchie" and "Quanto costano le repubbliche", in which republican states are compared to monarchies in order to highlight their greater efficiency,[47] or like this correspondence from Rome, in which members of the royal family are depicted humorously:

> At sunset, Queen Margherita, dressed in dark and accompanied by the Marchioness Mortadella of Bologna and by the Princess Panettone of the Earls of Stracchino of Milan, visited the main basilicas, followed by a cheering throng.[48]

In the idea of a united nation carried on throughout the Risorgimento, the "unredeemed" territories of Trento and Trieste were claimed as Italian and, as such, the multilingual and multicultural identities of those regions were not equally acknowledged, as the other nationalities were not considered equally legitimate. Since irredentism has its roots in the myth of Risorgimento and in the concept of nation, it is another factor in the development and evolution of the myth of a Greater Italy, which would reach fuller definition in the period between the Italo-Turkish War (1911–1912) and the First World War.

The irredentist stance is observable in relation to three recurring elements within the discourse: the enhancement of markers of Italianness amongst some of the people within the Austrian empire; the celebration of the martyrs for the irredentist cause; and claims of persecution of Italians in the Habsburg territories. People who live on both sides of the Gulf of Trieste are presented as Italians:

we would not know what to call otherwise people who speak the language of Dante, and do not differentiate physically and morally from those who live on the western part of the Adriatic.[49]

The "Italian" character is emphasised (and differentiated from the other identities and nationalities of the region) also through commemorations of the martyrdom of young irredentists like Guglielmo Oberdan. As well as news from the territory of Trieste being reported in the column "Notizie Italiane", the newspaper tends to represent the Italophone irredentist population in the Austrian territories as victims of Austrian violence: "the crusade of the Austrian police against anything that is Italian continues".[50]

In its very short life, *L'Italo-Australiano* represents the first space for the development within Australia of a narrative produced by, addressed to, and concerning Italians in Australia. Whereas it claimed it would represent the interests of the Italians in that part of the world, its agenda and ideological discourse were in fact the expression of a particular interpretation and understanding of such interests. In this newspaper's narrative are different traits related to *italianità* that would appear again in later Australian Italian-language newspapers. The newspaper attempts to delineate space and characteristics that define a collective Italian identity in Australia. In fact, the evolving myths of the Risorgimento and Greater Italy are the two most visible characters of a growing nationalistic attitude that, while diminishing the internationalist ideals, progressively designates the Italian presence in Australia in terms of relationship with otherness. *Italianità* begins to be defined here through processes of association (with British-Australian workers, as well as with Italians throughout the world) and opposition (by affirming what Italians are not, and who does not belong to the community). Furthermore, these traits in *L'Italo-Australiano* must be considered as product and representation of particular transnational interrelationships that developed within the transcultural field which the newspaper's discourse itself, as a means of reinforcement and propagation of such interrelationships, had contributed to creating.

Transnational spaces—as contexts of cultural interaction and transculturalism—are not homogeneous, as "languages, cultural formations, social practices collide".[51] They can be spaces of conflict and power struggles, because of "the entanglement and co-presence of trajectories and people previously separated by geographical and historical factors" and, as such, they impact on the processes that affect migrants' lives and issues of identity.[52] Hence, moving from the assumption that ethnic-language media play a role in dealing with these issues, it is crucial to analyse the functions Italian-language newspapers had in the processes of collective identification involving the Italian communities in Australia.

The experience of *L'Italo-Australiano*, albeit short, contributed to the development of narratives that have attempted "to make intelligible a sense of belonging"[53] amongst Italians—in relation to the building of collective memories; as such, it may help in investigating the extent to which the ideological discourse of such media has influenced the way in which Italian communities today look at their cultural heritage, at their history and present of migration, and at those of other peoples.

NOTES

1. Gianfranco Cresciani, "'Socialismo per La Generazione Presente': Rifugiati Politici Italiani e Movimento Socialista Australiano" ['Socialism for the Present Generation': Italian Political Refugees and the Australian Socialist Movement], *Italian Historical Society Journal* 20, no. 2012 (2012): 32.
2. "Il Perché" [The whys and wherefores], *L'Italo-Australiano*, 12 January 1885. Unless otherwise noted, all translations are my own.
3. Stuart Hall, "The Work of Representation", in *Representation : Cultural Representations and Signifying Practices* (London: Sage, 1997), 13–69. See also: David Morley and Kuan-Hsing Chen, ed., *Stuart Hall: Critical Dialogues in Cultural Studies* (London: Routledge, 1996), 131–150 and 158–9.
4. Michel Foucault, *The Archaeology of Knowledge*, trans. A. M.Sheridan Smith (London: Routledge, 1969); Michel Foucault, "On the Archaeology of the Sciences: Response to the Epistemology Circle", in *Aesthetics, Method, and Epistemology, Volume 2*, ed. James D. Faubion (New York: New Press, 1998), 302–327; Stuart Hall, "Encoding, Decoding", in *Culture, Media, Language: Working Papers in Cultural Studies, 1972–79*, ed. Stuart Hall, Doothy Hobson, Andrew Lowe and Paul Willis (London: Hutchinson, 1980): 128–138.
5. Benedict R. O'G Anderson, *Imagined Communities: Reflections on the Origin and Spread of Nationalism* (London: Verso, 1991).
6. Suvendrini Perera, "Introduction: Fatal (Con)Junctions", in *Asian & Pacific Inscriptions: Identities, Ethnicities, Nationalities*, ed. Suvendrini Perera (Bundoora, Vic.: Meridian, 1995), 2.
7. Donna Gabaccia, *Italy's Many Diasporas* (London: UCL Press, 2000), 14–34 and 187–191; Donna Gabaccia, "L'Italia fuori d'Italia", in *Storia d'Italia. Annali 24. Migrazioni*, ed. Paola Corti and Matteo Sanfilippo

(Torino: Einaudi, 2009), 225–48; Choate, *Emigrant Nation: The Making of Italy Abroad* (Cambridge, MA: Harvard University Press, 2008).

8. G. L. Buxton, "1870–90", in *A New History of Australia*, ed. Frank Crowley (Melbourne: Heinemann, 1974), 166–174 and 184–207; Caroline Alcorso, "Early Italian Migration and the Construction of European Australia 1788–1939", in *Australia's Italians: Culture and Community in a Changing Society*, ed. Stephen Castles, Caroline Alcorso, Gaetano Rando, and Ellie Vasta (North Sydney: Allen & Unwin, 1992), 1–17; Cresciani, "'Socialismo per La Generazione Presente'": 25–26.

9. Renato Zangheri, *Storia del socialismo italiano. Dalla rivoluzione francese ad Andrea Costa [Volume] 1* (Torino: Giulio Einaudi Editore, 1993), 269–333; Mark I. Choate, *Emigrant Nation*, 154–158; Emilio Gentile, *La Grande Italia: The Myth of the Nation in the Twentieth Century* (Madison, WI: University of Wisconsin Press, 2009), 32–35 and 62–72.

10. T. H. Irving, "1850–70", in *A New History of Australia*, ed. Frank Crowley (Melbourne: Heinemann, 1974), 138–152; Alcorso, "Early Italian Migration and the Construction of European Australia 1788–1939", 3–12; James Jupp, *From White Australia to Woomera The Story of Australian Immigration* (West Nyack, New York: Cambridge University Press, 2002), 5–10; Joseph Pugliese, "Race as Category Crisis: Whiteness and the Topical Assignation of Race", Social Semiotics 12, no. 2 (2002): 149–168, https://doi.org/10.1080/103503302760212078; Ann Curthoys, "Liberalism and Exclusionism: A Prehistory of the White Australia Policy", in *Legacies of White Australia: Race, Culture and Nation*, ed. Laksiri Jayasuriya, Jan Gothard, and David Walker (Crawley: University of Western Australia Press, 2003), 8–32; Francesco Ricatti, *Italians in Australia: History, Memory, Identity*, Palgrave Studies in Migration History (Basingstoke, Hampshire: Palgrave Macmillan, 2018), 53–71.

11. Alcorso, "Early Italian Migration and the Construction of European Australia 1788–1939", 5–9; Tito Cecilia, "Gli italiani in Australia, 1788–1940: una cronistoria", in *Italo-australiani. La popolazione di origine italiana in Australia*, ed. Stephen Castles, Caroline Alcorso, Gaetano Rando, and Ellie Vasta (Torino: Fondazione Giovanni Agnelli, 1992), 35–37; Gianfranco Cresciani, "Italians Discover Australia 1788–1900", in *The Italians in Australia* (Cambridge, UK: Cambridge University Press, 2003), 26–50; Fabio Baggio and Matteo Sanfilippo, "L'emigrazione italiana in Australia", *Studi Emigrazione/Migration Studies* 48, no. 183 (2011): 477–99. For a statistical analysis of Italian migration related to the period considered, see: Charles Archibald Price, *The Method and Statistics of Southern Europeans in Australia* (Canberra: Research School of Social Sciences, Australian National University, 1963), 62–97.

12. Alcorso, "Early Italian Migration and the Construction of European Australia 1788–1939", 4.
13. Ricatti, *Italians in Australia*, 54. On Italian migrants' racial categorisation in different contexts of migration, as well as on the origins of the *internal* racial hierarchisation of Italians, see also: Joseph Pugliese, "Race as Category Crisis: Whiteness and the Topical Assignation of Race"; Aliza S. Wong, *Race and the Nation in Liberal Italy, 1861–1911: Meridionalism, Empire, and Diaspora*, (New York: Palgrave Macmillan, 2006), 47–77; Dewhirst, "Colonising Italians".
14. Australian Bureau of Statistics, "Australian Historical Population Statistics" (cat. no. 3105.0.65.001), 2019, https://www.abs.gov.au/AUSSTATS/abs@.nsf/Lookup/3105.0.65.001Main+Features12016?OpenDocument.
15. Alcorso, "Early Italian Migration and the Construction of European Australia 1788–1939"; Cecilia, "Gli italiani in Australia, 1788–1940: una cronistoria"; Gianfranco Cresciani, "The Italians in Sydney", *Sydney Journal* 1, no. 1 (March 2008).
16. Cresciani, "'Socialismo per La Generazione Presente'": 25–26. On the Anglo-Italian Treaty (1883–1940) see: Catherine Dewhirst, "The Anglo-Italian Treaty. Australia's Imperial Obligations to Italian Migrants, 1883–1940", in *Italy and Australia: An Asymmetrical Relationship*, ed. Gianfranco Cresciani and Bruno Mascitelli (Ballarat, VIC: Connor Court Publishing, 2014), 81–113.
17. "Italians in Sydney. The Chinese of Europe", *The Australian Star*, 8 December 1887. By using the term "wall-eyed celestial", the author refers to Chinese people through a stereotypical and offensive image association (enhanced by the use of the absolutising singular).
18. Curthoys, "Liberalism and Exclusionism".
19. Jupp, *From White Australia to Woomera*, 8.
20. Curthoys, "Liberalism and Exclusionism".
21. "Italians in Sydney", *The Australian Star*, 16 December 1887.
22. "Italians in Sydney", *The Australian Star*, 16 December 1887. About Sceusa's defence of the "Italian race", see also: Francesco Sceusa, *Hail Australia! Morituri Te Salutant!* (Sydney, Jarrett & Co., 1888), https://nla.gov.au/nla.obj-570166992.
23. Salvatore Costanza, *Socialismo, emigrazione e nazionalità tra Italia e Australia* (Trapani: Corrao, 1995); Gianfranco Cresciani, "Sceusa, Francesco (1851–1919)", in Australian Dictionary of Biography (Canberra: National Centre of Biography, Australian National University, 1988), http://adb.anu.edu.au/biography/sceusa-francesco-8351; Cresciani, "'Socialismo per La Generazione Presente'".
24. See for example: "Dall'Australia. Un po' di geografia. Le elezioni e i socialisti" [From Australia. Some geography. The elections and the socialists],

Avanti!, 15 March 1897. The socialist newspaper *Avanti!* was first published in Rome in 1896. For a short biography on these Italian socialist migrants, see: Cresciani, "'Socialismo per La Generazione Presente'": 43–45; Costanza, *Socialismo, emigrazione e nazionalità tra Italia e Australia*, 107–123. On Pietro Munari, see: Ezio Maria Simini, "Un Operaio Agli Antipodi: Pietro Munari, Italiano in Australia", *Altreitalie*, no. 14 (1996): 52–70. On Giuseppe Prampolini, see: Fabio Grassi, "Un socialista tra l'Italia e l'Australia", *Affari Sociali Internazionali* 1, no. 1 (March 1973): 101–14.

25. Costanza, *Socialismo, emigrazione e nazionalità tra Italia e Australia*, 120.

26. Costanza, *Socialismo, emigrazione e nazionalità tra Italia e Australia*, 63–76; Simini, "Un Operaio Agli Antipodi: Pietro Munari, Italiano in Australia".

27. Cresciani, "'Socialismo per La Generazione Presente'".

28. I Figli del Popolo [The sons of the people], *L'Italo-Australiano*, 5 May 1885.

29. "Il Perché", *L'Italo-Australiano*, 12 January 1885. The producers were aware that not all the Italians in Australia approved of the newspaper's approach: "It [*L'Italo-Australiano*] will not be related to any political party, but rather [it will be] the organ of all the Italians in Australia, or at least of the majority of them" ("L'Italo-Australiano", 1 June 1885).

30. "Agli Italiani di Sydney e Australia" [To the Italians in Sydney and Australia], *L'Italo-Australiano*, 12 January 1885.

31. "Il Perché", *L'Italo-Australiano*, 12 January 1885.

32. Joseph Pugliese, "Migrant Heritage in an Indigenous Context: For a Decolonising Migrant Historiography", *Journal of Intercultural Studies* 23, no. 1 (2002): 5–18, https://doi.org/10.1080/07256860220122368.

33. "Il Perché", *L'Italo-Australiano*, 12 January 1885.

34. Pugliese, "Migrant Heritage in an Indigenous Context". On Italians and whiteness, see also: Joseph Pugliese, "Race as Category Crisis: Whiteness and the Topical Assignation of Race"; Ricatti, *Italians in Australia*, 53–59.

35. W. G. McMinn, *Nationalism and Federalism in Australia* (Melbourne: Oxford University Press, 1994), 99–127; Costanza, *Socialismo, emigrazione e nazionalità tra Italia e Australia*, 71–88.

36. "Advance Australia!", *L'Italo-Australiano*, 3 March 1885. The title is in English, but the article is in Italian.

37. "Advance Australia!", *L'Italo-Australiano*, 3 March 1885.

38. "Advance Australia!".

39. Marilyn Lake, "Race and Gender in Australia", in *Gendered Nations: Nationalisms and Gender Order in the Nineteenth Century* (Oxford: Berg, 2000), 159–76; Ann Curthoys, "Disputing National Histories: Some

Recent Australian Debates", *Transforming Cultures Ejournal* 1, no.1 (March 2006): 6–18, https://doi.org/10.5130/tfc.v1i1.187.

40. Ricatti, *Italians in Australia*, 3 and 35–39; see also: Ellie Vasta, "Italian Migrant Women", in *Australia's Italians: Culture and Community in a Changing Society*, 140–54.
41. "Le mine d'oro di Solferino" [Solferino gold mines], *L'Italo-Australiano*, 1 June 1885.
42. "Aurei consigli" [Golden advice], *L'Italo-Australiano*, 1 June 1885.
43. Cose Locali [Local issues], *L'Italo-Australiano*, 1 July 1885.
44. On the myth of Garibaldi, see: Lucy Riall, *Garibaldi: Invention of a Hero* (New Haven: Yale, 2007). On martyr cults and religious symbols and narratives transposed onto secular and nationalistic discourse in nineteenth-century Italy, see: Lucy Riall, "Martyr Cults in Nineteenth-Century Italy", *The Journal of Modern History* 82, no. 2 (2010): 255–287, https://doi.org/10.1086/651534; Alberto Mario Banti, "Deep Images in Nineteenth-Century Nationalist Narrative", *Historein* 8 (2012): 54–62, https://doi.org/10.12681/historein.37.
45. Gentile, *La Grande Italia*.
46. Cose Locali, *L'Italo-Australiano*, 1 May 1885; "V. Garibaldi", I Figli del Popolo, *L'Italo-Australiano*, 1 June 1885.
47. "Quanto costano le monarchie" and "Quanto costano le repubbliche" [How much monarchies cost; How much republics cost], *L'Italo-Australiano*, 1 June 1885.
48. "Our Rome letter", *L'Italo-Australiano*, 1 May 1885. The title is in English, but the article is in Italian. The aristocracy accompanying the Queen is here ridiculed through association with typically rich, northern-Italian food: "mortadella", a smooth-textured pork sausage; "panettone", a kind of spiced cake; and "stracchino", a soft cheese.
49. Cose Locali, *L'Italo-Australiano*, 1 May 1885.
50. "Trieste", Notizie Italiane [Italian news], *L'Italo-Australiano*, 12 January 1885. See also Sceusa's oration at the commemorations for Garibaldi's death, reported in *L'Italo-Australiano*, 6 June 1885.
51. Ilaria Vanni Accarigi, "The Transcultural Edge", *Portal : Journal of Multidisciplinary International Studies* 13, no. 1 (2016): 3, https://doi.org/10.5130/portal.v13i1.4829.
52. Vanni Accarigi, "The Transcultural Edge", 4.
53. Pugliese, "Migrant Heritage in an Indigenous Context", 6.

CHAPTER 4

Australia's Early Russian-Language Press (1912–1919)

Kevin Windle

Russian immigration to Australia began with a trickle at the close of the nineteenth century and accelerated markedly in the years following the failed revolution of 1905, reaching a peak in the three years preceding the outbreak of war in 1914. Writing in June 1914, the Imperial Russian consul in Australia, Alexander Abaza, estimated the total number of Russians resident in Australia at approximately 11,000, the majority in Queensland. He divided them into two groups:

> those who have come with the best of intentions, in the hope of better earnings; these are the great majority; and felons, political criminals and people of extreme socialist views who have fled Russia. This latter group is relatively few in number, but presents a great danger because it consists of comparatively educated people who spare no effort to acquire the greatest possible influence over all our fellow-countrymen who come here.[1]

K. Windle (✉)
School of Literature, Languages and Linguistics, The Australian
National University, Canberra, ACT, Australia
e-mail: Kevin.Windle@anu.edu.au

© The Author(s) 2020
C. Dewhirst, R. Scully (eds.), *The Transnational Voices of
Australia's Migrant and Minority Press*, Palgrave Studies in the
History of the Media,
https://doi.org/10.1007/978-3-030-43639-1_4

61

Some of the "felons" were fugitives from Siberian exile and penal colonies, who numbered about 500.[2] Statistically speaking, such numbers seem barely significant, but one of the more prominent immigrants, the Bolshevik journalist Fedor Sergeeff ("Artem"), claimed in October 1913: "In this town [Brisbane] there are perhaps a hundred of us Russians, but we generate more noise and trouble than ten thousand Englishmen."[3] As for the influence of the "felons" on their more peaceable fellow-countrymen, this was cause for growing official concern as manifestations of radicalism and disaffection became more frequent in the later years of the Great War. Documents from the Queensland Police Department show that Artem and some of his comrades were being monitored as early as January 1914.[4] The malign influence can be seen in action in an unpublished parable-like story by one of the holders of "extreme socialist views", the journalist Alexander Zuzenko, which shows how a Russian immigrant with no interest in politics, exposed to a brutal work environment and the urgings of a persuasive radical (the narrator), is reborn as a "stern-faced, angry proletarian" and provoked to murder a bullying charge-hand.[5]

At different times between 1912 and 1919, the influential "felons" published no fewer than seven weekly or fortnightly Russian newspapers. All were produced in Brisbane, the principal centre of Russian settlement. A small number ran for over two years, but most proved to be of shorter duration. Some were legal and could be distributed through the postal service; some had legal sanction withdrawn; and others never received it. Most are extant today, though few if any in complete runs. In a few cases, no copies appear to have survived in public collections.[6] These newspapers were products of a very particular national group at a time of war and violent social upheaval in Russia. This meant that they tended to be radical in their political orientation, increasingly so as war and revolution took their course, hence their difficulties with the law. The War Precautions Act (WPA) of 1914 delivered the Australian government special powers in many areas, including censorship of publications and mail—both of which constrained the efforts of would-be journalists, especially those in the Russian community. The WPA and its associated regulations would later lead to a ban on the display of the red flag, and thus to the "Red Flag riots" of March 1919, a watershed in the history of Russian radicalism in Australia.[7]

In wartime, the leaders of the community and editors of Russian newspapers were seen as potential subversives, eager to foment sedition. Suspicion of their motives and their loyalties mounted as they spoke out against moves to introduce compulsory conscription and opposed the war effort. All their communications, public statements, and publications were subjected to careful vetting. In November 1917 the Bolsheviks seized power in Russia, and soon, in Zuzenko's words, "The waves of the Russian revolution reached out and shook Australia," bringing increased public antagonism to the Russian community.[8] Animosity reached new heights when the new rulers in Moscow signed a peace treaty with Germany, in effect capitulating to the enemy and freeing German divisions for action in the west. In the face of increasing official harassment and surveillance, a mood of militancy swelled in Australia's Russian community and found expression in its newspapers. The crisis came on 23 March 1919, when the Russian community took the lead in what became known as the Red Flag procession, parading the banned red flag through the centre of Brisbane and calling for social justice and an end to the WPA. A week of serious rioting ensued as large numbers of returned soldiers, with much public support, turned on the Russian Association and its premises, determined to "burn the Bolsheviks out".[9] The riots and their aftermath are reflected in the community's Russian-language press, and indeed contributed to its demise.

This chapter builds on previous accounts of the early days of the Russian community in Australia, making use of recent studies of particular Russian-language newspapers of that period and biographical investigations of some of the community's leaders. Raymond Evans gave his pioneering work the sub-title "A Study of Intolerance", and indeed, the Australia of a century ago was on the whole unwelcoming to ethnic minorities.[10] Louise Ann Curtis has explored the official measures (censorship and surveillance) deployed to combat the "sedition" perceived to be taking hold in the Russian community of the time.[11] While attitudes in twenty-first-century Australia are no longer what they were in 1919, questions concerning free expression and censorship in the "ethnic" press, as in the English-language media, linger and are not amenable to easy resolution.

First Steps: Artem and His Allies, 1912–1917

Australia's first Russian-language newspaper was the weekly *Ekho Avstralii* [*Echo of Australia*] (June–September 1912), produced and edited by Artem, who had arrived in Queensland in 1911, having fled from a penal colony in Siberia. He would leave Australia on hearing of the February revolution in 1917 and achieve renown for his work as a close ally of Lenin in Russia, until his early death in 1921. His *Echo* was the organ of the Union of Russian Emigrants (URE), founded in Brisbane in early January 1911 with the aim of assisting new arrivals from Russia with little knowledge of English.[12] Artem wrote in the issue of 25 July of the mistrust directed at them by Australian workers and the upper classes alike, so that they felt "like hunted wolves in an unfamiliar forest".[13] According to B. S. Elepov and S. A. Paichadze, *Echo* had a print run of 300 copies.[14] Artem, who saw it as his mission to organise the amorphous masses, was responsible for energising the URE as a political force and later renaming it the Union of Russian Workers (URW).[15] His editorial in *Echo* No. 1 stated that the newspaper's purpose was to assist Russian workers in "the crucial matter of successfully selling their labour" and "to protect Russian-speaking workers in Australia".[16] Its general tone was thus made apparent, and official hostility was guaranteed. In September 1912 the Queensland government took legal action and closed it down by court order, as an unregistered newspaper.[17]

Although Artem's loyalties lay firmly with the Bolsheviks, this did not preclude the publication in *Echo* of material by supporters of other political persuasions. The contributors included the free-thinking former Tolstoyan Nikolai Il´in—never a Bolshevik—whose poem in the issue of 23 August 1912 is nonetheless not untypical of the tenor of much material. It concludes with the lines:

> Bards, where are you? // Events do not wait. // Do you really hear only groaning? // The masses are already marching to the sound of the Marseillaise; // and the tyrants' rotten thrones are trembling.[18]

Some 14 months after the demise of *Echo*, on 29 November 1913, a new Russian newspaper, *Izvestiia Soiuza russkikh emigrantov* [*News of the Union of Russian Emigrants*] made its appearance. According to a police report, it was sold for threepence to URE members and in later years contained "pro-German and anti-recruiting articles".[19] Artem was deeply involved, but by no means alone. His collaborators included Pavel Grey, Ivan Grey, Peter Utkin, Ivan Kuk (John Cook), and the poet Sergei Alymov. The leading article in the first issue, signed "P. Grey", painted a dreary picture of the life of Russians in Australia: they are described as isolated, unable to speak English, often far from any fellow-countrymen, able to find only labouring jobs at which they might work ten hours a day, with few diversions beyond cards, drink, and, if they were lucky, the cinema.[20] According to Grey, they led "empty lives of monotony and deathly tedium". Petr Utkin, then Secretary of the URE, developed this theme: the Russians were shunned by local workers and lived "gloomy, sickly, pitiful lives" in hermit-like seclusion.[21] Grey's leading article went on to state the aims of the paper:

> Our newspaper must be dedicated to the interests of the working masses and its line must be revolutionary-socialist, since the majority of the Russian emigrants are undoubtedly in sympathy with that line.

Alymov contributed a suitably stirring poem: "The drums are beating like heralds of death ... We're calling you on to a better life ... Rise up. Do not sleep!"[22]

The newspaper and its successors also encouraged the work of the Australian Society of Aid to Political Prisoners in Russia, which raised funds and forwarded them to a central collection point in Krakow (then part of the Austro-Hungarian Empire).[23] In the early days of the Great War, the newspaper clearly stated its position with regard to that war: it shared the view of the Russian Social Democratic Party, which called "not for agitation in favour of peace, but in favour of civil war against Russian Tsarism and international capital".[24]

Although based in Melbourne (the then-national capital), Consul General Abaza read the newspaper with mounting concern, and in December 1915 wrote to Benjamin Macdonald, the Tsar's honorary consul in Brisbane, urging him to take up the matter with the Queensland authorities. The newspaper, he wrote, was "nothing but a farrago of disloyal and socialistic nonsense".[25] Abaza felt it should "be absolutely suppressed in the interest of the Russian colony itself", and he went on: "You know yourself how uneducated the majority of Russian immigrants to this country are, and consequently how easily they can be led astray by a vile rag of that description." The "vile rag", now renamed *News of the Union of Russian Workers*, was duly suppressed in February 1916, but almost immediately reappeared, with little appreciable difference in content or policy, under a new title: it would now be called *Rabochaia zhizn'* [*The Worker's Life*] and run for a further two years.

The departure of Artem and some of his close collaborators for Russia after the February revolution of 1917 brought changes of personnel. The editorship and secretaryship of the URW passed to Peter Simonoff, who ensured that the content and tone continued with minimal change, lending support to pacifist, trade-unionist, and socialist causes. Simonoff, who often signed as "A. Simens", wrote eloquently against conscription and the Nationalist government of William Morris Hughes.[26]

Despite this, on occasion *The Worker's Life* found support in unexpected quarters. A secret memorandum addressed to the Prime Minister's Department in April 1917 by the founder and head of the Counter Espionage Bureau, George Steward, about the URW and its newspapers, took issue with the views of the Russian Foreign Ministry.[27] The Russian newspaper, which enjoyed "a circulation of about 1200 copies per week", had as its object "merely to convey current news to Russian subjects who are not conversant with the English language". Abaza had written that the URW was "a danger to the community". This was investigated, wrote Steward, and "found to be without any foundation", most likely based on the reports of a highly dubious informant. His accompanying letter stated his emphatic opinion that "up to the present time this Association is not in any respect a menace to the Commonwealth."[28]

Within a matter of months, however, events in Russia would affect the standing of the URW in the wider community and its press would be viewed with less favour. Once again Abaza brought his influence to bear and succeeded in securing the suppression of the newspaper in late 1917 under the War Precautions Act, just at the time when he himself was forced from office by the fall of the Provisional Government.[29]

The closure of *The Worker's Life*, at a time when its readers were eager for news of the momentous events in their homeland, drew protests from some in the Russian community. Alexander Zuzenko, then working in Halifax in north Queensland, sent a telegram to the state premier on 2 January 1918, making plain his view and that of his comrades.[30] Zuzenko's deficient English skills conspire with the telegraphic medium to undermine intelligibility, but there can be no doubt that the writer and his constituency felt strongly about the matter and earnestly wished to see their newspaper replaced:

> Only sole Russian newspaper in Australia workers life printed in Brisbane is suppressed on account not having Russian censor. We group our russian workers laboring Halifax district in number of 36 men come all together on meeting 1 jan in Halifax carried resolution of protest against violence action biggest majority of ours cannot speak and read English only from our labor newspaper workers life we can get the news printed in russian many of ours going after few months back to russia it is not to good if they take away from

this country lost believing of freedom of Australia and turn over understanding of suitableness labour government for workers we asking your permission again on free will printing ours newspaper.

As for "not having Russian censor", the writer was mistaken: the censor's office could and did monitor the contents, and was even more vigilant when replacements eventually arose.

The Press and Revolution: Simonoff, Zuzenko, Klushin, 1917–1918

From December 1917, for a period of five months, Australia's Russian population had no newspaper in its own language. However, in the early months of 1918, plans took shape to inaugurate a new newspaper to replace the defunct *Worker's Life*. The initiative came from the last editor of that newspaper, Simonoff, who was no longer in a position to hold office in the URW or to edit a newspaper owing to his elevation to the office of consul representing the Bolshevik regime in Australia.[31]

Znanie i edinenie (*Knowledge and Unity*) made its debut in the last week of May 1918, under the editorship of Nikolai Lagutin. The military authorities responsible for censorship of the press noted that:

> proofs were submitted and censored. The editor has exercised reasonable care in the selection of matter and, although portions were disallowed, the general tone of the issue was such as to convey the impression that the lesson taught by the suppression of the Worker's Life had not been forgotten.[32]

Perhaps for that reason Simonoff was sorely disappointed with its quality, and admonished Lagutin in no uncertain terms:

> Frankly speaking I am astounded. What devil made you print all that rubbish? ... You know yourself for whom the paper is intended – for the workers, who are not uncompromisingly behind the Bolsheviks. Explain the ideals and aims of the Bolsheviks and attack those of their opponents. ... Remember that what you publish must be in the form of accounts of current events and articles on current events – not historical matter.[33]

On reading this, the censor commented that Simonoff appeared to "overlook the fact that the local Censorship has a Russian Interpreter".[34] However, in August 1918 the secretaryship and editorship passed to

Zuzenko, who had been at odds with Lagutin and had objected to the "mutilation" of his contributions.[35] When Zuzenko was at the helm, Simonoff showed more understanding of the limits on his freedom of action: to a comrade in Mount Cuthbert he wrote, "Zuzenko is now secretary and will probably manage affairs better than Lagutin, ... but it is impossible to expect too much from the paper, as the censorship cuts it unmercifully."[36]

While Lagutin was preparing to publish *Knowledge and Unity*, a rival body had broken away from the URW and was planning a newspaper of its own. This was the "Group of Russian Workers" (GRW), a faction which arose shortly after Simonoff's appointment to the office of consul, and whose *raison d'être* was to oppose that appointment. The GRW was headed by the intellectual Konstantin Klushin (also known as Orloff). Its secretary for a brief period was the sailor Herman Bykoff (also known as A. Rezanoff), but before any publishing plans could be brought to fruition, Bykoff had parted company with Klushin and left the GRW. In addition to the censor's records, we have Bykoff to thank for insights into personal and political relations within the community. His extravagantly farcical play, "How We are Learning Self-Management and Control", written in early 1919,[37] lampoons his comrades in both the URW and GRW, and offers quotations or near-quotations from their writings, with footnotes to authenticate them. Thus, when Rip-the-Sails (Zuzenko, in his anarchist persona) utters surprising self-discrediting statements, the playwright inserts a supporting footnote: "article by A. Z-ko-M-ko, in *Knowledge and Unity* No. 16, also *Ninth Wave*."[38]

The leaders of the GRW took care to consult the censor's office before launching their own organ on 23 June 1918, under the title *Listok Gruppy rossiiskikh rabochikh* (hereafter *Listok*), with a parallel title in English: *The Paper of the Russian Group of Workers*. Its content, mostly written by the editor, Klushin, shows that he viewed it as a platform from which to pillory Simonoff as one with little understanding of Bolshevism, and to argue that he was ill-suited to his consular post. At the same time, Klushin castigated the URW as a body which denied its members freedom of speech and thought, imposing unity at the expense of individual rights and personal autonomy.[39] *Listok* was not destined for a long life, principally because the parent body, the GRW, went into swift decline. Bykoff had defected even before the publication of the first issue. Others followed, and before long there was talk of reunification with the URW, while Simonoff remained in his consular post—still unrecognised by the Australian and British governments.[40]

Knowledge and Unity, under Zuzenko's editorship, outlived *Listok*. Since no copies have survived, our limited knowledge of it derives from Bykoff's writings and references and quotations in intercepted correspondence. The censor followed its contents assiduously and disallowed some of them, while acknowledging that Zuzenko was "a very fine article writer".[41] In November 1918, Zuzenko, under the pseudonym Matulichenko, was expressing frustration at the limits imposed. In *Knowledge and Unity* No. 20 (27 November 1918), he wrote: "Of course we are not allowed to write about the war or socialism or anarchy or to translate anything from the *Worker* or the *Standard*," and elsewhere complained that "twelve columns, more than half the paper" were cut from No. 15.[42] Many contributions would have alarmed the censor: "Petruchino" (actually V. Petruchenia) is quoted as writing, "The revolutionary Russian worker has shown how to conduct the fight … What has been done by the Bolsheviks in Russia will be done here and everywhere else."[43] Zuzenko also used the newspaper to promote his idea of federating Russian groups throughout Australia in a unified body, and thus boosting the influence of the socialist Russian community in the country at large.[44]

It is clear that, despite the restrictions imposed by the censor, the primary audience of *Knowledge and Unity* received it with enthusiasm. Readers wrote to Zuzenko to voice their support. W. Tweed (V. Tyutin/Tiutin) of Mourilyan, for example, so admired Zuzenko's "magnificent" article entitled "The Ninth Wave" that he produced an English version which he sought to publish.[45] In September 1918, Zuzenko and Simonoff were both barred from publishing and speaking in public, but this did not bring the closure of *Knowledge and Unity*, which was, we may presume, among the intended results. Zuzenko's fiancée Civa Rosenberg took it over—in name only. In reality, all editorial work remained firmly in Zuzenko's hands. The disguise did not deceive the censor or the authorities: passages such as the following, marking the Armistice of 11 November, were plainly Zuzenko's work:

> Peace has been declared, so do not sleep, brothers … It is time to get ready …They have been trying all the time to publish false rumours about Bolshevism and … the most gallant of men, Lenin and Trotsky. Why should we be living here imprisoned in Australia? We are all brothers fighting one enemy "Capitalism". We are fighting for liberty and for the red flag.[46]

Sentiments such as this, no doubt, inclined the authorities to proscribe the newspaper with all speed. In December, it was closed down by government order. Zuzenko, however, was not to be easily silenced.

LAST GASP: ZUZENKO, BYKOFF, 1919

Knowledge and Unity reappeared at the end of December 1918, but no longer in Russian; from this point on it would be in English. The censor, perhaps caught off guard by this development, let pass some rousing calls to arms—such as "THE OBJECTIVE IS THE COMPLETE ABOLITION OF THE CAPITALIST SYSTEM"—over the signature of Civa Rosenberg.[47] In reality the author and editor was Zuzenko, who would marry Rosenberg in February 1919.[48] The disturbances of March 1919 and subsequent arrests marked the end of their involvement with the newspaper, which passed into the hands of the Social Democratic League.

However, even before the ban on the Russian *Knowledge and Unity*, Zuzenko—ever energetic and combative—had been hard at work preparing a new paper in Russian. It would appear on 23 December 1918, with the title *Deviaty val* [*Ninth Wave*] and run for only four issues, none of which appears to have survived. Fragments of its contents can be seen in the intercepted correspondence and the censor's notes.[49] Sergeant A. M. Short of the Commonwealth Police, aided by his interpreter, Leo Berke (or Berk), reported its first issue and cited the masthead, "Unofficial newspaper by editor Cane Mamena" (i.e., Sanya Mamin, one of Zuzenko's pseudonyms).[50] The leading article, in prose characteristic of "Mamin", set the truculent tone:

> The editor is put in prison, in his place steps another person and continues the work, viz: – the publication of the illegal Russian paper – this has begun. Carry on! Friends, the last battle, the battle against evil has begun. Capital and power are smashed every week. They are mortally wounded and in the agony of death they are biting and infecting themselves with their own poison.[51]

The first issue of *The Ninth Wave* caused indignation when the editor identified "traitors" in the Russian community. Berke, a returned soldier and opponent of the revolutionaries, named in No. 1, made clear to Sergeant Short that he feared for his safety. Klushin too found himself accused of being an *agent provocateur*—a claim which he termed a "pack of lies", while an ally wrote of "deliberate falsehood" by "Mamin".[52]

Nevertheless, *The Ninth Wave* found an eager readership in some quarters. From Ingham, in the Queensland cane fields, G. Bolotnikoff wrote to Zuzenko to report that issue No. 1 was "read by every Russian here".[53] He was particularly interested in a speech by Lenin, reproduced in the newspaper, and expressed the view that Australia would soon experience "a strong thunder-storm of revolution". The censor treated such communications with all seriousness, noting "the power a newspaper has in the bush", where "the Russian is dangerous" and "lack of any other diversion gives him an attentive audience".

From the correspondence it is clear that Bykoff, who had by now rejoined the URW, was collaborating with Zuzenko on *The Ninth Wave*, but their differences plainly made for serious complications. Bolotnikoff's enquiry about Lenin and his policies received a lengthy reply not from Zuzenko but from "Arov" (Bykoff), who set out to clarify some matters of ideology, pointing out that Zuzenko had "got a proper dressing down" for writing about Lenin without the knowledge of the URW.[54]

Bykoff's participation notwithstanding, *The Ninth Wave* remained very much Zuzenko's personal mouthpiece, if not megaphone, but while he might have liked to see it replace *Knowledge and Unity* as the organ of the URW, he found himself out of step with his comrades and failed to attract wider support. Bykoff, despite the evidence of his collaboration, wrote in a postscript to his unpublished article "Russian Australia":

> I criticized *The Ninth Wave* for failing to reflect the ideas of Soviet Russia, and the Union voted by an overwhelming majority to refuse material support for a newspaper which did not express the views of a majority in the Union.[55]

After four issues, by mid-February, *The Ninth Wave* had gone the way of its predecessors, having faced numerous difficulties, including funding and the seizure of its type.[56] In March came the Red Flag demonstration and riots, the events which would bring the URW to national prominence, call forth a frenzy of anti-Russian feeling in the broader population, bring the returned soldiers out in force, and have irreversible consequences for the participants and their publishing ventures.

In early 1919, while drafting "Russian Australia" and the play "Self-Management", Bykoff was also making plans for a new newspaper, *Fakel* (*The Torch*). His intention, he makes clear, was to gain permission to publish legally, and the draft materials state that this would be a "strictly non-party" newspaper, in which a variety of opinions could be expressed. "Our modest aim", he wrote:

> is to point out to our comrades the need for knowledge as a pre-condition for mutual understanding and unification on principles of workers' solidarity and labour co-operation.[57]

In a draft of a leading article for No. 1, he wrote that the Soviets in Russia admitted:

> Bolsheviks and Mensheviks, Right SRs and Left Maximalists, anarchist-communists, social evolutionists, and even Plekhanovites and Leninists etc., i.e. all who recognise the Soviet state authority of the toiling people.[58]

He lodged an application for permission in early March, anticipating no difficulty, even stating in a letter, that "permission is granted already." The censor's notes point out that this is incorrect.[59] The paper was never launched.

Nabat [*The Tocsin*], the last Russian newspaper of this turbulent period, published by "The Group of Communists, Brisbane"—and described in its first leader as "our small illegal newspaper"—had the shortest life. There were two issues: the first dated 6 August 1919, the second undated but evidently from late September. No. 1 achieved limited circulation; No. 2 was prepared but may never have gone to press.[60] The main theme is the Red Flag procession of 23 March and its aftermath, the delayed response no doubt due to the difficulties in which the editors found themselves. The leading participants (the editors) had little time at liberty between the riots and their deportation. In fact much of the writing must have been done in prison. Both issues present a kind of post mortem, carrying a full account of the event and news of the subsequent arrests and deportations. Its contributions are unsigned or have bylines like "Red Demon", "Red Hedgehog", "A Russian Worker", but the content and phrasing clearly identify Bykoff and Zuzenko as the principal authors and editors, and some participation by Lagutin cannot be ruled out.[61] The reports and commentary admit that the URW has suffered a defeat: a brave "handful of Russian workers" was unable to hold out against the prevailing forces of ignorant reaction. The writers appeal for unity and solidarity against British cultural arrogance and conceit, and for renewed efforts to rouse the local workers from their apathetic torpor. One of the few signed contributions is Zuzenko's valedictory letter (No. 2, September 1919), posted when the ship carrying him to Egypt called at Hobart.[62] He urges his fellow-countrymen to continue the struggle and not lose heart.

The second and last issue of *The Tocsin* closes with a series of defiant slogans: "Long Live the Social Revolution", "Long live the Russian Socialist Soviet Republic", "LONG LIVE THE SOVIETS!"

By late 1919 the Russian-language press in Australia had become more militant than in earlier years, and at the same time less accessible to its readers. Since the closure of the Russian-language *Knowledge and Unity* in December 1918, they had had *The Ninth Wave* until February, and two issues of *The Tocsin*. Both were illegal, and able to reach few readers; indeed, *The Tocsin* No. 2 (September 1919) may have reached none at all. With *Knowledge and Unity* now in English only, readers with limited English had no newspaper to follow, and the deportation or departure of the most active journalists in the community meant that there would be no replacement.

The community's press, viewed collectively, makes one thing abundantly clear: the revolutions in Russia, eagerly awaited by many, had not brought unity of purpose. The censor gloated in January 1919: "The harmony which extreme Socialism was supposed to bring is further away than ever."[63] And, indeed, one is struck by the deepening discord among the leading figures, in their newspapers as elsewhere. All welcomed the end of Tsardom, and many liked to think of themselves as Bolsheviks, but the "Bolshevik consul" had to contend with opponents like Klushin, quick to find evidence that he was no Bolshevik. In turn, Bykoff would quote Klushin to prove that he (Klushin) espoused principles alien to those of the new leadership in Moscow. Bykoff presented himself as a true Bolshevik among impostors, but some of his Utopian statements about the Soviets allowing all groups and parties to be represented seem in retrospect to show an uncertain grasp of developments in Russia. As Dmitrii Volkogonov has reminded us, it was not long before the slogan "All power to the Soviets" had been replaced by "All power to the Bolshevik Party", or, as Mikhail Tomsky is reputed to have put it in 1922: "We have many parties, but unlike foreign countries, we have one party in power, and the others in jail."[64] Of Zuzenko, Bykoff claimed that his "expostulations … plainly show that he has not grasped the meaning of the revolution which has taken place in Russia."[65] Indeed Zuzenko continued to declare himself an anarchist and seemed ambivalent in his attitude to Bolshevism, embracing the revolution, but at moments fiercely denouncing its leaders. He would later write that he finally abjured his anarchist past only in 1920, when he heard Lenin and Trotsky speak at the All-Russian Congress of Trade Unions in Moscow.[66]

Given the distance and the state of communications with Russia at the time, it is perhaps not surprising that what Bykoff in *The Tocsin* called "the glorious social revolution"[67] was open to such varied interpretations— including some which would soon appear jejune—and the root of much dissension. One signal event in Brisbane, however, made allies of antagonists and rivals: Zuzenko and Bykoff joined forces to lead the Red Flag procession, and supported each other in the aftermath. *The Tocsin* clearly shows the two working in harmony. Bykoff and Klushin found themselves thrown together in the cells of Darlinghurst Detention Barracks, Sydney's military prison, and deported, with others, in September 1919.

Many in the Russian community were also united in their wish to return to Soviet Russia. To them, deportation was not an unwelcome outcome. They had wished to return earlier but the opportunity was denied them, hence Simonoff's many representations as consul on their behalf. The Russian press and intercepted correspondence often reflect this heartfelt wish. Bykoff had written in an editorial for *The Torch*, "sooner or later we will return there",[68] and many saw themselves as "prisoners" in an alien land.

With Zuzenko, Bykoff, and Klushin deported, the heyday of the radical Russian press was over. *Knowledge and Unity* had already changed its language, and thus its readership. Simonoff issued his magazine *Soviet Russia*, also in English, for an Australian readership. Of those involved in the production of Russian newspapers in Australia, as far as is known, only Zuzenko continued to ply the trade of journalist in later life: in Moscow in 1923–1924, he wrote for *Na vakhte* [*On Watch*] and occasionally *Gudok* [*The Whistle*]; in the USA for *Novoe russkoe slovo* [*New Russian Word*], and later the newspaper of the Baltic Shipping Line, with which he sailed as master mariner until Stalin's Great Purge ended his life in 1938.[69] Bykoff's literary gifts were also employed in the service of the Soviet Communist Party, in occasional articles on the history of the labour movement. Sergei Alymov, whose verse had once graced the pages of Artem's earliest newspapers, would become known to millions in the USSR as the lyricist responsible for some forgettable propaganda ditties, but did not escape a term in a labour camp on the White Sea, which led him to contribute to a celebrated volume in praise of Stalin's White Sea Canal and secure early release.

In Australia, the Russian community itself would soon undergo far-reaching change. The revolution would bring a new cohort of immigrants, fleeing not from Tsarist oppression, but the far harsher Bolshevik regime. Later Russian newspapers published in Australia would reflect this very different orientation, almost exclusively anti-Bolshevik. Such an orientation was of course unexceptionable to Australian governments, and the question of suppression did not arise. A century on from the deportation of Zuzenko and Bykoff, in a country which prides itself on "embracing diversity" and encouraging the use of many languages in the press and other media, much has changed. Yet the issue of press censorship and the handling of extremist publications, when these provide a platform for "hate speech" and incitement to violence, are unlikely to go away soon.

NOTES

1. Abaza to Bentkovskii, June 13, 1914, in Alexander Massov, Marina Pollard and Kevin Windle, ed., *A New Rival State? Australia in Tsarist Diplomatic Communications* (Canberra: ANU, 2018), 316. Abaza cites a total of 12,000 Russians in Australia and New Zealand, with 1000 in New Zealand.
2. Ibid.
3. Artem (Sergeev, F.A.). *Stat'i, rechi, pis'ma* [Articles, Speeches and Letters] (Moscow: Izdatel'stvo politicheskoi literatury, 1983), 126.
4. Criminal Investigation Branch to Commissioner of Police, January 5, 1914. Queensland State Archives (QSA): A/45328 ID318868.
5. Zuzenko, Alexander, "Zakon klyka i dubiny" [The Law of the Fang and the Cudgel], no date. University of Queensland, Fryer Library, Poole-Fried Collection, 336, Box 8, Folder 10. In English in Kevin Windle, "Murder at Mt Cuthbert: A Russian Revolutionary Describes Queensland Life in 1915–1919," *AUMLA*, 110 (2008): 53–71.
6. This chapter is based on primary sources to the extent that this is possible, resorting where they are unavailable to secondary sources.
7. Raymond Evans, *The Red Flag Riots: A Study of Intolerance* (St Lucia: University of Queensland Press, 1988); Kevin Windle, *Undesirable: Captain Zuzenko and the Workers of Australia and the World* (Melbourne: Australian Scholarly Publishing, 2012).
8. Windle, "Murder at Mt Cuthbert," 67.
9. *Daily Standard*, "Their Way. Riotous Ex Soldiers. Revolt against the Law," March 25, 1919, p. 5.
10. Evans, *The Red Flag Riots*.
11. Louise Ann Curtis, "Red Criminals: Censorship, surveillance and suppression of the radical Russian community in Brisbane during World War I," Doctor of Philosophy thesis, Griffith University, 2010.

12. Criminal Investigation Branch to Commissioner of Police, June 12, 1911. Queensland State Archives (QSA): 14812 ID86529.

13. *Ekho Avstralii*, July 25, 1912, quoted in A.I. Savchenko, "Bol'sheviki i rossiiskaia trudovaia emigratsiia v Avstralii 1907–1917 gg." [The Bolsheviks and the Russian Workers' Community in Australia 1907–1917]. In *Nauchnaia konferentsiia po izucheniiu Avstralii i Okeanii, 19-aia: tezisy dokladov* [Nineteenth Scholarly Conference on Australia and Oceania: Abstracts] (Moscow: Nauka, 1988), 158.

14. B. S. Elepov and S. A. Paichadze, *Geopoliticheskii kharakter rasprostraneniia russkoi knigi: k postanovke voprosa* [The Geo-political nature of the Dissemination of Russian Books: towards a framing of the question] (Novosibirsk: GPNTB SO RAN, 2001), 56.

15. The Russian titles *Soiuz russkikh emigrantov* and *Soiuz rossiiskikh rabochikh*, when translated, lose a significant distinction: *russkii* = ethnically Russian; *rossiiskii* = pertaining to the Russian state, having citizenship, but not necessarily of Russian ethnicity.

16. Aleksandr Savchenko, "Pervye russkie gazety v Avstralii," [The First Russian Newspapers in Australia] *Avstraliada*, 15 (1998): 12.

17. Curtis, "Red Criminals," 44, 106.

18. N. Il'in, *Ekho Avstralii*, August 23, 1912, p. 2. In another contribution, Il'in impugned his erstwhile mentor Tolstoi and his pacifist principle of non-resistance to evil. N. Il'in, "Neprotivlenie pered sudom vyshnim," [Non-resistance before the highest court] *Ekho Avstralii*, July 18, 1912, pp. 2–3.

19. Sergeant O'Hara to Commissioner, Queensland Police, February 12, 1916. QSA: A/45329 ID317879.

20. P. Grei, *Izvestiia SRE*, November 29, 1913, p. 1.

21. Petr Utkin, "K russkim ot russkoi organizatsii," *Izvestiia SRE*, November 29, 1913, pp. 3–4.

22. Sergei Alymov, "Pesn' barabanov" [The Song of the Drums], *Izvestiia SRE*, November 29, 1913, p. 4.

23. A. M. Chernenko, *Rossiiskaia revoliutsionnaia emigratsiia v Avstralii (1900–1917 gg.)* [The Russian Revolutionary Emigration in Australia (1900-1917)], (Dnepropetrovsk: Dnepropetrovsk State University, 1978), 32–34.

24. P. Simonov, "Russkii rabochii i voina," [The Russian Worker and the War], *Izvestiia SRE*, February 4, 1915, p. 1.

25. Abaza to Macdonald, December 7, 1915, QSA: A/45329 ID317879

26. For example, P. Simonoff, "Konskripshen i Giuz," [Conscription and Hughes], *Rabochaia zhizn'*, December 5, 1917, p. 3.

27. On Steward's career see Chris Cunneen, "Steward, Sir George Charles Thomas (1865–1920)", *Australian Dictionary of Biography* (Canberra:

National Centre of Biography, Australian National University, 1990) http://adb.anu.edu.au/biography/steward-sir-george-charles-thomas-8657 (accessed November 20, 2019).

28. Steward to Secretary, PM's Department, April 24, 1917, Suspected Persons – Russians. NAA: A1606 A35/1.

29. See Chernenko, *Rossiiskaia revoliutsionnaia emigratsiia*, 57; Curtis, "Red Criminals," 44.

30. Soosenko to Prime Minister of Queensland, January 2, 1918. QSA: ID 862638, PRE/A578.

31. On Simonoff's stormy career as unrecognised consul of the unrecognised Soviet state, see Kevin Windle, "Trotskii's Consul: Peter Simonoff's account of his years as Soviet representative in Australia (1918–1921)," *Slavonic and East European Review* 93 (2015): 493–524; idem, "Pervyi konsul Sovetskoi Rossii v Avstralii P. F. Simonov i ego druz′ia i nedrugi" [The First Soviet Russian Consul in Australia: P. F. Simonov, his friends and foes] 114, *Klio*, No. 6 (2016): 176–188; and Iurii Artemov, *Russkaia revoliutsiia v Avstralii i seti shpionazha* [The Russian Revolution in Australia and Espionage Networks] (St Petersburg: Aleteiia, 2017).

32. Censor's Notes, Week ending May 29, 1918, QF1073. NAA: A6286 1/29.

33. Simonoff to Lagutin, July 18, 1918, QF1469. NAA: A6286 1/46.

34. Censor's Notes, Simonoff to Lagutin, July 18, 1918, QF1469. NAA: A6286 1/46.

35. Zuzenko to Simonoff, August 8, 1918, QF1701. NAA: A6286 1/58. The censor observed that all involved were "agitators of the worst type" "spreading the poison amongst their fellow workers".

36. Simonoff to Zaremba, September 10, 1918, QF1861. NAA: A6286 1/62.

37. "O tom, kak my uchimsia samoupravleniiu i kontroliu" [How We are Learning Self-Management and Control]. NAA: BP4/1, 66/4/2165. See Kevin Windle, "Unmajestic Bombast: The Brisbane Union of Russian Workers as Shown in a 1919 Play," *Australian Slavonic and East European Studies* 19 (2005): 29–51.

38. "O tom," 5. NAA: BP4/1, 66/4/2165. A. Z-ko = Alexander Zuzenko; M-ko = Matulichenko, one of Zuzenko's several aliases.

39. For more detail on *Listok*, see Kevin Windle, "*Listok Gruppy rossiiskih rabochikh*: a 1918 Brisbane Russian Newspaper," *Australian Slavonic and East European Studies* 32 (2018): 52–78.

40. See Windle, *Undesirable*, 38-39; and Windle, "Trotsky's Consul".

41. Tweed to Zuzenko, Censor's Notes, October 19, 1918, QF2274. NAA: A6286 1/76. See also censor's notes to Galch[enko] to Zuzenko, August 5, 1918, QF1540: "Zuzenko is a scholar and spoken of as a ready writer." NAA: A6286 1/50.

42. Matulichenko, Week ending November 27, 1918, QF2441, NAA: A6286 1/81; Zuzenko to Tyutin, September 29, 1918, QF2019, NAA: A6286 1/68. The text and the censor's notes do not specify which material was permitted and which was expunged.
43. Intelligence Report, 1st Military District (December 11, 1918), QF2538. NAA: A6286 1/86.
44. Article signed by Zuzenko, week ended October 2, 1918, QF1963. NAA: A6286 1/66.
45. Tweed to Zuzenko, Censor's Notes, October 19, 1918, QF2274. NAA: A6286 1/76.
46. *Knowledge and Unity*, November 12, 1918, quoted in Raymond Evans, "Agitation, Ceaseless Agitation," in *Russia and the Fifth Continent: Aspects of Russian-Australian Relations* ed. John McNair and Thomas Poole (St Lucia: University of Queensland Press, 1988), 144.
47. Civa Rosenberg, "To Our Australian Comrades," *Knowledge and Unity*, December 31, 1918, p. 2
48. See Windle, *Undesirable*, 51–54.
49. The title *The Ninth Wave* comes from a Russian saying which describes the ninth wave as the most powerful and destructive.
50. Sgt Short to Commissioner, December 26, 1918. NAA: BP4/1 66/4/1817.
51. C. Kalinin, January 10, 1919, Censor's notes, QF2941. NAA: A6286 1/100.
52. Ibid.
53. Bolotnikoff to Zuzenko, March 6, 1919, QF3368. NAA: MP95/1/0.
54. Arov to Bolotnikoff, March 11, 1919, QF3408. NAA: A6286 1/114.
55. "Rus´ avstraliiskaia, iz zapisnoi knizhki 'trampera'," vii, NAA: BP4/1, 66/4/2165. For an English version, see Kevin Windle, "Hades or Eden? Herman Bykoff's *Russian Australia*," *Australian Slavonic and East European Studies* 26 (2012): 24; also Kevin Windle, "A Crude Orgy of Drunken Violence," *Labour History* 99 (2010): 167.
56. Gamanoff to Cherbakoff, March 2, 1919, MF2628. NAA: A6286 3/96.
57. "Peredovitsa" [Editorial], 2, NAA: BP4/1 66/4/2165.
58. "Nashi zadachi" [Our Tasks], 5. NAA: BP4/1 66/4/2165.
59. Soviet of Souse to Gooseff, March 6, 1919. NAA: A6286 1/112.
60. The typescript materials for No. 2 are held in the Central State Museum of Modern Russian History, Moscow (1913/Biu 313-12A).
61. For fuller treatment of *Nabat*, see Kevin Windle, "Nabat and its Editors," *Australian Slavonic and East European Studies* 21 (2007): 143–164; Windle, "Crude Orgy," and Windle, "An Anarchist's Farewell," *Australian Slavonic and East European Studies* 30 (2016): 87–112.

62. "Pis'mo t. Zuzenko" [Letter from Comrade Zuzenko], *Nabat*, [September 1919], p. 11.
63. Censor's notes, Simonoff to Robertson, January 23, 1919, QF2951. NAA: A6286 1/100.
64. Dmitrii Volkogonov, *Lenin: A new biography*, trans. Harold Shukman (New York: Free Press, 1994), 82; Boris Bazhanov, "Pobeg iz nochi." *Kontinent*, 8 (1976), 264.
65. "Rus' avstraliiskaia," xi; Windle, "Hades or Eden," 23.
66. See Windle, *Undesirable*, 91–92.
67. "Razgrom S.R.R." (The Crushing of the URW) *Nabat*, [September 1919], p. 4; Windle, "Crude Orgy," 176.
68. "Peredovitsa," NAA: BP4/1 66/4/2165.
69. See Windle, *Undesirable*.

CHAPTER 5

Respectability and Disloyalty: The Competing Obligations of *L'Italiano*'s Editors

Catherine Dewhirst

On 10 May 1940, as part of a wartime precautionary response, Australia's military officials identified the names of specific migrants for internment, including 1135 Italians and naturalised Italian-born British subjects.[1] Notwithstanding the detention of some hundreds of those of enemy-state origins (who were considered a serious threat to national security at the outbreak of the Second World War, nine months earlier), the May contingency list reflected similar fears. News ricocheted across the Dominions that British intelligence suspected Hitler's victories over Denmark, Belgium, and the Netherlands were due to Axis saboteurs—the "Fifth Column"—and that internments had begun.[2] Public opinion about the widespread activity of fifth columnists in Australia contributed as much to

C. Dewhirst (✉)
University of Southern Queensland, Toowoomba, QLD, Australia
e-mail: catherine.dewhirst@usq.edu.au

© The Author(s) 2020
C. Dewhirst, R. Scully (eds.), *The Transnational Voices of Australia's Migrant and Minority Press*, Palgrave Studies in the History of the Media,
https://doi.org/10.1007/978-3-030-43639-1_5

the Commonwealth government's response, as did the measures already in place to prohibit the liberties of sectors of the population under the National Security (Aliens Control) Regulations of 1939.[3] On 11 June 1940, the day after Mussolini declared war on Britain and France, the Regulations resulted in police raids on the businesses and homes of enemy aliens and foreign-born British subjects, and the internment of those on the May list for the defence and public safety of the nation.

Queensland police began a series of raids, including at the premises of the Italian migrant newspaper business, *L'Italiano* (1930–1941), in Brisbane where they seized official documents, correspondence, and copies of the newspaper's weekly editions.[4] They then arrived at the home of the editor, Cristofaro Albanese (1903–?), taking his personal papers and some belongings. A second raid on Albanese's home occurred three months later on 25 September 1940, resulting in his arrest for internment and Albanese's predecessor, Cesare Baucia (1892–1957), was "capture[d]" and interned on 14 April 1942 (two months after the fall of Singapore and the growing fear of a Japanese invasion).[5] Although the police confiscated a further "23 packages" from the newspaper's director, Australian-born Norman Morris Colless (1898–1952) in June 1942, the Commonwealth Security Service in Canberra began taking a more serious interest in *L'Italiano* a year later. Director-General of Security W. B. Simpson requested Queensland's Security Service to produce reports on the confiscated evidence.

There was some hesitation from Brisbane. J. M. Jones, the interpreter, seemingly required a minimum of four months to examine the large body of material, including 900 other individual cases, before compiling a full report.[6] But the Director-General was only interested in documents relating to *L'Italiano* because the newspaper had "received correspondence from, [*sic*] all parts of the Commonwealth [...]. This would apply particularly to interstate matter as 'L'ITALIANO' had a wide circulation."[7] In his short report on 7 of the 23 packages, Mr Jones named 33 Italian migrant men living across the 3 eastern states as implicated in a suspected Fascist ring, including Baucia and Albanese; advising the Director-General:

> there is a possibility that letters written at a time when the Fascists [1939–1940] were showing themselves in their true colours and were definitely anti-British, may yield some information of interest. [...] Extracts from some of the material already examined could with profit be added to

individual files. These letters [to the editor] from among the mass of correspondence so far examined are the only ones that call for attention.[8]

It appears that his advice was ignored, but the Director-General instead requested the files of one of the men mentioned in the report: Melbourne-based commercial agent Cavaliere Gualtiero Vaccari, who was partly responsible for expanding the sales of *L'Italiano* from Queensland to New South Wales and Victoria.[9]

Such attention by the Commonwealth authorities was to be expected, given the regulations to control propaganda under the Act of 1939 by prohibiting enemy-alien newspapers.[10] The view by 1942 was that Italians could not be trusted: officials and the general public believed that they represented a ready "workforce", especially in Queensland (due to their higher population and density), and would quickly mobilise to follow the orders of an occupying regime and overturn democracy.[11] Gianfranco Cresciani describes the views in official records and letters sent in by members of the public as "rampant paranoia" from such descriptions as "the [volatile] Italian temperament", the "subversive talk" of Italian-speaking groups in public, the "deep and cunning" and "oily" individuals, and their "raucous voices", "standing in rings all up the street".[12] The image of a threat to public order and the choice of discriminatory wording with racial overtones (evoking an early version of today's "hate speech") suggest the motivations of personal grudges and business competition, rather than good citizenship.[13] Indeed, from her investigation of internment policy and its impact, Kay Saunders found that enemy-alien groups were targeted on the basis of their "ethnic origin", not "political ideology or religious affiliation"; much of the anti-foreigner discourse also having more to do with ethnicity than ideology.[14]

Copies of *L'Italiano* did not survive the war, which explains the minimal scholarly attention it has received.[15] Yet, from the oral histories he conducted in the 1950s, W. D. Borrie describes it as one of "the two most important [Italian-language newspapers]" in Queensland.[16] The second newspaper his informants spoke of was the *Italo-Australian* (1922–1940) in Sydney, but there was a third in Melbourne, *Il Giornale Italiano* (1932–1942). Since the 1980s' public access to official archival files, Cresciani's analysis qualifies the latter as "the major channel of Fascist propaganda", but notes that both the *Italo-Australian* and *L'Italiano* were also pro-Fascist.[17] What made many Italian migrants receptive to Fascism, he states, was the combination of racial tensions with their exclusion from mainstream politics and an "inferiority complex".[18] Fascism offered an alternative means for support in this context, funding public events—often infused with nostalgic connections to the homeland—to promote membership. Italian migrant clubs, associations, and newspapers thus became "subsidiary societies" to the Fascist cause, which insidiously directed "political and social behavior".[19] At a time when Fascism had a degree of acceptance over the more threatening socialist and anarchist groups, the Australian government showed itself amenable to the Italian Consulate's requests about obstructing anti-Fascist newspapers; the government banned *Il Risveglio* (1927), *L'Avanguardia Libertaria* (1930–1932), and *La Riscossa* (1929–1931).[20] David Brown goes somewhat further, placing the "widely read" *L'Italiano* within a socio-political landscape of fractured Italian communities throughout Queensland—they were torn between Fascism and anti-Fascism.[21] However, he cautions against interpreting Italians' support for Fascism on the basis of class, arguing that Italians worked in with Fascism "for a variety of reasons", which mirrored the social order within their communities.[22] Both Cresciani and Brown agree that financial reasons lured Italians to Fascism more than political belief.[23]

This chapter explores how the two editors of *L'Italiano*, which was launched as a non-political and non-sectarian newspaper, attempted to navigate economic and ideological forces to serve their Italian-Australian readership. They, like other Italian migrants, found themselves in a paradoxical position, wedged between a deep sense of respectability and loyalty (as family and ethnic community members and workers) and the constant reminders from mainstream society and the Italian Consulate of scorn and disloyalty (via racial stereotyping and political threat). From a migrant perspective, "respectability" can be understood as forming part of *sistemazione*—the process of adjusting family, home, and work within a new society—while "loyalty" speaks more to the reputation of good citizenship, which was brought into question by Australian and Italian officials. The binary between respectability and disloyalty reflects a process operating across nation-building and through the interplay of ethnicity and race, which was exacerbated for Italians by both Italian Fascism and the climate of war.

Rarely do we gain insight into the daily workings of a newspaper business beyond the information in its broadsheets. However, Baucia's and Albanese's life stories and voices come through in the business letters they wrote, the responses they received, copies and drafts of the newspaper's articles, and the investigations conducted for their internment from their official wartime files. *L'Italiano*'s case reveals how wider economic and political tensions imposed on business competition and contributed to intra-community relations.

COMPROMISING COMMUNITY INTERESTS

Central to any migrant newspaper in Australia are the constructs of ethnicity and race. Ethnic group identity and racial ideologies emerged in the context of Western colonisation, imperialism, and the nineteenth-century global migrations. Overall, an estimated 20 million people left Italy after unification in 1861 and up to the end of the interwar years.[24] Australia's population was always minute in comparison with the larger transoceanic settler societies. According to the 1933 census, out of a population of 6,629,839, there were 17,658 Italians living in Australia, although the figure of 26,756, based on shipping records, suggests a substantial flow of temporary settlers.[25] By contrast, in 1930 the United States had a population of 822,658 Italians.[26] The Italian migrant press emerged spontaneously in Australia, as it had around the world, out of a need to provide individuals with basic information, news from the homeland, the world, and the new society, and a sense of community in the face of local difficulties. However, the nationalising of Italians abroad formed part of Italy's foreign affairs agenda from the 1890s and specifically in the early twentieth century when the Emigration Law of 1901, which established the Emigration Commission (1901–1928) and the Italian Colonial Institute (1906–1927), came into effect. In other words, Italy turned its commercial and political attention to cultivating ties with Italian migrant associations and newspaper enterprises as part of its dual colonial programme; that is, colonising African states and Italian diasporic networks.[27] Mussolini's regime was to continue this trend.

Australia's Italian migrant communities may be best understood from developments in the United States' immigration history where a national identity, tied to republicanism, asserted a level of exclusive power. Here, the dominant group of white Anglo-Saxon Protestants defined the nation's non-Indigenous and non-Black cultural "others" as "foreigners"; they were *ethnic* immigrants, unequal to the "special peoplehood".[28] According to Kathleen Niels Conzen, David Gerber, Ewa Morawska, George Pozzetta, and Rudolph Vecoli, a restrictive meaning of nationality developed over time, differentiating the "mainstream" from the "sidestream ethnoculture", including a "process of negation" between these two sectors, but amongst the migrant minority groups as well.[29] At the same time ethnicity underwent reinventions and renegotiations with the result that minority communities began assimilating somewhat, yet also asserted their ethnicity as a counterpoint to being negatively categorised.[30] The fact that the "melting pot" of the American peoplehood included growing ethnic groups problematised the national ideal. Eduardo Bonilla-Silva's theory of "racialized social systems" further helps to explain how inequality operated structurally across ideological, political, economic, and social layers.[31] As he explains, when differences of "subordination and superordination" qualify a society's social relations and include a discourse of race, ideological and structural racism converge.[32]

Racial antagonism against Italians was expressed in Australia from the 1890s up to the First World War, and it re-emerged over the 1920s and 1930s.[33] This is clear from a sense of panic that officials and the general public expressed in the 1920s over Australia being flooded by thousands of Italians and other Southern Europeans when the United States passed immigration restrictions on "undesirable" Southern Europeans in 1921 and 1924. Much of the Australian public reacted by pointing to the inferior status of non-British migrants, who it was believed would threaten jobs and moral standards.[34] As the international crisis loomed over the 1930s, there was little tolerance for ethnic differences.

It is interesting to note that, prior to 1935, Mussolini was lauded in the Australian press, not because of his Fascist government but for his leadership in having saved Italy from a perceived worse fate.[35] This seems to have given many Italian migrants a false sense of pride which newspaper editors used to attack prejudice and discrimination. Nevertheless, Fascist propaganda—already active through the Italian consular corps and some prominent leaders of both the Italian and Australian communities since the mid-1920s—attracted those seeking advancement within their communities.[36] While many Italians were cajoled into joining the local *Fasci all'estero* (Fascist branches abroad) by the allure of socialising and celebrating non-political cultural events, Italian businessmen were prepared to tolerate the emergent political ideology for the sake of gaining commercial contacts and opportunities.[37] The structure of the *fasci* also facilitated notions of respectability and worthiness, which was particularly important due to the residue of anti-Italian hostility over the 1920s and 1930s. But Italy's invasion of Abyssinia in 1935 gave rise to further aggression in Europe and had implications for the diaspora. By this time, Fascism represented a competing national ideology because it had already infiltrated the Italian migrant communities.

Of the 34 Italian migrant newspapers printed over Australia's history since 1885, there were eight active in the 1930s, only three of which managed to survive the outbreak of the war, albeit briefly. In Sydney, the *Italo-Australian* followed a liberal approach but embraced Fascism once the *Fasci all'estero* had become established in the country. The *fasci* first sprang up before Mussolini's March on Rome but only became part of the regime's foreign and emigration policies a year after Mussolini dissolved the Emigration Commission and replaced it with the General Bureau of Italians Abroad on 28 April 1927.[38] From this time, Italy's consular and other officials began promoting the *fasci* throughout the Italian-Australian communities for membership growth, sometimes threatening the loss of business if Italians did not join.[39] The first *fascio* was established in Melbourne in 1926.[40] Four years later Norman Morris Colless launched *L'Italiano*, providing Queensland's Italians with their own newspaper.[41] *L'Italiano* initially gained a reputation for being anti-Fascist under the editorship of Baucia until he resigned at the end of 1935, but it became classified as pro-Fascist when Albanese took over soon after. It is not therefore surprising that the respective editors of these three newspapers, former editors, and the directors of the *Italo-Australian* and *Il Giornale Italiano* were interned.

L'ITALIANO'S ANTI-FASCIST REPUTATION

Cesare Baucia was born in Alessandria, Piedmont, and migrated to Australia in 1924. He headed to Ingham's sugarcane fields for work, returning to Brisbane six months later to run a restaurant and he took up other jobs, including at T. C. Beirnes Department Store. He naturalised in 1930 after securing the position of editor for *L'Italiano*, becoming a Justice of the Peace (JP) the following year. However, Baucia's internment initially had more to do with *Il Giornale Italiano*. After resigning as editor of *L'Italiano* five years later, he joined his wife, Ida Dadesso Baucia, in Melbourne for their daughter, Magda, to attend university, and he found work in the electrical trade. He was soon offered a position as advertising representative for *Il Giornale Italiano* in Queensland, which he took and returned to Brisbane, leaving his wife and daughter in Melbourne. Once Australia entered the war, he resigned from the newspaper, but he came to the attention of the Commonwealth government because he unwittingly offered his services to the Australian Military's censorship as an Italian interpreter or to work with Intelligence.[42] It was not only his activities in Queensland during his employment with *Il Giornale Italiano* that made him suspicious. A case was then constructed about his former role as editor for *L'Italiano*.

Amongst the official concerns contributing to the case against Baucia was a list of circumstantial evidence noting him as having been "actively engaged in the interests of various Fascist organisations and activities".[43] Having fought in the First World War back in Italy, he had joined Australia's Italian National Association of Ex-soldiers as well as the Italian Chamber of Commerce. As investigations show, he had also attended a number of Brisbane *facio* events, including a luncheon in Townsville for Consul-General Amedeo Mammalella in 1939 with six high-ranking officials.[44] The new editor of *L'Italiano*, Cristofaro Albanese, had been present as well, with both representing their employers, respectively. Furthermore, Baucia had been the organiser of a ceremony and gift for Archbishop James Duhig (an Italian white marble fountain, a replica of one of Andrea del Verrochio's famous Renaissance masterpieces) on behalf of Italian migrants for defending them in the Australian press. Most of these activities were linked to his employment with *Il Giornale Italiano*. However, the many telegrams and letters in his possession, dating back to his time as editor of *L'Italiano*, also attested his knowledge of pro-Italian activities, including letters from the well-known anti-Fascist and Communist, Constante Danesi, a cane-cutter and chef from Innisfail, which the Queensland Security Service interpreter commented on:

> The letters show a fairly close friendship existed between the two men, although Danesi's views were definitely anti-Fascist whereas Baucia through his many associations with leading Fascists was probably a sympathiser of Fascism.

And, Baucia and his family were close friends with the secretary of the Brisbane *fascio*, Dr Giovanni Battaglia, and his wife.[45] "It is difficult to believe", the interpreter commented, that Baucia "could have served faithfully such a violently pro-Fascist paper as 'Il Giornale Italiano' over a period of 3 or 4 years without having become a convert to Fascism".

Baucia's file includes copies of some of Battaglia's regular letters to the *Italo-Australian* and *Il Giornale Italiano* (and by implication *L'Italiano*) for publication about Brisbane's *fascio*'s news. In 1932 Battaglia reported on the combined national celebrations for the March on Rome (28 October), Italian Day and the King's birthday (4 November), and National Unity and Armed Forces day (20 November), held as a picnic at Bishop Island.[46] This report reveals how Fascism capitalised on memories and love of the homeland for a major propaganda exercise. Drawing together a large number of Brisbane's Italian families and some Australians, everyone was given a small "tricoloured cockade" badge for the boat trip after which, it was reported, the singing began. Battaglia describes the effect on the passengers:

> It was truly moving to see the Italians of Brisbane, united together for the first time in the same boat, with the same aim and the same flame in their hearts: The Motherland! To study that psychological moment in the faces of the Italians was truly interesting. What the music of the national hymns [*sic*] aroused in some was like the voice of the blood awakened after a long lethargy, in other faces was profound emotion even to the extent of tears, in others extreme joy, and in others the sign of the sweet nostalgic sadness like a memory of maternal lullabies, or of an ancient hearth with the vision of native mountains. As remarked by an old resident [...] 'never were there so many Italians together or so much enthusiasm'.[47]

Combining ethnic culture with national identity in the ambience of a crowd may have softened some to the fascist ideology (there was no mention of vehement anti-Fascists disrupting the day as there had been at other times), but this picnic represents the classic display of invention. As Eric Hobsbawm explains, the threefold workings of invented traditions rely on "social cohesion" or "membership" (national origins and migrant status), the parameters of "legitimizing institutions" or "authority" (the Italian Consulate and the *Fasci*), and shared "beliefs, value systems and conventions of behavior" (ethnicity).[48] It was from such questionable connections that Baucia would be interned.

In preparing to arrest Baucia in 1942, officials believed that there was no question about his fifth columnist potential. One report describes him as a clear suspect: "[l]iving in poor circumstances, owing to sending money to Italy for many years. Student of various philosophies. Type of man who would be used by Battaglia and Quaglia to do the spadework for the Fascio".[49] Another points to the threat of his associates: "his past association and activities and his alleged connection with an organisation spreading pro-German propaganda amongst the foreign community in Brisbane, he is regarded as a definite menace to the interests of National Security."[50] The claim that he was promoting Nazi Germany was something more serious:

> Reliable information brands BAUCIA as a definite Fascist one who is definitely disloyal to this country and who never loses an opportunity to spread the propaganda among other Italians less capable of judging for themselves, that Hitler cannot eventually fail to win the War, and that they must accordingly fit themselves for a victorious conclusion.[51]

A political cartoon accompanies the documents in Baucia's file, titled the "Prix de la tolérance/Preis der Toleranz/The price of tolerance", reminiscent of the late nineteenth-century anti-Semitic discourse and an essential component of the Nazis' anti-Jewish propaganda (see Fig. 5.1).

The cartoon (of unknown origin) pictures a vulnerable Britannia—half-naked, sexualised, and unconscious if not blind—being crucified, in this case on a Jewish Star of David, with the caricature of a rabbi holding an enlarged yad, from which spring flails, representing ideas. One of the ideas on the flails, "cinema press", helps to locate the image in the era of the 1920s and 1930s. The artist highlights the first line of the Hebrew script in the Torah itself, "dumißt", which in German (*du misst*) may translate as "you give up on".[52] The origins of the image are potentially British, directed to those living in France, Germany, but mainly Britain—given the English words flowing from the yad as if to warn of a Jewish conspiracy funding the dismantling of democracy and British values, if not also the Empire, were people to be "tolerant" of such ideas. This was a malicious attempt to discredit Baucia, potentially passed onto the government by an informant to support the pro-German accusations made about him. Whatever its origins and source, its effect was damning and likewise warned the viewer of how "tolerance" of nine seemingly Jewish concepts would be sufficient to overthrow civilisation.

The only evidence linking the cartoon to Baucia is a report repeating sentiments in which he was understood to have been "a member of a pro-German organisation which is engaged in spreading pro-German propaganda among the foreign community in Brisbane".[53] The German organisation remains nameless, but seven other Italians who met at various inner-city Brisbane cafés were also implicated.[54] In the investigation, Sergeant Harrison remarked that "two thoroughly reliable naturalised

Fig. 5.1 "Pris de Tolérance/Preiz de Toleranz/The price of tolerance". Baucia, Cesare - Queensland investigation case file", National Archives of Australia. NAA, BP242/1, Q25546. Courtesy of the National Archives of Australia

Italians" supplied this information. It is unusual for an informant to be named in internment records, but Silvio Marchisotti was one of the two who told police that he had been associating with the eight men deliberately in order to gain "information relative to subversiveness, which might be of benefit to Australia".[55] According to Marchisotti, these were men of some influence in the community and the ringleaders were Igino Costa and Cesare Baucia.

Little is known about Baucia's work at *Il Giornale Italiano*, but he had been very dissatisfied during his time as editor for *L'Italiano* due to his strained relations with the owner, Norman Morris Colless. Behind the scenes of the newspaper's daily operation, Baucia complained that he had been given little autonomy to do his job and that his writing was compromised. After resigning in 1935, he wrote to the Italian Royal Consulate General:

> I have the pleasure in finally being able to inform you that to my great joy I have left "L'Italiano" of Brisbane, and have finished with being dependent on an Australian who, only because he paid me, claimed my complete sub-

mission. A while ago I wrote to [Consul-General] Com. VITALI about the matter. When I was with L'Italiano I had to write what the owner ordered me to; now I am glad to be free and to be able, like all the others, to speak my own words. Precisely for this I decided to leave the employment and I have suffered rather than continue to be the servant of exploiters and false friends.[56]

No Italian editor, particularly a naturalised British subject, was bound to report to the Consul-General about employment matters, but this letter indicates that Baucia had already sought advice about his predicament, and possibly his rights, from an authority he trusted. As Baucia explained more clearly to his associate and friend Constante Danesi, he "was tired of supporting an ignorant, egotistical and lying master, who, although receiving a great benefit from the Italians, has never done anything for them, but has always thought of his own pocket as he does at present".[57]

Baucia's relations with Colless suggest there were other agendas at play. Indeed, Cresciani states that, "if a newspaper was totally subservient to the consular political dictates, it was rewarded with a subsidy."[58] *Il Giornale Italiano*, alone, received £500 per annum from the Italian Consulate. In writing to Colless after Baucia had resigned, Danesi drew Colless's attention to one of Danesi's own articles, printed in 1933, on Italo Balbo's flight from the United States, in which he had included some criticism against Fascism from the *Manchester Guardian*.[59] This article had prompted the Consul-General to withdraw the Italian Navigation Company's regular advertisement and, consequently, marked *L'Italiano* as another anti-Fascist newspaper. Danesi attempted to make Colless understand that Italians were not interested in Fascist politics: "Is it true or not that the 'Italiano' although it states on its front page that it is nonpolitical and nonsectarian etc. carries on a philo-fascist policy and propaganda? is it true or not that many of the readers of the Italiano not pay?" By this time, Albanese had already begun to steer the newspaper towards compliance with the Fascist line. But Danesi also rhetorically asked Colless: "Is it true or not that Mr. Baucia was sent away from the paper, because he loved democracy too much, through the pressure of the followers of Lojola [*sic*], and [was] replaced with one of their recommendations?" Raimondo Rajola was a family relative of Albanese.

Fascist Influence over Business Competition

Cristofaro Albanese was born in Torre del Greco, Naples, in 1903 and emigrated to Australia in 1925 with qualifications in business and languages.[60] He arrived in Melbourne, where he worked initially in the Italian Consulate before moving to Sydney for an administrative job for Raimondo Rajola, also from Torre del Greco. He travelled to Fiji in 1926 to work in his uncle G. Rajola's jewellery business, returning to Sydney a year later. He then went back to Italy for seven months over 1929–1930, where he and Rosalia d'Aniello possibly became engaged, but he returned to Sydney to continue work with Rajola until he took on the editorship of L'Italiano in 1935. Rosalia arrived in Brisbane two years later, having married Albanese by proxy.[61] By the time he had applied for naturalisation in 1939 (signed by Colless, JP)—granted in 1940—the couple had two boys under the age of three, Francesco and Salvatore, and on Cristofaro's internment, Rosalia was five-months' pregnant with their third son, Carlo.

Albanese appears to have been central to L'Italiano's increasing business to the extent that, once interned, one of the newspaper's executive members, Mr Abercrombie, met with a major of the Northern Command on behalf of Colless to seek Albanese's release on bond. When told that this was not possible, he asked "whether facilities could be granted to Albanese to write articles and do the work of preparing matter for publication" in L'Italiano whilst interned:

> there was no man in Australia capable of replacing him. [...] The work called for a man of high scholastic attainments as well as that intimate knowledge of the psychology of Italians which could only be found in one of their compatriots. [... because] their readers were very critical.[62]

The Northern Command refused. Yet, as correspondence in Albanese's internment records suggests, he wrote brilliantly, had a knack for securing subscriptions, and dealt efficiently with those interested in the newspaper and any detractors.

The case against Albanese's suspected Fascist loyalties is surprisingly not simple. Although he had taken a conciliatory approach to Fascism well before the outbreak of war, there were conflicting views about his politics. One inspector wrote:

Albanese is of opportunist type and has had left-wing political associations but was never trusted by these bodies owing to membership of the Fascist Party. On 8th August [1939], Albanese was interviewed at the office and stated that he had been a member of the Fascio but now renounced all convictions and proposed applying for naturalisation. He then gave certain information regarding Fascist activities in North Queensland, which partly confirmed previous advice.[63]

In his appeal hearing, Albanese said he had become a member of the Fascist Party in Italy but only for a few months and did not consider himself a Fascist.[64] He even admitted having joined the March on Rome, and boasting about this to Melbourne's Consul, but telling the tribunal he had abandoned the march a few days later, not reaching Rome. And, from a summary investigative note in his file, another view was:

Is at present editor of the Italian paper, published in Brisbane, "L'Italiano", which is definitely non-Communist, and owned by Colless family, who believe Albanese to be a Fascist, or at least non-political. Reliable information in the North shows that Albanese, although posing as a Fascist, is the central figure of Northern Communists. Shrewd, cunning, and entirely untrustworthy. Extremely anti-British and uses his Fascist connections in this direction being friendly with prominent churchmen.[65]

This contradictory report is better understood from the perspective of the central anti-Fascist figure in North Queensland, Constante Danesi, whose influence across the Italian migrant communities was extensive.

Danesi felt that *L'Italiano* had changed substantially under Albanese, writing to Baucia in 1938: "I dreamed of a different 'Italiano', of a paper independent of Fascist Consular Authorities, that would continue along the lines on which you had established it—that is a fusion of Italian and Australian elements. [...] In what hands has the paper fallen after so much labour! The present Editor has a subtle, hypocritical and filthy Fascist policy."[66] Danesi's regular updates from Queensland's northern Italian communities were often printed in *L'Italiano* whilst Baucia was editor but seem to have conflicted with Albanese. In one of Danesi's articles—focussed on criticising the anti-Italian tactics of Queensland's Premier Forgan Smith (on which Albanese agreed)—he also commented on how Fascism had emerged in Italy. The article went to print with a scolding remark from Albanese that Danesi's "dictatorial attitude in asking for the publication of his writings is completely out of place".[67] As he clarified,

L'Italiano could "publish any letter or article whatever written by readers, provided that the writers have not the sole purpose of insulting in a senseless fashion, this or that regime or any individual, be he leader of a government or a workman".

However, Albanese went further in his reproach against Danesi's article in the same edition, making an example of him to the reading public (and Consul-General): "Sig. Danesi is right in asserting that Fascism was a consequence of the war, but he should have added that if Italian Socialism had been a national party (like British Labour) instead of an international party, Italy today would not have Fascism but Socialism. And this, being national, would be called National Socialism; in a word, exactly that which exists in Germany and which is an almost exact copy of Fascism."[68] For Danesi, this deliberate "malicious criticism" showed how Albanese "has wished to mystify my writing by not dealing with the true spirit or content of what I had written".[69] While this tension reveals Albanese's anti-Socialist views, it also suggests the threat Danesi posed, symbolising the wider division across the Italian migrant communities.

Albanese addressed the implications of his editorial approach in his appeal hearing for release from internment. *Il Giornale Italiano* was "an opposition paper", he explained, whose director and editorial team classified *L'Italiano* as anti-Fascist, but he had worked hard to alter this view:

> I have been called an anti-Fascist, and anti-Communist and God knows what. They tried to put the Italian Consul against me personally and the paper and to a great extent they succeeded. I tried, just for the paper, just for the sake of business – personally I did not care a scrap, to become friends with the Consul. […] It is business. My boss is an Australian. I told him it was for the sake of business. Those fellows tried to make the Consul believe everything and I had to put my own story.

The "story" Albanese told was one of transforming *L'Italiano*'s reputation. To be considered anti-Fascist meant financial penalties whereas taking a conciliatory stance to Fascism could enable the Brisbane-based business to compete against the Sydney and Melbourne newspapers for subscriptions and consular subsidies. When Colless asked Albanese to "tone it down" in one of his draft articles, Albanese cited up to 80 per cent of Italians in North Queensland as being Fascist or sympathetic to Fascism (a figure that had been fabricated and based on the views of a man called Zamboni):

it is quite evident that the fascist policy cannot be a drawback in the race for the acquisition of as many [subscriptions] as possible. [...] I am afraid I cannot "tone it down a bit" unless I want to lose the little bit of sympathy we enjoy among fascist people. [...] the true fact is that if the paper is condemned by those most fascist gentlemen [Consul, Consul-General] the inevitable result would be that the majority of Italians would not read "L'Italiano" fearing to be classified as antifascists, and hope of ever going [b]ack to Italy.[70]

L'Italiano attracted two Melbourne-based Italians, Francesco Pisano and Gualtiero Vaccari, who would assist Albanese in increasing its readership and sales to buffer *Il Giornale Italiano*'s dominant position. Their correspondence with Albanese helps to unravel why he cultivated ties with Fascism.

In 1937 Colless and Albanese received a proposal from Francesco Pisano, who had been working for *Il Giornale Italiano* as a sales representative but had recently resigned after being poorly treated. Pisano offered to promote *L'Italiano* beyond Queensland. This would become a mutually beneficial relationship, which allowed *L'Italiano* to expand, increase subscriptions, and begin to print a supply of news about Melbourne for the southern Italian communities. However, in responding to a letter from Pisano, Albanese clarified upfront that *L'Italiano* "is not a paper with political objectives, it does not intend to convert anyone to one or other political creed; but it will be noticed that it strives within the limits of possibility to clear the fog produced by the anti-Italian propaganda assiduously conducted by a great part of the Australian press".[71] It is important to understand this stance in terms of the fact that the two men did not know each other well, in addition to the context of the geopolitical tensions. The newspaper had nevertheless begun to court the Consul-General and Italians in Melbourne and Sydney. Albanese defined it as 100 per cent Italian, explaining to Pisano: "although not being actually Fascist, [I] took part among the Black Shirts who marched on Rome [...] a thing that I do not think can be affirmed by many others who don the Black Shirt only for opportunism." He later remarked to Consul-General Mammalella that this kind of "opportunism" was "political hypocrisy". Since Melbourne, like Sydney, had a greater number of *fascio* members than Queensland, as Brown points out, *L'Italiano* needed to deflect its anti-Fascist reputation for economic reasons.

Pisano opened another door for increasing *L'Italiano*'s business from Melbourne in 1938, this time by reaching into the Italian Catholic network of Father Ugo Modotti—whom he described as "a Jesuit in blood and bone"—to convince him of the value of the Queensland newspaper as "the most honest of the journalistic body of Australia..., quite the reverse of the criminals who direct the Giornale Italiano".[72] Approaching Modotti had been Gualtiero Vaccari's idea and the next step was to pay the priest a visit in order "to get him to engage in propaganda in his visits to his flock". A Fascist and ardent supporter of the Melbourne newspaper, Modotti was not interested in *L'Italiano*, particularly because he had recently glanced at one of its articles (Danesi's, in fact) and felt it was "far away from Church and from God" for its condemnation of Mussolini and the regime. Albanese (himself Jesuit trained) wrote to Modotti immediately to convince him otherwise, and using the art of persuasion presented himself as a true Fascist. He outlined his Catholic and Fascist credentials, explained that he had not joined the *fascio* because "I was disgusted by the fact that certain compatriots were Fascist and Masons at the same time" and "I thought that my participation in the Fascio in this country would not be of any benefit either to the Motherland or to myself."[73] He also explained how he approached Danesi, telling the priest: "I have done enough in the last two years to maintain that the Italians of North Queensland, an old seat of antifascism, have largely changed their opinions of both political and religious character." Then, referring to the Induction and Extreme Oath of the Jesuits and Danesi, he wrote:

> You know that there are circumstances in life when the end justifies the means, when to convert sinners it is necessary to frequent even taverns and places of sin, [...] when speaking of my own case, in order to convert an antifascist it is advisable to give him liberty of speech only to reply to him and so to show him that his thoughts are based on false reasoning.

He ended with a confession of his own "pride and arrogance" and asked for "pardon". Perhaps it was these efforts—of Pisano and Albanese—in courting Modotti's goodwill about shifting the perception that *L'Italiano* was a communist and anti-Catholic newspaper, but two years later, Vaccari wrote to Albanese that Modotti had begun vacillating from *Il Giornale Italiano*.[74]

In early 1940, during the critical countdown months before the raid on his home and his internment, Albanese heard from Vaccari. They had in fact already worked together at some stage, possibly when Albanese had first arrived in Melbourne. Vaccari's interest was in increasing *L'Italiano*'s sales in both Sydney and Melbourne by establishing "collaborators" (correspondents) to include a column dedicated to the news of "local events" in these cities.[75] Albanese explained that a former correspondent for Sydney only lasted a few months there because *era stato consigliato di non aver nulla a che fare con un giornale antifascista* ["he was advised never to have anything to do with an 'antifascist' newspaper"].[76] As such, *il povero Pisano fu varie volte messo alla porta da certi grossi calibri del fascismo locale* ["poor Pisano was shown the door various times by certain big shots of the local Fascism"].

Letters between Vaccari and Albanese focus on attracting the Melbourne readership of Modotti's parishioners and beyond for which, Vaccari noted, any news on Communism "definitely needed to be omitted [...] as to retain the direction favourable to Fascism which is pursued in your paper".[77] Vaccari remarked that "[a]t least nine tenths of our countrymen are not enrolled with the Fascist movement but are not opposed to it" and he wondered "to what extent Fascism may be favoured [in *L'Italiano*] without entirely renouncing our non-political principle".[78] In his reply, Albanese expressed concern that *L'Italiano* "should not give the authorities the right of defining it anti-fascist" and argued that "it is certainly possible to criticise individuals, or rather their actions, even if they are Fascists, but certainly it is not possible to criticise them because they are Fascists".[79] As with Pisano, Albanese outlined the newspaper's policy for the arrangement of a correspondent:

> This attitude of criticism on our part (or, at least that of our correspondent) must not necessarily mean our (or his) total adherence to the Fascist dogmas. We accept these as a maxim only when it appears to us that their absolutism may be justified by possible benefit of our people. All of which means that we intend to obey reasonably or relatively but not absolutely. And it means also, in practical terms, that we shall remain faithful to our non-political principles by avoiding the publication of material of an exclusively propagandist character.

By April, Vaccari reported that *L'Italiano* was now attracting a positive interest from the Consulate.[80] Still, there would be no subsidy for *L'Italiano*; it was sapped up by the *Italo-Australian* and *Il Giornale Italiano*.

A migrant newspaper can never tell the whole story of the communities it reaches. Through a reading Albanese's appeal hearing and business correspondence—limited also in their own way—it becomes apparent that he was a talented and ambitious businessman, the type of editor Colless was looking for. Through the efforts of a family member he quickly secured the job of *L'Italiano*'s second editor after Baucia left. The timing coincided with increasing Fascist propaganda, which led to a conciliatory approach for the sake of sales, given the competition for consular subsidies from the Italian migrant newspapers in Sydney and Melbourne, and later for potentially expanding *L'Italiano*'s readership into the southern states. From his correspondence with Pisano and Vaccari, Albanese clearly cared less about Fascist politics than business expansion, but he knew how to play along with the Fascists. Fascism was a "means to an end" for mutual benefits. Although constrained by a difficult relationship with Colless, Baucia's files show his tendency to give sufficient space to the Communist and anti-Fascist Danesi of North Queensland, where he himself had once worked. And, while Baucia's editorship coincided with the era before Mussolini's imperialist direction became widely known, gaining work with *Il Giornale Italiano* cast him as doubly suspicious. From the perspective of the Australian government and military officials, internment would dismantle the danger posed by both men, if not a suspected Fascist ring. There was never a Fifth Column, but similar effects of cultural, ideological, and structural racism persist today as shown in more recent reports on migrants and asylum seekers.[81] Yet the effect in the early 1940s underscored beliefs about the disloyalty of an ethnic minority population seeking respectability.

In the end, Cesare Baucia was released from internment in 1943 after ten months of incarceration, with a comment on his records stating: "Whilst in camp, he acted as a camp leader and his conduct in organising and controlling all the internees in his camp, was excellent. ...he showed anti-Fascist sentiments."[82] Cristofaro Albanese's situation was more complex because his wife and children were also interned and located in a separate camp. When the family was released in 1944, after three and a half years for Albanese, Rosalia was not recognised as an "alien" to be able to access the ration coupons for her family because her husband had naturalised; nor was she able to receive an identity card because Albanese's naturalisation documents had been revoked.[83] Exploring the life stories and voices of 2 of the 33 men listed in interpreter J. M. Jones's report on *L'Italiano* reveals how the newspaper's original apolitical, non-sectarian aims were compromised by attempts to balance competing business demands in a context of international crisis, and the tension between respectability and disloyalty within both Italian migrant communities and Australian society.

NOTES

1. Gianfranco Cresciani, *Fascism, Anti-Fascism and Italians in Australia, 1922–1945* (Canberra: Australian National University Press, 1980), 85; Gerardo Papalia, 'The Italian "Fifth Column" in Australia: Fascist Propaganda, Italian-Australians and Internment', *Australian Journal of Politics and History* 66, no. 2 (2020): 229–231.
2. Margaret Bevege, *Behind Barbed Wire: Internment in Australia during World War II* (St Lucia, Qld: University of Queensland Press, 1993), 51–53; Gianfranco Cresciani, "The Bogey of the Italian Fifth Column", in *Italians in Australia: Historical and Social Perspectives*, ed. Michael Arrighi and Gaetano Rando (Wollongong, NSW: Department of Modern Languages, University of Wollongong, Dante Alighieri Society, 1993), 68.
3. See: Paul Hasluck, *The Government and the People, 1942–1945. Volume I* (Canberra: Australian War Memorial, 1970a), 138; Paul Hasluck, *The Government and the People, 1942–1945. Volume II* (Canberra: Australian War Memorial, 1970b), 121.
4. Letter, Albanese to the Deputy Director of Security (Queensland), September 7, 1945, in "Cristofaro [or Christopher] ALBANESE and wife Rosalia", National Archives of Australia (NAA): BP242/1, Q16961. [All translations are from contemporary official interpreters unless otherwise noted.]
5. "Prisoner of War/Internee: Albanese, Cristofaro; Date of birth—06 November 1903; Nationality—Italian", NAA: MP1103/1, PWQ7298; "Prisoner of War/Internee; Baucia, Cesare; Year of birth—1892; Nationality—Italian nbs", NAA: MP1103/2, Q8759.
6. Letter, Deputy-Director of Security, Queensland, to Director General of Security, Canberra, September 1, 1943, in "[L'Italiano – Newspaper], 1940–1944", NAA: A373, 6230.
7. Memorandum, Director General of Security to the Deputy-Director of Security, Queensland, June 28, September 8, 1943, NAA: A373, 6230.
8. Interpreter J.M. Jones, November 3, 1943, NAA: A373, 6230.
9. Letter, Director-General of Security, Canberra, to the Attorney General, Australia, September 24, 1943, in "VACCARI, Gualtiero", NAA: A6126, 58. The request related to the proposal of Vaccari as a liaison officer between Archbishop Mannix and Italian internees, which Prime Minister Curtin was enquiring about.

10. "Regulations Under The National Security Act 1939", *Statutory Rules 1939*, No. 88, September 13, 1939, Part VII, 24 (b) and (c) (i), (ii).
11. Bevege, *Behind Barbed Wire*, 159, 175–176.
12. Cresciani, "The Bogey", 71, 74, 76, 29, 80.
13. Cresciani, "The Bogey", 70–73. On 'hate speech', see: Ann Curthoys, "The Reconstruction of Hate Language", in *Hate Speech and Freedom of Speech in Australia*, ed. Katharine Gelber and Adrienne Stone (Annandale, NSW: The Federation Press, 2007), 20–33.
14. Kay Saunders, ""Discovering" the Subversive and Saboteur: The Disjuncture between official records of internment policy and practice and the remembered experiences of internees in Australia in the Second World War", *Oral History Association of Australia Journal* 13 (1991): 6–7.
15. Anecdotal evidence suggests that *L'Italiano*'s broadsheets are possibly in a box deep within one of the military archives or storage areas. Personal communication, Amedeo Tosco, who was told as much by an archivist, August 28, 2001.
16. W. D. Borrie, *Italians and Germans in Australia: A Study of Assimilation* (Melbourne: F. W. Cheshire, 1954), 120.
17. Cresciani, *Fascism*, 77–78.
18. Cresciani, *Fascism*, 4.
19. Cresciani, *Fascism*, 33, 155.
20. Cresciani, *Fascism*, 99, 101–102, 107–108.
21. David Brown, "Fascism within the pre World War II Italian population of Queensland: a study of community processes and interaction", *Queensland History Journal* 93 (2017): 30–32.
22. Brown, "Fascism", 35.
23. Cresciani, *Fascism*, 141; Brown, "Fascism", 35.
24. Ercole Sori, *L'emigrazine italiana dall'Unità alla seconda guerra mondiale* [Italian Emigration from Unity to the Second World War] (Bologna: Il Mulino, 1979), 19.
25. Australian Bureau of Statistics, Census of the Commonwealth of Australia, *Census Bulletin No. 15, Summary of the Commonwealth of Australia* (Canberra: L. F. Johnson, 1933), 8; Borrie, *Italians and Germans:* 51–52.
26. U. S. Department of Commerce, *Fifteenth Census of the United States: 1930. Population. Special Report of Foreign-Born White Families by Country of Birth by Head, Volume VI [Supplement]* (Washington: United States Government Printing Office, 1933), 6.
27. See Catherine Dewhirst, "Colonising Italians: Italian Imperialism and Agricultural 'Colonies' in Australia, 1881–1914", *Journal of Imperial and Commonwealth History* 44, no. 1 (2016): 28–29.

28. See Kathleen Niels Conzen, David A. Gerber, Ewa Morawska, George E. Pozzetta and Rudolph J. Vecoli, "The Invention of Ethnicity: A Perspective From the U.S.A.", *Journal of American Ethnic History* 12, no. 1 (Fall 1992): 3, 8.
29. Conzen, Gerber, Morawska, Pozzetta and Vecoli, "The Invention": 5–6.
30. Conzen, Gerber, Morawska, Pozzetta and Vecoli, "The Invention": 9–10.
31. Eduardo Bonilla-Silva, "Rethinking Racism: Towards a Structural Interpretation", *American Sociological Review* 62, no. 3 (June 1997): 471–473.
32. Bonilla-Silva, "Rethinking Racism", 474–476.
33. See Catherine Dewhirst, "Collaborating on whiteness: representing Italian in early white Australia", *Journal of Australian Studies* 31, no. 2 (2008): 38–40; Catherine Dewhirst, "The 'Southern Question' in Australia: The 1925 Royal Commission's Racialisation of Southern Italians", *Queensland History Journal* 22, no. 4 (2014): 321–325.
34. Dewhirst, "The 'Southern Question'", 321–322.
35. Roslyn Pesman Cooper, ""We Want a Mussolini": Views of Fascist Italy in Australia", *The Australian Journal of Politics and History* 39, no. 3 (1993): 349, 351–353.
36. Cresciani, *Fascism*, 141, 144–147.
37. Brown, "Fascism": 27–29; David Brown, ""Gathered around the Sign of the Littorio": The Italo-Abyssinia Conflict and Its Impact on Italian Fascism in Queensland, 1935–1939", *Spunti e Ricerche*, Special issue "150 Years of Italians in Queensland", edited by Catherine Dewhirst, Claire Kennedy and Francesco Ricatti, 24 ([2009] 2011): 57–59.
38. Philip V. Cannistraro and Gianfranco Rosoli, "Fascist Emigration Policy in the 1920s: An Interpretive Framework", *The International Migration Review* 13, no. 4 (1979): 677, 686–687.
39. See Brown, "Fascism": 30–32.
40. Cresciani, *Fascism*, 14–15, 43.
41. In 1917 Norman Morris Colless had been destined for the 3rd Light Horse Brigade after he enlisted for the Australian Imperial Force at the age of 22 and a half years. He never saw action as he was discharged on a technical irregularity, having enlisted just short of 18 years. While this was sufficient grounds for discharging him, there were also medical reasons, including having contracted gonorrhea within a couple of weeks of being stationed at Broken Hill, with recurring bouts of the disease. "Colless Norman Morris: SERN DEPOT: POB Brewarrina NSW: POE Broken Hill NSW: NOK S Colless Nellis Monar", NAA: B2455, COLLESS N M.
42. Report, Inspector R.F.B. Wake to Inspector in Charge, Commonwealth Investigation Branch, 17 October 1940; Sergeant R.P. Harrison, "Cesare Baucia", January 6, 1942 in "Baucia, Cesare—Queensland investigation case file": NAA: BP242/1, Q25546.

43. Captain John Stevens, Reasons for Recommending Detention and Summary of File, January 10, 1942, NAA: BP242/1, Q25546.
44. Letter, Interpreter R.M. Kemp, Visit of the Italian Consul General, June 1939, January 23, 1942, NAA: BP242/1, Q16961.
45. Report, Inspector R.F.B. Wake to Inspector in Charge, Commonwealth Investigation Branch, October 17, 1940; Dr Battaglia, Fascio Festival, November 9, 1933, NAA: BP242/1, Q25546.
46. Letter, Battaglia to the "Italian Journal", Sydney, December 5, 1932, NAA: BP242/1, Q25546.
47. Letter, Battaglia to the "Italian Journal".
48. Eric Hobsbawm, "Introduction: Inventing Traditions", in *The Invention of Tradition*, ed. Eric Hobsbawm and Terence Ranger (Cambridge: Cambridge University Press, 2000), 9.
49. Captain Stevens, Intelligence Summary, n.d., NAA: BP242/1, Q25546. Captain Filiberto Quaglia was a shipping manager.
50. Captain Stevens, Reasons For Recommending Detention, NAA: BP242/1, Q25546.
51. Sergeant Harrison, Cesare Baucia, NAA: BP242/1, Q25546.
52. NAA: BP242/1, Q25546. The inference reflects the well-established belief in 'disloyalty' from the threat of anti-national and anti-imperial ideologies assigned to 'foreign' migrants and radicals. See Raymond Evans, *Loyalty and Disloyalty: Social Conflict on the Queensland Homefront, 1914–18* (Sydney: Allen & Unwin, 1987), 174, 180–181. My thanks go to Associate Professor Richard Scully for discussion and insights about the image.
53. Excerpt in Appendix J.a, November 27, 1941, Summary of File, January 10, 1942, NAA: BP242/1, Q25546.
54. The other Italians were Igino Costa, Simone Bellave, Pietro Montecucco, Paolo Piccio, Amleto Ambrosi and Guido Pietrobelli, whose meeting places were Roma Café in Queen Street, D'Ambrosi's Café and Sorbello's Café in Leichhardt Street, Central Club in Elizabeth Street, and Piccio's residence at Kangaroo Point.
55. Report, Sergeant Harrison, Pro-German sentiments of members of the Italian community, September 30, 1941, in "PIETROBELLI, Guido [Italian— born 1894]—Queensland investigation case file", NAA: BP242/1, Q49369.
56. Letter, Baucia to the Consul-General, Sydney, March 12, 1936, NAA: BP242/1, Q25546.
57. Excerpt in Appendix C.6, October 19, 1938, Summary of File, 10 January 1942, NAA: BP242/1, Q25546.
58. Cresciani, *Fascism*, 83.
59. Letter, Danesi to Colless, October 12, 1938, NAA: BP242/1, Q25546.

60. Letter, Albanese to the Camp Commandant, Gaythorne, n.d., NAA: BP242/1, Q16961.
61. "Brides Welcomed at Midnight", *The Courier Mail*, May 7, 1937, p. 15.
62. Minute Paper, Major Morton on interview with Mr Abercrombie, *L'Italiano* executive, n.d., NAA: BP242/1, Q16961.
63. Dossier, Inspector R.F.B. Wake, n.d., NAA: BP242/1, Q16961.
64. Appeal Hearing transcript, n.d., NAA: BP242/1, Q16961.
65. "Christopher (or Cristofaro) Albanese", n.d., NAA: BP242/1, Q16961.
66. Letter, Danesi to Baucia, October 14, 1938, NAA: BP242/1, Q25546.
67. Article, "The Italians and the Sectarian Calumnies"; September 14, 1938, NAA: BP242/1, Q25546.
68. Article, "Speaking of Coherence"; September 14, 1938, NAA: BP242/1, Q25546.
69. Letter, Danesi to Colless, October 12, 1938, NAA: BP242/1, Q25546.
70. Letter, Albanese to Colless, November 18, 1938, NAA: BP242/1, Q16961. Brown discusses the low *fasci* membership numbers, showing that it was unpopular in North Queensland: Brown, "Gathered around": 58. The man Albanese referred to may have been Brisbane resident Edward Zamboni, who was also interned.
71. Letter, Albanese to Pisani, September 23, 1938, NAA: BP242/1, Q16961.
72. Letter, Pisani to Albanese, September 23, 1938, NAA: BP242/1, Q16961.
73. Letter, Albanese to Modotti, October 26, 1938, NAA: BP242/1, Q16961.
74. Letter, Vaccari to Albanese, March 9, 1940, NAA: A373, 6230.
75. Letter, Vaccari to Albanese, February 7, 1940, NAA: A373, 6230.
76. Letter, Albanese to Vaccari, February 10, 1940, NAA: A373, 6230. [My translation.]
77. Letter, Vaccari to Albanese, February 7, 1940, NAA: BP242/1, Q16961.
78. Letter, Vaccari to Albanese, February 20, 1940, NAA: BP242/1, Q16961.
79. Letter, Albanese to Vaccari, March 2, 1940, NAA: BP242/1, Q16961.
80. Letter, Vaccari to Albanese, April 11, 1940, NAA: A373, 6230.
81. Cresciani, "The Bogey", 81. See also: Curthoys, "The Reconstruction of Hate Language", 29–31; Waleed Aly, "Curse of Australia's silent pervasive racism: The polite racism of the educated middle class is much worse than ugly tirades that go viral on YouTube", *The Sydney Morning Herald*, April 5, 2013, https://www.smh.com.au/opinion/curse-of-australias-silent-pervasive-racism-20130404-2h9i1.html; "'UN concern over *'inhumane'* *detention* centres for *asylum seekers*", *The Sydney Morning Herald*, November 11, 2013, https://www.smh.com.au/politics/federal/un-concern-over-inhumane-detention-centres-for-asylum-seekers-20141111-11k3j0.html (accessed December 14, 2019); "Cruel, and no deterrent: why Australia's policy on asylum seekers must change", *The Conversation* http://theconversation.com/cruel-and-no-deterrent-why-

australias-policy-on-asylum-seekers-must-change-117969   (accessed January 3, 2020).

82. Memorandum, Deputy Director D.A. Alexander, Commonwealth Department of Migration, October 4, 1949, NAA, BP242/1, Q25546.
83. Letter, Albanese to the Commonwealth Investigation Bureau, June 15, 1944, NAA: BP242/1, Q25546.

CHAPTER 6

Zionism, Assimilationism and Antifascism: Divergent International Jewish Pathways in Three Post-War Australian Jewish Magazines

Max Kaiser

In the immediate post-War period, Jewish communities worldwide sought to draw political lessons from the events of the Holocaust, the rise of fascism and the Second World War. At the same time, diasporic Jewish communities were struggling to create new political frameworks to understand the establishment of the state of Israel.[1] In Australia, these conditions produced an intense level of cultural and political debate in the Jewish community, which played out across a variety of Jewish newspapers and magazines. These debates revolved around alternate trajectories for Jewish politics, as various tendencies put forward distinct visions for how Australian Jews could best navigate the contemporary political situation.

M. Kaiser (✉)
University of Melbourne, Parkville, VIC, Australia
e-mail: Kaiserm@unimelb.edu.au

© The Author(s) 2020
C. Dewhirst, R. Scully (eds.), *The Transnational Voices of Australia's Migrant and Minority Press*, Palgrave Studies in the History of the Media,
https://doi.org/10.1007/978-3-030-43639-1_6

107

This chapter examines three major Jewish magazines of this period: *The Zionist* (1943–1952), *The Australian Jewish Outlook* (1947–1948) and *Unity* (1948–1951). These magazines were, to a certain extent, in dialogue with each other and had significant overlap in their concerns. However, they reflected divergent perspectives on Jewish politics, representing Zionist, antifascist and assimilationist ideas, respectively.

Australian Jews were (and still are) divided by class, ethnicity, length of settlement, gender and large differences in religious practice and affiliation (to say nothing of their geographic location in different Australian states and territories, towns or cities).[2] Thus we need to historicise the concept of the "Jewish community" rather than taking it as a given or using it as shorthand to describe all Jews in Australia. According to Hsu-Ming Teo, the process of becoming a singular "ethnic community" in Australia is not simply a "natural" collective response to having a shared minority language or culture. Instead, various groups and individuals "governed by different economic interests, gender inequality, and [regional] ethnocentrism" are brought together in response to discrimination, assimilatory pressures and social marginalisation.[3] This process of "ethnicisation" is reinforced by business, political and cultural institutions that discursively construct the ethnic group as a method of exploitation, governance and representation.[4] Utilising the framework of "ethnicisation" as a historical process assists us in understanding the constructed nature of "the Jewish community".

As with other "ethnic communities" in Australia, the idea of "the Jewish community" can be apprehended as a result of historical processes of resistance to racialisation and social discrimination, as well as a technique of governance and management of difference. As such, Jewish people are not passive objects defined solely by a changing governmental racial discourse. They deploy notions of race, religion and ethnicity in order to shape their own positioning within Jewish and non-Jewish discourses. Eric Goldstein suggests that "ethnicisation" is not a top-down process, but one shaped by multiple, contesting ideas and practices.[5] Following Goldstein and Michael Staub, this chapter suggests that the formation of "ethnic identities" in this context is just as much shaped through "intraethnic" political conflict as through "interethnic conflict".[6]

Fascism and war in Europe set the stage for Jewish intraethnic conflict to emerge in 1940s Australia. According to census figures, the Jewish population in Australia more than doubled in the years between 1933 and 1961, rising from 23,553 (with a majority being Jews of British descent) to 59,343.[7] This was largely the result of German and Austrian refugees arriving in the late 1930s and Holocaust survivors arriving from Eastern Europe in the late 1940s and the 1950s.[8] Almost all of the post-war migrants settled in Melbourne and Sydney, cementing these cities as the major Jewish population centres, and the main locations of major political and cultural developments.[9] As Suzanne Rutland puts it, this influx "radically transformed every aspect of Jewish life in Australia".[10] A "Jewish community" in Australia was created by what both W.D. Rubinstein and Rutland deem a "revolution" in Jewish communal affairs across Australia in the early 1940s.[11] The major factors prompting these changes were the Holocaust and the challenges thought to be facing Jews on a transnational level from an intensified international antisemitism.[12] The "revolution" was precipitated by the influence of the new Jewish immigrants, the rapid emergence of a widespread intra-Jewish political solidarity and an embrace of a Jewish identity that transcended religion.[13] The result of this "revolution" was to facilitate the large expansion of Jewish communal institutions and create the semi-democratic representative structures of Australian Jews—including a national representative body, the Executive Council of Australian Jewry in 1944—that remain significantly unaltered to this day.[14]

Along with the creation of new political structures came the substantial development of the Australian Jewish press, which played a significant part in driving communal change. The 1940s saw a flowering of periodicals and magazines that engaged in a common conversation about the politics and plight of Jewish people in Australia and internationally.[15] In this sense, the 1940s saw the emergence of what Benedict Anderson terms an "imagined community": a group of people who did not necessarily know each other personally, but saw themselves as part of the same public through engagement and investment in a common media, social and political groups, cultural, educational and welfare institutions, and political representation.[16] While there remained state-based weekly Jewish newspapers as well as dozens of local synagogue and club newsletters, the magazines surveyed in this chapter aimed to be national publications that would inform Jewish debate across an imagined Australian Jewish public—the creation of this public meant that "the Jewish community" became a site that can be conceptualised as an arena of political contestation.

The Jewish periodicals that partially constituted this arena, analysed here, are examples of what has been deemed the "ethnic press" in Australian scholarship. This literature began with Miriam Gilson and Jerzy Zubrzycki's foundational 1967 sociological survey, *The Foreign-language*

Press in Australia.[17] Gilson and Zubrzycki assess the role of the ethnic press as functioning to socialise migrants into life in Australia, and acting "as an agency of social control within the ethnic group".[18] Both of these functions partially apply to *The Zionist*, *The Australian Jewish Outlook* and *Unity* but provide a limited framework for analysing the contents of these magazines. While Gilson and Zubrzycki's study remains important, it is a prime example of the proto-multicultural sociological studies of this period, that aimed to defend and justify the autonomous activities of ethnic groups in Australia to an Anglo audience by emphasising their function in preparing "the immigrant population for good citizenship".[19] As noted above, this chapter focuses on intraethnic conflict surrounding assimilation and cultural and political positioning. This approach complicates a straightforward analysis of ethnic press sources as maintaining or policing group identity and assisting socialisation or acculturation into Australian society. The texts analysed here are treated as evidence of the heavily contested nature of how these processes played out in the Australian Jewish community, highlighting how this contestation was always deeply informed by international events and debates.

Robert Mason suggests that it is precisely by turning to transnational history that we can start to overcome the limitations of existing multicultural and ethnic histories.[20] He argues that we need to take the transnational constitution of these ethnic communities seriously: physically through the process of migration, but also ideologically and epistemologically. Mason quotes the editors of the collection, *Transnational Ties* (2008), as stating that "transnational history is not a case of tracing the movement of certain individuals, but of investigating such individuals' 'imaginative reach'".[21] Thus a transnational framing can foreground migrants' past political and cultural experience as well as depict an ongoing "transnational dimension of political self-constitution".[22] Mason suggests that the diversity of migrant culture and politics exceeds the limits of ethnic and multicultural institutional structures [and histories] that "emphasise depoliticised ethnicities at the expense of other facets of migrants' lives".[23] An essential part of writing histories of the migrant press is to understand and take seriously the worldviews, epistemologies and transnational ideological connections that shape and are shaped by migrants. Such a framing assists us to break with "the frame of the nation-state" as the site of politics.[24] In this chapter the transnational dimension of the Australian Jewish political imagination therefore takes centre stage.

THE REVOLT AGAINST ASSIMILATION

Through the 1930s the Zionist movement in Australia contested the conservative and assimilationist politics of the Jewish establishment in
Australia. As explored below, this establishment emphasised a fundamental
Jewish allegiance to the British Empire and emphasised inconspicuousness
as the only viable strategy to address antisemitism.[25] In the post-war, post-
Holocaust years, the Australian Zionist movement stepped up its attack on
these ideas.[26] After a long, if uneven, sponsorship by the British under the
mandate system, the Zionist movement turned increasingly against the
British in its quest for unlimited immigration to Palestine and ultimately
for an independent state.[27] This meant Zionist activists in Australia had to
distinguish themselves from the previous, hegemonic Jewish Australian
identification as loyal subjects of the British Empire.[28] The emergence of
The Zionist (1943–1952), as the official monthly magazine of the Zionist
Federation of Australia and New Zealand, itself represented the growing
professionalisation, ambition and popularity of the Australian Zionist
movement.[29] The monthly publication of *The Zionist* was a large step up
from the "rather humble", "roneod" weekly bulletin it replaced, and
reflected the rising fortunes of Australian Zionism in the context of the
new situation in Palestine, the ongoing war and the mass murder of
European Jewry.[30] *The Zionist's* publication in Melbourne reflected the
strength of Zionist politics in Victoria, as compared to other states.[31]
Under the editorship of Aaron Patkin, *The Zionist* represented a forth-
right, if relatively pluralistic, Australian Zionism.[32]

After the war an uneasy alliance developed between Australian Zionists
and Jewish leftists who were associated with the Jewish Council to Combat
Fascism and Anti-Semitism (JCCFAS). A like-minded group of Central
European refugees, men from established Eastern European families, and
Anglo-Australian Jews, founded the JCCFAS in Melbourne in May
1942.[33] As historian David Rechter states, the JCCFAS "represented in
institutional form the broad-based antifascist leftism enjoying considerable vogue both within the Jewish community and in society at large".[34] It
combined the practical activity of monitoring and responding to specific
incidences of antisemitism with a larger propaganda effort that consis-
tently linked the threats of antisemitism, fascism and reactionary politics
more generally.[35] While the JCCFAS was not a communist front organisation, it was influenced by Communist Party of Australia members and
ideology.[36] The Soviet Union, tentatively from 1945 onwards—but

particularly after UN Ambassador Andrei Gromyko's May 1947 speech—
reversed its longstanding anti-Zionism and supported the establishment of
Israel.[37] Communist parties worldwide thus embraced the independence
struggle.[38] The international Jewish left envisioned the plight of the *Yishuv*
(Jewish settlement in Palestine) within the framework of global post-war,
anti-imperialist struggles for de-colonisation and national independence.[39]
The JCCFAS, in the events leading up to the establishment of the state of
Israel, were its strong proponents, seeing a defence of the *Yishuv* as inex-
tricable from the fight against antisemitism.[40] Thus, during the immediate
post-war period the Jewish antifascist left and the Zionist movement seemingly had common cause. Both movements were struggling to define a
Jewish politics involving a certain measure of collective rights and autonomy, as the only viable option to combat the global rise of antisemitism
and express solidarity with oppressed Jews internationally. This was in
stark contrast with the establishment assimilationist view of Jewishness as
simply a private matter of religion.[41]

"For God, for King and for Country": The Assimilationist Backlash

An epiphenomenon of this political struggle within the Jewish community
was the formation of *The Australian Jewish Outlook* (1947–1948) (hereafter *AJO*), a short-lived journal established to counter the growing influence of Zionism within the Jewish community.[42] The *AJO* had a national
audience, but was published in Perth where Zionism had yet to become as
dominant as in the eastern states. It was set against both anti-British
Zionism and communism.[43] Its primary anxiety around Zionism was that
it would lead to a dis-identification of Jews from a fundamental political
and national loyalty to Australia and, by extension, the British Empire.
The *AJO* denied that "the Australian Jew is a homeless or Stateless exile;
it insists that Australian Jews, either born or naturalised, live in Australia as
Australian citizens by right and not by sufferance, and must accept to the
fullest degree the obligations of citizenship equally with all other
Australians".[44] The *AJO*'s reference to "exile" here was a response to the
widespread Zionist notion of *shelilat hagalut* or "negation of exile".[45]
Developed through the early twentieth century, this notion suggested that
a diasporic or exilic existence of the Jewish people was no longer possible
or desirable, and that a territorial concentration and a re-establishment of

Jewish sovereignty were necessary to return the Jewish people to their full political and cultural potential. In a world situation defined by modern nationalisms, Jewish life in "exile" was judged to be dangerous, distorting and unnecessary.[46]

Daniel Weiss has suggested that this Zionist concept of the "negation of the *galut*" suffered from a misapprehension of the Jews' supposedly then exilic existence. Weiss defines the pre-modern rabbinical conception of *galut* as referring to a "nation in exile", the politically bounded nature of a Jewish collectivity with three key features: a universal geography; lack of ties to any particular territory; and lack of ultimate political allegiance to the law or military defence of any nation where Jews were situated.[47] As suggested by the *AJO*, Weiss argues that the political rights bestowed upon Jews as individuals in modern Western nation-states had already in effect negated the situation of *galut*.[48] The "negation of the *galut*" through the political emancipation of Jews was most famously phrased during the French Revolution as: "The Jews should be denied everything as a nation, but granted everything as individuals".[49] The *AJO* was in agreement with this formulation; for them the historical debate on the global place of the Jews was essentially done and dusted. They emphasised a "non-political", religious version of Jewish identity and an ultimate and primary allegiance to Australia and the British Empire.[50] Much to their chagrin (as suggested above), in the 1940s this subject became one of live debate.

The post-war Jewish community actively debated the political implications of various definitions of Jewishness. For the *AJO*, Jews were a non-politically defined religious group; for the Zionists and territorialists, Jews were a nation. For the Jewish antifascist left, Jewishness meant none of the above. In December 1947, the *AJO* featured a debate on how to define what Jewishness was. There were three major articles: "The Case for the Racial Group" by David J. Benjamin; "The Case for the National Group" by S. Stedman, the editor of the territorialist *Australian Jewish Forum* (1941–1949); and "The Case for the Religious Group" by Phillip Masel.[51]

Masel's opinion was reflective of the *AJO*'s editorial line. He suggested that Jews could not be defined as a common race, as they have "intermingled with all the other racial groups of the world" producing everything from "Jews of essentially Nordic appearance" to "communities of black Jews".[52] Masel disputed the argument that Jews in Palestine were building an all-encompassing Jewish nation, suggesting that they were in fact building a new type of nationality: "[j]ust as the Jew is different from the Israelite of the past, so the Israelite of the future will be different from the Jew of today. The Jew must be a member of the religious group; the Israelite of the future may or may not be".[53] For Masel there was only one characteristic that defines the modern Jew: "It is solely his religious faith".[54] Unlike in the USA, a Jewish discourse about a racial Jewishness was marginal in post-war Australia.[55] In Benjamin's definition race was not biological; he held that "race does not depend entirely on descent".[56] His very loose definition of race was not entirely distinct from the religious definition. He suggested that Judaism as a religion, coupled with a feeling of common descent and the inheritance of Judaism through the ages, made Jews into a race.[57]

Stedman built his definition of Jews as a nation on the basis of a contemporary and historical assessment of the political self-definition and external treatment of Jews. He disputed a purely religious definition of Jewishness by pointing to the example of Jews living in *kibbutzim* (communal farms) in Palestine who, while not observing what was traditionally thought of as religious practice, were "carrying into practice the very essence of the Jewish religion".[58] These collective farmers had come "to Palestine with the sole intention of rebuilding the National status which has been trampled under foot by oppressors of Jewry".[59] Stedman went on to claim that the Jews had been recognised by the Balfour Declaration and by Napoleon Bonaparte as a nation; and now the Soviet Union treated the Jews as a nation and assigned them their own territory and state (*Birobidjan*). Finally, Stedman suggested that what bound Jews together as a nation was "our common history and culture, common suffering in the face of centuries-long persecution". He claimed that the Holocaust had also occasioned a new sense of Jewish transnational political solidarity that reflected a turn towards a politics of Jewish nationhood.[60] Although Stedman's definition of a nation conflated a number of differing political definitions in an ahistorical manner, his view was reflective of an increasingly dominant Zionist historiography of Jewish nationhood.[61]

Writing in *The Zionist* in June 1947, Patkin underlined a stark choice between assimilationism and Jewish nationalism. In his historical account, any resistance to assimilation, from the *Haskalah* (Jewish Enlightenment) onwards, was evidence of Jewish nationalism. This account was contained in a withering critique of the *AJO*, as a "medley of ignorance and treachery towards those who in this crucial hour of our history are at one with the people".[62] For Patkin there was no contradiction between Australian Jews "enjoying the rights and privileges of full citizenship" in Australia and the fact that "the Jewish people as a group is homeless or Stateless".[63] To counter this homelessness, Jews as a group needed to "claim the reconstitution of Palestine as a Jewish 'National Home,' i.e., a Jewish State".[64] In Patkin's rendering Jewish collective politics was synonymous with Zionism, the only answer to Jewish oppression was Jewish nationalism. Jewish antifascists offered another option.

AN "INTERNATIONALLY DISTRIBUTED PEOPLE": JEWISH ANTIFASCISM'S THIRD OPTION

Unity magazine was published between 1948 and 1951. It was a sophisticated forum for debate, opinion and analysis, representing a high point of Jewish antifascist and leftist thought. The Unity association was founded in 1945, inspired by the Melbourne JCCFAS. Most people involved in the Unity association were active in the socialist Zionist movement, had some association with the Communist Party or had communist sympathies.[65] It began publishing the magazine in May 1948 before members of the association formed the Sydney Council to Combat Fascism and Anti-Semitism (SCCFAS) later that year.[66] The magazine differed from other Jewish publications: it was not a newspaper, nor was it affiliated with a synagogue or a stream of Jewish religion.[67] It was an independent magazine, governed by its own editorial committee, rather than being the organ of a political organisation or youth movement, though it had close ties and affinities with both the Melbourne-based JCCFAS and its Sydney equivalent. Notably, the magazine was published in Sydney rather than in Melbourne where the JCCFAS was stronger and had more influence and followers.[68] This allowed the magazine to be somewhat independent from the JCCFAS's everyday campaigns and concerns, and thus able to attract a broader range of readers and writers. It also allowed *Unity* to posit itself as a national Jewish magazine, appealing to and rhetorically addressing all Jews in Australia.

Unity was firmly enmeshed within a transnational politics of Jewish antifascism. This Jewish antifascism was born from the international Popular Front against fascism. The "Popular Front" here denotes the movements and ideas generated through the international Communist movement's strategy of working within broad cross-class and cross-political tendency coalitions to defeat the international threat of fascism.[69] This new orientation on the global left had a significant effect on Jewish left politics internationally.[70] Both the Jewish and non-Jewish left's emphasis during this period on fighting fascism meant a change in Jewish left politics to reflect the understanding that fascism attacked Jews *as Jews*. Therefore, fascism could be fought through the mobilisation of Jewish culture, identity and international intra-Jewish solidarity. This politics came to international prominence with the entry of the Soviet Union into the Second World War and the impact of the Holocaust on a worldwide Jewish consciousness.

The politics of *Unity* were shaped by frequent reprints, and engagement with the ideas from two prominent English language Jewish antifascist left magazines, *New Life* (1947–1948, UK) and *Jewish Life* (1946–1956, USA).[71] As such *Unity's* intervention into the Australian Jewish press debate on Jewishness was a reprint from *New Life* of Hyman Levy's article, "What is a nation?"[72] Levy, utilising a materialist analysis, suggested that Jews did not qualify as a nation, but nor could they be defined simply as a religious group.[73] Jews were dispersed throughout the world, he argued, and lived in a large variety of societies, cultures and economic systems:

> In spite of the common tradition and history, religious and secular, they tend naturally to adopt the customs and social habits of the people among whom they live... There are many bonds of unity and sympathetic understanding, many cultural bonds of a traditional nature originating in past and in present history, but it would be the veriest of confusions to identify these with what is clearly a very different thing – the sense of national unity... There is, however, most definitely a sense of united consciousness among Jews, of unity of understanding, but to label this as a sense of national consciousness would be a violation of history and of common-sense... Those who, with blinkered vision, cannot see Jewry as other than single nation must wring their hands in despair as they witness [what they see as] the disintegration of Jewry everywhere throughout the world except in the particular spot where they imagine the true essence of nationhood is being preserved and developed. What they are, in fact, doing is to react in despair to the disintegration of their own narrow outlook on the growth and expansion of Jewry. Those, on the other hand, who are conscious both of unity and of diversity in Jewry can witness with delight the rich and varied forms in which this internationally distributed people express themselves in culture; music, literature, art, and in language, contributing in a unique way to the pattern of civilisation and at the same time reflecting like many facets of a diamond of their own intrinsic beauty.[74]

Jewishness, in this rendering, was a historically determined, legitimate and important collective identity.[75] Its diasporic nature was a positive rather than a negative. The answer to antisemitism was not nationalism but, as Levy put in another article republished in *Unity*, to "see that freedom and equality for Jewry come with freedom and equality for other oppressed people".[76] This was an underlying philosophy of *Unity* and indeed the transnational Jewish antifascist left as a whole during this period. Levy's reference to "the particular spot where they imagine the true essence of nationhood is being preserved and developed" is clearly a derisory reference to the *Yishuv* as the centre of a Jewish nation. While Levy's article was a rejection of Jewish nationalism, it did not preclude a transnational, transhistorical identification or solidarity in line with a Jewish antifascist Popular Front politics. Whilst the Jewish antifascist left rejected Jewish nationalism, they did not seek—like the *AJO* did—to confirm a "negation of the *galut*" via political assimilation in Western nation-states. Jewishness in their rendering had a strong political, rather than only cultural or religious, valence but it transcended an allegiance to particular nation-states or nationalist ideologies, including Australia, Israel and other figurings of Jewish nationalism.

As far back as 1945, the editor of *The Zionist*, Aaron Patkin had been critical of the JCCFAS' association of the fight against antisemitism with the struggle against fascism and reactionary ideology. For Patkin this sort of political fight was pointless whilst the root cause of "Jewish homelessness" remained.[77] In other words, Patkin suggested that the only cure for antisemitism was Zionism. This fundamental tension in approaches re-emerged after 1948, when the expedient alliance between Australian Zionists and the Jewish antifascist left broke down. In the late 1940s Zionism came to dominate more and more spheres of Australian Jewish life, becoming the most powerful Jewish political faction and ideology.[78] By around 1950, as the Jewish left became more critical of Israel, and Israel aligned itself more firmly with the USA and West Germany in the Cold War, Patkin and the Zionist movement joined the anti-communist crusade against the JCCFAS.[79]

As put, decades later, by one former JCCFAS member—Sam Goldbloom—the convergence of Zionism and anti-communism in the Jewish community meant that, in the 1950s, to be anything other than one hundred per cent supportive of Israel or supportive of the Australian government of the day—to harm the goal of the community being an "Israeli outpost in the South Pacific"—became unacceptable.[80] While the old assimilationist leadership, as represented by the *AJO*, had been edged out, Zionism's new congruence with anti-communism in international politics meant it became a route towards a new form of political quiescence in the Australian Jewish community. This was reflected in the drastic reduction in substantial Jewish periodicals in Australia, as magazines such as *Unity*, *The AJO*, the *Australian Jewish Forum* and even *The Zionist* all folded by the mid-1950s.[81] If the 1940s saw the invention of the Australian Jewish community as an arena of vigorous political contestation, the following decade saw the consolidation of just one hegemonic political orientation.

The rise of Trump and the extremism of Israeli politics have brought major changes to US Jewish politics, which have recently seen a dramatic increase in "intraethnic" contestation, particularly over the rise of the far right, and Zionism. One indication of this is the successful relaunch of the left-wing *Jewish Currents* magazine. As part of his presidential campaign, Bernie Sanders wrote an opinion piece for the magazine in 2019, which, in an echo of Hyman Levy, praised a new generation of Jewish activists for seeing "the fight against antisemitism and for Jewish liberation as connected to the fight for the liberation of oppressed people around the world".[82] *Jewish Currents* started publishing as *Jewish Life* in 1946, and was a large influence on *Unity*, and Jewish antifascist politics in Australia more generally. While a significant challenge to established Jewish politics in Australia is yet to fully emerge, Sanders' editorial is evidence that, as Stuart Hall puts it in his gloss on Antonio Gramsci, "social forces which lose out in any particular historical period do not thereby disappear from the terrain of struggle; nor is struggle in such circumstances suspended".[83]

NOTES

1. See World Jewish Congress, *Papers from the World Jewish Congress Second Plenary Assembly*, 1948, http://www.bjpa.org/Publications/details.cfm?PublicationID=22287 (accessed June 21, 2017).
2. Suzanne Rutland, *Edge of the Diaspora: Two Centuries of Jewish Settlement in Australia* (Rose Bay, NSW: Brandl & Schlesinger 1997), 340–346; P.Y. *Medding, From Assimilation to Group Survival: A Political and Sociological Study of an Australian Jewish Community* (Melbourne, Canberra, Sydney: F.W. Cheshire, 1968), 20–21.

3. Hsu-Ming Teo, "Multiculturalism and the Problem of Multicultural Histories: An Overview of Ethnic Historiography", in *Cultural History in Australia*, ed. H. Teo and R. White (Sydney: Allen and Unwin 2003), 149.
4. Teo, "Multiculturalism and the Problem of Multicultural Histories", 149. In Michael Kakakios and John Van Der Velden's account, "the massive increase of the migrant working mass, and the hegemonic problems this has created for the state since the 1960s, gave birth to "ethnicity" as an outward ideological projection of the community bourgeoisie". Michael Kakakios and John van der Velden, "Migrant Communities and Class Politics: The Greek Communities in Australia", in *Ethnicity, Class and Gender in Australia*, ed. Gill Bottomley and Marie De Lepervanche (Sydney: Allen and Unwin, 1984), 163.
5. Eric L. Goldstein, *The Price of Whiteness: Jews, Race and American Identity* (Princeton, NJ: Princeton University Press, 2006), 204–208.
6. Michael E. Staub, *Torn at the Roots: The Crisis of Jewish Liberalism in Postwar America* (New York: Columbia University Press, 2002), 18.
7. Rutland, *Edge of the Diaspora*, 256.
8. It is notable that census questionnaires in Australia have only ever defined Jewishness as a matter of religious identification. Medding, *Assimilation to Group Survival*, 18–19; Rutland, *Edge of the Diaspora*, 256. There was also significant immigration of Jews from Russia, Palestine and particularly Poland before the 1930s. Rutland, *Edge of the Diaspora*, 147–148.
9. Rutland, *Edge of the Diaspora*, 254.
10. Rutland, *Edge of the Diaspora*, 256.
11. Rutland, *Edge of the Diaspora*, 324–327; W.D. Rubinstein, "The Revolution of 1942–1944," *Australian Jewish Historical Society Journal* 11, Part 1 (1990): 142–153.
12. Rubinstein, "The Revolution of 1942–1944" 146–149.
13. Rubinstein, "The Revolution of 1942–1944".
14. These representative bodies are not elected via universal suffrage. They consist of delegates from Jewish organisations. Proposals for individual democratic franchise were defeated in this period. See, Rubinstein, "The Revolution of 1942–1944", 152; Rutland, *Edge of the Diaspora*, 352–357.
15. Rutland, *Edge of the Diaspora*, 212; Marianne Dacy, *Periodical Publications from the Australian Jewish Community: A Union List*, 5th edn (Sydney: University of Sydney, Archive of Australian Judaica, 2007).
16. Benedict Anderson, *Imagined Communities: Reflections on the Origin and Spread of Nationalism* (London: Verso, 1983).
17. Miriam Gilson and Jerzy Zubrzycki, *The Foreign-Language Press in Australia* (Canberra: Australian National University Press, 1967).
18. Gilson and Zubrzycki, *Foreign-Language Press*, 127–128. Gilson and Zubrzycki's study explicitly excludes the Chinese and Jewish press. They

cite Percy Joseph Mark's *The Jewish Press in Australia, Past and Present* (Sydney, 1913) as "unfortunately out of date". Gilson and Zubrzycki, *Foreign-Language Press*, vii. Mark's volume was eventually succeeded by Suzanne Rutland, *Pages of History: A Century of the Australian Jewish Press* (Darlinghurst, NSW: Australian Jewish Press, 1995). For a more sociological survey, since outdated, see Mark Braham, "The Jewish Press in Australia", in *The Ethnic Press in Australia*, ed. Abe (I.) Wade Ata and Colin Ryan (Melbourne: Academia Press and Footprint Publications, 1989).

19. Gilson and Zubrzycki, *Foreign Language-Press*, 157.

20. Robert Mason, "Australian Multiculturalism: Revisiting Australia's Political Heritage and the Migrant Presence", *History Compass* 8, no. 8 (2010): 817–827.

21. Desley Deacon, Penny Russell and Angela Woollacott, eds., *Transnational Ties: Australian Lives in the World* (Canberra: ANU E Press, 2008), cited in Robert Mason, "Australian Multiculturalism", 819.

22. Ghassan Hage, *Alter-Politics: Critical Anthropology and the Radical Imagination* (Melbourne: Melbourne University Publishing, 2015), 92.

23. Mason, "Australian Multiculturalism," 820.

24. Michael Rothberg, *Multidirectional Memory: Remembering the Holocaust in the Age of Decolonization* (Stanford, CA: Stanford University Press, 2009), 20.

25. Medding, *Assimilation to Group Survival*, 70.

26. Rutland, *Edge of the Diaspora*, 295–310.

27. This began with the 1939 MacDonald White Paper, restricting Jewish immigration. However, the *Yishuv's* fortunes were inextricably tied to the British Empire in the Second World War, somewhat dampening protests until after the war. Rutland, *Edge of the Diaspora*, 307–310. For the role of the British in facilitating Zionist colonisation, see Rashid Khalidi, *The Iron Cage: The Story of the Palestinian Struggle for Statehood* (Boston: Beacon Press, 2006), 31–64.

28. The Australian intelligence services were thus concerned not only with communist activism within the Jewish community but also with Zionist organising, see "REFERENCE COPY, "Jewish Unity Association," (1941–1949)", A6122, 155, National Archives of Australia.

29. Early issues accompanied a mass membership campaign for Zionist organisations that, in Victoria for instance, aimed to enrol "the majority of the adult Jewish population". "Zionist Work in Australia and New Zealand," *The Zionist*, October (1943).

30. "The Weekly Bulletin," *The Zionist*, September (1943).

31. Rutland, *Edge of the Diaspora*, 303.

32. For a biographical sketch of Patkin, see Vivien Altman, "'The Spark in the Ash'", *Australian Jewish Historical Society Journal* 23, part 1 (2016):

79–92. For a portrait of Australian Zionism and its growing fortunes during this period, see Bernard Keith Hyams, *The History of the Australian Zionist Movement* (South Caulfield, Vic.: Zionist Federation of Australia, 1998), 66–101.

33. David Rechter, "Beyond the Pale: Jewish Communism in Melbourne", Masters thesis, University of Melbourne, 1986, 81–82.

34. Rechter, "Beyond the Pale," 82.

35. Rechter, "Beyond the Pale," 110.

36. Rechter, "Beyond the Pale," 100.

37. For a discussion of the intersection between Popular Front politics, a changing communist position on Palestine and the shift in Soviet foreign policy, see Paul Kelemen, *The British Left and Zionism: History of a Divorce* (Manchester & New York: Manchester University Press, 2012), 86–106. For an examination of the change in Soviet policy, see Laurent Rucker, *Moscow's Surprise: The Soviet-Israeli Alliance of 1947–1949* (Cold War International History project, Woodrow Wilson International Center for Scholars, 2005). For Gromyko's speech, see Andrei Gromyko, "Palestine at UNO: Extracts from the Speech Made by Mr. Andrei Gromyko at the General Assembly of UNO on May 14th", *New Life* 1, no. 5 (1947).

38. For an account of how the Soviet Union's support for Israel allowed the communist David Martin to briefly edit the *Sydney Jewish News* see David Martin, *My Strange Friend: An Autobiography* (Sydney: Pan Macmillan, 1991), 213–214.

39. For example, see: "Safeguard the Jewish State!", *Jewish Life* 2, no. 3 (1948); Ber Mark, "Voice of the Oppressed: World Congress of Intellectuals in Wroclaw, Poland, August, 1948", *Unity: A Magazine of Jewish Affairs* 1, no. 6 (1949).

40. See Burgoyne Chapman, "The Vindication of [ ]", *Australian Jewish News*, 21 July 1950; Philip Mendes, "The Australian Left's Support for the Creation of the State of Israel, 1947-48", *Labour History* 97 (2009): 137–148. It is understandable why the JCCFAS drew these two issues together. While there were no antisemitic riots around the issue as there were in Britain the period saw an upshot in antisemitism in the Australian press and as Norman Rothfield then put it "there was undoubtedly an attempt by anti-Semitic groups in this country to utilise the situation in Israel for the purpose of creating ill-feeling towards the Jews in Australia". Quoted in Norman Rothfield, *Many Paths to Peace* (Fairfield, Vic.: Yarraford Publications, 1997), 23.

41. As Hannah Arendt suggests, the category of "Jewishness" as something quantifiable and subject to internal contestation was only possible as a result of modern Jewish emancipation and assimilation. Hannah Arendt,

The Origins of Totalitarianism (Orlando: Harcourt Books, [1951]; repr., 1976), 83–84.

42. For an extended account of the fortunes of this journal, see Louise Hoffman, "A Review of the Jewish Press in Western Australia", *Journal of The Royal Western Australian Historical Society* 8, no. part 2 (1978).

43. The *AJO* were against what they called "political Zionism", which aimed at the creation of an independent Jewish State. They were in favour of "Zionism as a humanitarian and cultural movement designed to facilitate the migration to Palestine of Jews who, because of racial and religious discrimination, cannot or will not live in the country of their birth or adoption". "The "Australian Jewish Outlook": Editorial Policy Outlined", *Australian Jewish Outlook* 1, no. 1 (1947), 2.

44. "The "Australian Jewish Outlook": Editorial Policy Outlined."

45. Shalom Ratzaby, "The Polemic About the "Negation of the Diaspora" in the 1930s and Its Roots", *Journal of Israeli History* 16, no. 1 (1995): 19–38; Donna Robinson Divine, "Exiled in the Homeland", *Shofar: An Interdisciplinary Journal of Jewish Studies* 21, no. 2 (2003): 66–81.

46. Ratzaby, "Polemic About." See also Amnon Raz-Krakotzkin, "Exile Within Sovereignty: Toward a Critique of the 'Negation of Exile' in Israeli Culture", *Theory and Criticism*, 4 and 5 (1993): 23–56, 113–132.

47. Daniel H. Weiss, "A Nation without Borders?: Modern European Emancipation as Negation of Galut", *Shofar: An Interdisciplinary Journal of Jewish Studies* 34, no. 4 (2016): 72. This notion of nationhood does not imply a modern concept of nation as produced by modern nationalism.

48. Weiss, "A Nation without Borders?".

49. Cited in Weiss, "A Nation without Borders?" 80. For a discussion of Jews and the French Revolution, see Maurice Samuels, *The Right to Difference: French Universalism and the Jews* (Chicago and London: The University of Chicago Press, 2016), 17–49. For a discussion of Jewish emancipation and the emergence of modern antisemitism, see Patrick Wolfe, *Traces of History: Elementary Structures of Race* (London & New York: Verso, 2016), 85–111.

50. The origins of this ideology lie with the maskilim of the Haskalah or Jewish Enlightenment who venerated the state, seeking to turn Jews into individual state citizens above all else. David Biale, *Power and Powerlessness in Jewish History* (New York: Schocken Books, 1986), 98–117.

51. David J. Benjamin, "The Case for the Racial Group," *The Australian Jewish Outlook* 1, no. 8 (1947), 10; Philip Masel, "The Case for the Religious Group," *The Australian Jewish Outlook* 1, no. 8 (1947), 12–13; S. Stedman, "The Case for the National Group," *The Australian Jewish Outlook* 1, no. 8 (1947), 11–12. On territorialism see Adam Rovner, *In the Shadow of Zion: Promised Lands before Israel* (New York: New York

University Press, 2014); Clive Sinclair, "The Kimberley Fantasy", *Wasafiri* 24, no. 1 (2009): 33–43.

52. Masel, "The Case for the Religious Group," 12.
53. Masel, "The Case for the Religious Group," 13.
54. Masel, "The Case for the Religious Group". For a discussion of the transformation of the idea of Judaism into a "religion" rather than a political entity, see Leora Batnitzky, *How Judaism Became a Religion: An Introduction to Modern Jewish Thought* (Princeton, NJ: Princeton University Press, 2011); David N. Myers, *Resisting History: Historicism and Its Discontents in German-Jewish Thought* (Princeton, NJ: Princeton University Press, 2003), 24.
55. See Eric L. Goldstein, *The Price of Whiteness*, 165–206.
56. Benjamin, "The Case for the Racial Group," 10.
57. Benjamin, "The Case for the Racial Group".
58. Stedman, "The Case for the National Group," 11.
59. Stedman, "The Case for the National Group".
60. Stedman, "The Case for the National Group".
61. For a discussion of Zionist historiography, see David N. Myers, *Re-Inventing the Jewish Past* (New York & Oxford: Oxford University Press, 1995).
62. A. L. Patkin, "An "Australian Jewish Outlook"", *The Zionist*, June (1947), 21.
63. Patkin, "An "Australian Jewish Outlook"", 19.
64. Patkin, "An "Australian Jewish Outlook"". While, as noted above, the movement internationally was turning against the British, even in 1947 Patkin was still angling to position Zionism as congruent with British imperial loyalty claiming that it "enabled Britain to obtain the Mandate for Palestine and to gain a firm hold in the Mediterranean". Patkin, "An "Australian Jewish Outlook"", 21.
65. "REFERENCE COPY, "Jewish Unity Association," (1941–1949)", A6122, 155, National Archives of Australia.
66. After the formation of the Sydney Council, the magazine continued to be published by the Unity association. All other political work was undertaken by the SCCFAS. Nate Zusman, ""Unity" a Magazine of Jewish Affairs," *Australian Jewish Historical Society Journal* 9, part. 5 (1983): 341–355.
67. There were two major Jewish weekly newspapers in Melbourne at the time, both of which had substantial Yiddish supplements, the *Australian Jewish News* and the *Australian Jewish Herald*. In Sydney there was *The Hebrew Standard of Australasia* and the *Sydney Jewish News*. There was a plethora of contemporary publications affiliated with social and sporting clubs, political organisations and synagogues. For a comprehensive listing of Australian Jewish periodical publications, see Dacy, *Periodical Publications*.

68. The driving force behind the establishment of the magazine was its editor Hyam Brezniak who lived in Sydney, see Suzanne Rutland, "Creating Intellectual and Cultural Challenges: The Bridge", in *Feast and Fasts: Festschrift in Honour of Alan David Crown*, ed. Marianne Dacy, Jennifer Dowling, and Suzanne Faigan (Sydney: Mandelbaum, 2005); Hyam Brezniak, interview by Hazel de Berg, 29 April, 1975, National Library of Australia, Hazel de Berg collection.

69. Duncan Hallas, *The Comintern* (London: Bookmarks, 1985), 123–159; Stuart Macintyre, *The Reds: The* Communist Party of Australia from Origins to Illegality (St Leonards, NSW: Allen & Unwin, 1998), 244–328.

70. Matthew B. Hoffman and Henry F. Srebrnik, "Introduction", in *A Vanished Ideology*, ed. Matthew B. Hoffman and Henry F. Srebrnik (Albany: State University of New York Press, 2016), 10–11.

71. For an extended discussion of the genesis of this politics and of *New Life* and *Jewish Life* see Max Kaiser, ""A new and modern golden age of Jewish culture": shaping the cultural politics of transnational Jewish antifascism", *Journal of Modern Jewish Studies* 17, no. 3 (2018): 287–303.

72. Hyman Levy, "What Is a Nation?," *Unity: A Magazine of Jewish Affairs* 1, no. 2 (1948), 17.

73. Levy's analysis of what constituted a nation was informed by Joseph Stalin's 1913 definition of a national group, see Joseph Stalin, "Marxism and the National Question", in *Marxism and the National and Colonial Question* (Moscow: Co-operative Pub. Society of Foreign Workers in the U.S.S.R., 1935), 3–53.

74. Hyman Levy, "What Is a Nation?". Levy expanded upon this in his 1958 booklet *Jews and the National Question* (London: Hillway Publishing Company, 1958).

75. The Jewish left historical materialist account of Jewish history was set out comprehensively in a series of articles by Moses Miller published in *Jewish Life* disputing a nationalist (or religion based) Jewish historiography, see Moses Miller, "Zionism and the State of Israel : 1," *Jewish Life* 3, no. 7 (1949). For Miller both a nationalist and a religious interpretation of Jewish history were founded on an idealist conception of a national or divine will as historical subject, discounting material factors.

76. Hyman Levy, "A Letter to Jewish Intellectuals", *Unity: A Magazine of Jewish Affairs* 1, no. 3 (1948).

77. A.L. Patkin, "Note", *The Zionist*, October (1945).

78. For instance, see M. Kusher, "The Jewish Cultural Conference: Critical Comments," *Australian Jewish Forum* 8, no. 71 (1948).

79. A. L. Patkin, "Press Review: The "Unity"", *The Zionist*, April (1950). See Max Kaiser, "Between Nationalism and Assimilation: Jewish Antifascism in

Australia in the Late 1940s and Early 1950s", Doctor of Philosophy thesis, University of Melbourne, 2019, 145–187.

80. Sam Goldbloom, interview by Suzanne Rutland, 12 April 1988, CY MLOH 437/135, Suzanne Rutland collection, State Library of New South Wales.
81. Dacy, *Periodical Publications.*
82. Bernie Sanders, "How to Fight Antisemitism", *Jewish Currents,* November 11, 2019, https://jewishcurrents.org/how-to-fight-antisemitism/ (accessed November 20, 2019).
83. Stuart Hall, "Gramsci's Relevance for the Study of Race and Ethnicity", in *Stuart Hall: Critical Dialogues in Cultural Studies,* ed. David Morley and Kuan-Hsing Chen (London & New York: Routledge, 1996), 423.

CHAPTER 7

Literary Ambitions: The Polish-Language Press in Australia

Katarzyna Kwapisz Williams and Mary Besemeres

Introduction

In 2018 the Polish-language press celebrated 90 years in Australia. The first Polish-language periodical in Australia, *Stronica Polska* (Polish Page), was published in 1928 as part of *The Muses' Magazine* (Brisbane) and edited by a musician Stefan Polotyński. Having appeared in 10 of the 14 issues of the magazine, it had the longest run of all foreign-language sections.[1] From 1942 *Wiadomości Polskie* (Polish News) was published by the Polish Consulate General in Sydney. In fact, according to Gilson and Zubrzycki, before 1948 there were only two foreign-language periodicals published in Australia, and *Wiadomości Polskie* was one of them. As they

K. Kwapisz Williams (✉)
Center for European Studies, The Australian National University,
Canberra, ACT, Australia
e-mail: kasia.williams@anu.edu.au

M. Besemeres
School of Literature, Languages, and Linguistics, The Australian National
University, Canberra, ACT, Australia
e-mail: Mary.Besemeres@anu.edu.au

© The Author(s) 2020   127
C. Dewhirst, R. Scully (eds.), *The Transnational Voices of
Australia's Migrant and Minority Press*, Palgrave Studies in the
History of the Media,
https://doi.org/10.1007/978-3-030-43639-1_7

explain, the publication of this bulletin "foreshadowed a new phase in the development of the foreign-language press in Australia which was to begin less than three years after the end of the war".[2]

The production of *Wiadomości Polskie* was a significant achievement by individuals from the Polish community in Australia, given that printing newspapers in languages other than English at the time was a major challenge. In the 1930s publishing work in foreign languages was believed to be dangerous because it was thought to perpetuate the "isolation of immigrants by inducing them not to learn the language in their country of adoption" and to encourage "the existence of group colonies".[3] Since the policy at that time in Australia was to prevent group settlement of foreigners, anything that might encourage this—like foreign-language media—was considered not "useful from Australian point of view".[4]

Although Arthur Calwell, the Minister for Immigration 1945–1949, agreed to the establishment of several foreign-language newspapers, the official support for publications in languages other than English was limited. In 1950, Major General Sir Frederick Gallagher Galleghan (1948–1949) suggested at the Australian Citizenship Convention that migrant newspapers should be banned, because "permitting publication of foreign language newspapers" meant that "migrants would continue to read and speak the language of the country of their origin".[5] This idea was opposed by Calwell on the grounds that it "would be unfair to older people to expect them to change their whole surroundings, and, at the same time, be out of contact with their own language".[6] However, he conceded that perhaps the publisher should print at least 25% of the paper in English.

Soon, however, it became clear that migrant newspapers in Australia would not follow this rule and that the government would be unable to police it. Moreover, it was becoming obvious that minority language newspapers play a significant role not only in maintaining ties with a migrant community's homeland, but also in informing the community about national affairs. Thus, in 1954 then-Immigration minister Harold Holt released the foreign-language press from the requirement to publish a portion of each newspaper in English. Two years later foreign-language newspapers gained the same legal status as other Australian newspapers. Among those who believed that foreign-language media was crucial for developing ties between migrants and their host country was Polish-Australian sociologist Jerzy Zubrzycki, later known as a "father of multiculturalism". In the study Zubrzycki conducted with Miriam Gilson, the authors insisted that foreign-language media plays the role of a "two-way integration", which means that it enables two cultures to learn from each other, "whereby the multilingual culture, which we have never had before, might be encouraged in this country".[7] The content analysis conducted by Gilson and Zubrzycki of nine papers, including two in Polish (1956, 1958–1959) showed that "assimilation while maintaining the European heritage, has become more important for most papers than the retention of special cultural identity among their readers".[8]

The foreign-language press served as an important platform supporting migrants who were trying to acculturate in Australia, for example, by highlighting the advantages of naturalisation and learning English. Jan Dunin-Karwicki, the editor of *Wiadomości Polskie* Polish News, believed that "the task of absorbing into Australian community such a great number of new settlers, in such a short time and, most of all, in such a smooth way, would not be possible for any government organisation if not for the assistance of the ethnic press".[9] He also maintained that "Most of these papers, with few exceptions, in an unbiased manner, try to present the issues of the Australian politics, trade unions, etc., on a distinctly non-partisan base".[10] Yet, there were other commentators who did not share this view and critiqued Polish-language media for being too indifferent to readers' needs. Interestingly, referring to *Wiadomości Polskie* and *Tygodnik Polski* (Polish Weekly), Marian Kałuski notes a "strange tendency" to *avoid* anything that might help Poles to adapt more readily to life in the new country. According to him, these periodicals reflect the "mentality of many politically-minded Polish Australians [...] for whom Poles are only staying in countries like Australia until the communists in Poland have been overthrown".[11] Moreover, in contrast to Dunin-Karwicki, Kałuski claims that in the end, the political bias of the Polish-language press, its ignorance of Australian affairs and refusal to recognise that many Polish migrants were trying to assimilate and already reading only in English, resulted in its ultimate failure to keep its readership.[12]

Indeed, a limited readership has often been considered the most serious problem of the Polish and generally foreign-language press in Australia. Although in 1953 the *Herald* (21 February 1953) reported the existence of 67 foreign-language press titles, a decreasing number of readers, together with high production costs and falling sales,[13] had dire consequences for the foreign-language media. In fact, out of nine newspapers published in Polish in the early 1950s, only three survived until the mid-1960s (*Polish News; Polish Weekly; Our Way*). Nevertheless, with over 150 individual periodical titles published up until the 1990s,[14] the

Polish-language press seems to be a unique phenomenon among minority language periodicals in Australia. It represents a hidden history of Polish-language culture in Australia and its literary ambitions.

In this chapter we highlight the abundance of cultural and literary forms and themes featured in most of the Polish-language periodicals and the relatively high number of sophisticated writers. We examine the cultural and literary content of some of the periodicals and discuss the problems the editors' literary ambitions resulted in. We draw attention to the specific social function of these periodicals and propose to look at their intellectual and literary content as an indication that these periodicals served predominantly as a means of self-expression,[15] reinforcing the identities and sense of belonging[16] of a dislocated diasporic intelligentsia, and that this function might have been at times more important to editors than dealing with issues of interest to the broader migrant community. We thus argue that the highly literary content of much of the post-war Polish-language media reflects what Joanna Kujawa has called, referring to the history of Polish immigration to Australia—"the history of exiled intellectuals".[17]

We use the phrase "Polish-language press" to refer to regular and irregular periodicals produced and read by Polish immigrants in Australia. Polish immigrants to Australia are often described as a group as the "Australian Polonia", that is "a community of permanent settlers who [...] retained enough elements of their distinct identity to be considered a part of the Polish emigrant diaspora".[18] Yet, since the term "Polonia" is rather ambiguous and often interpreted to mean all people of Polish ancestry who live outside Poland,[19] we do not rely on it here. Neither do we use the term "Polish diaspora" which includes second- and third-generation immigrant descendants who cultivate some elements of Polish identity, but who have not been significantly involved in the development of the Polish-language press in Australia. We prefer to use the term "Polish-language press" to cover a range of weekly, fortnightly, monthly and irregular periodicals and their supplements published predominantly in Polish, although sometimes including texts in English. These periodicals were published for and—importantly in the context of this chapter—*by* Polish immigrants in Australia.[20]

CREATED "BY FINE WITS FOR CONNOISSEURS OF VARIOUS SORTS"

While it can be safely assumed that the Polish-language press was crucial in assisting migrants with both adapting to life in Australia and maintaining ties with Poland, the actual role of the press is difficult to determine. Although before the Second World War, small but active intellectual circles of Poles and Polish Jews had already emerged in Australia, the Polish-language press developed most intensively following the post-Second World War wave of immigration, when Australia accepted about 65,000 Polish-born refugees who made up the largest group among Displaced Persons (DP). More specifically, Kałuski points to 1955–1965 as the period of the most intensive development of the Polish-language press in Australia.[21] This is the development initiated and carried out by the first wave of post-war immigrants who were often considered—and indeed often declared themselves to be—uneducated manual workers.[22] In fact, while many DPs had no chance of higher education due to the war, some received professional training, completed their degrees or at least started their tertiary education or professional career before the war. Some had to conceal their qualifications in order to make themselves acceptable for an assisted scheme to come to Australia as highly needed labourers.[23]

As a result, in a very large group of young migrant labourers, often described as uneducated and unqualified, many talented, both accomplished and aspiring artists, writers, translators came to Australia. This first wave of post-war migrants contributed to the most intensive development of the Polish press in Australia and created a press with a significant literary and intellectual dimension. Although the Solidarity-era wave of immigration (1980–1991) from Poland brought 15,000 political migrants to Australia, of whom half had tertiary education, this wave did not have anything like the role of the post-war wave in creating a Polish-language press in Australia.

Although, as Lencznarowicz writes, "the majority of correspondents and columnists were self-taught when it came to journalism",[24] among regular contributors to Polish-language media were also professional journalists. One of them was Edmund Jakubowski, who was a member of the editorial board of *Wiadomości Polskie* and worked for the newspaper until 1988. Under the pen name E. Żagiell, he also wrote for the Paris-based Polish émigré journal, *Kultura*, the London-based journal, *Orzeł Biały*, the Mannheim newspaper, *Ostatnie Wiadomości* and Melbourne's *Tygodnik*

Katolicki. Among those who wrote for *Wiadomości Polskie* were the professional journalist Władysław Polak, the lawyer and columnist Adam Nasielski, the Polish literature specialist Bolesław Karpowski, the journalism graduate Andrzej Chciuk and the journalist Ryszard Krygier. In 1952, the professional organisation, Związek Dziennikarzy RP, Syndykat Australia (Union of Journalists of the Republic of Poland, Australian Branch) was formed.[25]

The achievements of these individuals extended beyond the Polish community in Australia. Chciuk's works were published in prestigious Polish émigré outlets round the world.[26] Krygier formed the Australian Committee (Association from 1957) for Cultural Freedom, and created the literary-political magazine *Quadrant* under the editorship of the poet and critic James McAuley. For his achievements he was awarded an OBE in 1981. Polish-language periodicals were able to showcase an impressive array of writers who produced work of high quality. As Nasielski put it, satirically, these included:

> poets, ambassadors, consuls, generals, lawyers, historians, genuine prewar editors-in-chief, novelists, honest-to-God high school teachers, a doctor who discovered he had true literary talent and several local journalistic candidates of whom one passed the test of time and is now a mainstay of our well-organized and solid editorial team.[27]

The migrant intelligentsia included artists, writers and scholars educated in Poland, who, due to the language barrier they faced in Australia, mainly wrote for readers of Polish. Some of them already had work published in Poland, among them Andrzej Chciuk, Andrzej Gawroński, Leszek Paszkowski and Zbigniew Jasiński, known as "the poet of the Warsaw Uprising". Others who contributed poetry or fiction to Australian Polish-language newspapers included Krystyna Jackiewicz, Irena Lewulis, Zygmunt Przybyłkiewicz, Władysław Romanowski, Liliana Rydzyńska, Barbara Schenkel, Tadeusz Sobolewski, Ludwik Tabaczyński, Anna Wiciak-Suchnicka and Zdzisław Marek.

In 1972, Adam Nasielski wrote that only 10% of Poles living in Australia belong to Polish organisations and they are "the only potential readers of Polish Australian newspapers".[28] Two years later he rephrased his observation, stressing that the Polish émigré press in Australia was created by and for the elites—"by fine wits for connoisseurs of various sorts".[29] Similarly, Kałuski suggests that the popularity of cultural themes might have reflected editors' ambitions rather than readers' interests.[30] While it is hard to assess the social and cultural needs of the readers at that time, it seems that the aspirations of editors and writers were indeed highly intellectual. Lencznarowicz, although he does not agree with Nasielski and rather emphasises the "decidedly class-neutral" character of the Polish-language press,[31] observes that *Wiadomości Polskie* was "too difficult and uninteresting" for uneducated readers.[32] According to Father K. E. Trzeciak, the newspaper's editors refused to "place articles with the kinds of information newcomers from Europe desperately needed" and instead kept publishing artistic-literary essays.

To address this problem Trzeciak founded *Tygodnik Katolicki* in direct opposition to the style of *Wiadomości Polskie*, aiming for a use of language that would be "straightforward, understandable for someone with a few years of primary school education".[33] However, once Roman Gronowski took over editing *Tygodnik Katolicki*, it too became a newspaper addressed largely to an intelligentsia readership. Nasielski observes that the high standard of its articles was the reason for its low subscriptions and sales.[34] Similarly, Kałuski observes that standards were simply too high for the newspapers to reach more than a handful of readers. Generally, Nasielski saw these newspapers and magazines as "written by a select group for a fairly limited class of readers of above-average understanding and intelligence". This might be why, he continued, the Polish-language press had a much higher standing than many other Australian periodicals, as "cultured Polish editors"—as he puts it ironically—refused to give in to the demands of the market even if they sometimes envied their Australian colleagues and other editors their "blatant plunge to the lowest standard".[35]

The gradual distancing of younger generations with Polish heritage from older Polish Australians suggests that the intellectual activity of these editors, writers and poets was intended not so much for younger generations, as for the writers themselves. Cultural initiatives like the press provided an outlet and a sense of community for those immigrants who were unable to find a place for themselves in the new reality. Lencznarowicz writes about the group of intellectuals most closely involved in cultural and artistic production: "many of them could not regain their pre-war social footing, could not relate to Anglo-Saxon culture and customs, and had no common language with less educated fellow Poles".[36] Already in the interwar period in Australia, Połotyński warned that the intelligentsia "would find its vision of an ideal life ending abruptly inside a mine or cutting sugar cane".[37] Reflecting on her frustration at always being considered a foreigner in Australia, Barbara Schenkel confesses "To be an actress with an accent... it was impossible".[38] Periodicals could, then, partially recreate the social roles and social environment that these intellectuals had known in Poland. In Lencznarowicz's words, "journalists, writers, poets, diplomats, historians found a kind of refuge in Polish newspapers for the creativity they were often unable to express in the Australian environment".[39] Referring to *Wiadomości Polskie*, he notes that its contributors were able to recover, to some extent, a world of Polish history and culture which was still very much alive for them, and which they often contrasted both with the actual situation in Poland at the time, and with the Australian reality they faced.[40]

Through their writing they could also *create* new spaces of belonging. Lech Paszkowski—a journalist, writer and editor of historical papers and researcher of the history of Poles in Australia—said something that confirms his alienation from any existing country: "I feel European of Polish-Lithuanian origin".[41] Barbara Schenkel—a journalist, actor and writer of short stories and poems—found herself "on a path of war" with both Catholic and Jewish Polish communities in Australia, and disappointed with Australians: "About Australia she feels regret for her alienation, a 'certain [moral] hangover'. About Poland 'a tragic sadness'".[42] Both Paszkowski and Schenkel developed their skills working and writing for Polish-language weeklies and monthlies, and made significant contributions to cultural and intellectual life in Australia. Paszkowski published several books and a few hundred articles and essays in the Polish-language press in Australia, France and the UK, and Schenkel contributed significantly to multicultural literature and art in Australia.

While some of Kujawa's interviewees[43] focussed on cultural differences and tensions as the most important factor in their alienation, others found their belonging in an acceptance of their creativity (Skubiszewski), in recognition by professional organisations (Skubiszewski, Gotowicz, Kałuski) or in a social contribution and commitment to Australia (Smolicz, Zubrzycki).[44] For many young intellectuals and artists, for whom the war resulted in "a total crush of dreams",[45] Polish-language media provided a space for "a self-reflective discourse".[46] They facilitated the construction of what Smolicz called a "personal cultural system"—"a mediator between the culture of the group and the private world of the individual".[47] Distinguishing it from a set of cultural and social values of the whole ethnic group, he highlights the importance of the autonomous space in which individuals could redefine themselves and validate their own self-concepts.

Interestingly, a younger generation of Polish-Australian writers and artists (Walwicz, Kajetan and Koman) represents a more radical stance on belonging. They either consciously define themselves outside traditional parameters of belonging and even mock them or unconsciously (Kajetan, Koman) associate themselves with new parameters of belonging, such as change, adaptability and process.[48] While all three have contributed significantly to Polish culture in exile and to culture and the arts in Australia, they have not chosen to publish or feature in the Polish-language press but rather sought outlets for their creativity outside it.

Promoting Polish-language Arts

While in 1954 Ludwik Kruszelnicki lamented that *Tygodnik Katolicki* was written "for the ten educated ones" rather than "a thousand uneducated fellow Polish migrants",[49] most editorial teams emphasised their hope for the uniting role of their periodicals—to be, as Ludwik Tabaczyński hoped for the magazine *Echo*, "known to all Poles living in Australia or New Zealand" and to reach "every tent in the remotest wilderness, to become an airborne courier that unites friends scattered wide in this great country".[50] Artistic and cultural life was very important for the Polish community in Australia. A number of cultural societies and discussion fora arose, run usually by members of the local intelligentsia. Among them were Polskie Koło Kulturalno-Artystyczne (the Polish Cultural-Artistic Circle), Polskie Towarzystwo Muzyczne im. Chopina (the Chopin Polish Musical Society) and Związek Artystów Scen Polskich (the Union of Polish Actors) in Melbourne. There were also both professional theatres like Teatr Polski in Adelaide, and amateur theatres, satirical cabaret groups like Wesoła Kookaburra (Merry Kookaburra) in Melbourne or Zielony Kangur (Green Kangaroo) in Sydney, dance groups and musical ensembles.[51]

The Polish-language press played an equally important role in cultural life. Most of the periodicals carried work characterised by an abundance of cultural, literary and artistic forms and themes and published a relatively high number of sophisticated writers. The migrant press not only fostered Polish language but also promoted an interest in Polish history and literature. Clearly, the Polish-language press was not interested merely in conveying practical information, as foreign-language media has often been believed to be.[52] According to Lencznarowicz's research, many authors have pointed out the "cultural function of the media or of individual newspapers published by Polish immigrants and their descendants (…) in countries of migration".[53]

Referring to his close analysis of Polish-language media in Australia, Lencznarowicz stresses that for Polish immigrants "keeping Polish culture alive was a key goal".[54] Among the community's most important aims was maintaining a continued use of Polish. The publishers and editors of Polish-language newspapers had a clear awareness of this need for an active nurturing of Polish-language use. Periodicals such as *Forum, Wiadomości Polskie, Tygodnik Polski* cited as their main raison d'être a "strong commitment to an undiluted form of Polish language"[55] and to "an enriching of the native tongue".[56] Although the standard of Polish spoken by second- and third-generation Polish Australians gradually fell, until it reached the level of a kitchen Polish, in the 1976 Census, over 64,900 people claimed to regularly speak Polish.[57]

Yet, while maintaining a native language is the fundamental responsibility of an ethnolinguistic group such as the Australian Polonia, the actual function of the Polish-language press within the community seems to have been much more complex. The stated aims and assumptions of editors of the Polish-language press did not always correspond to its actual social function, and its thematic focus varied over time. The post-Second World War press editors felt that they had a special mission to foreground critical issues such as Poland's independence, Stalin's Katyń massacre, Soviet repressions and Siberian gulags. Thus, during its most prolific period, the focus was on Polish matters, particularly politics and history (e.g. in *Polish News* 72% of the content was focused on Poland and 5% on Australia), in the form of essays, regular columns, historical sketches, poetry and other literary forms. Referring to *Polish News* and *Polish Weekly*, Kałuski reports that Polish matters comprised 71.6% and 57.2% of the whole content. Cultural themes comprised 19.9% of the text in *Polish News* and 18.1% of *Polish Weekly*, compared to political themes, which dominated the content (34.3% and 34.5%, respectively).[58]

The results of Lencznarowicz's quantitative study of Polish-language newspapers, which aims to capture their role in Polish-Australian society, clearly indicate the significance of cultural themes. Under the category of "cultural subject matter", Lencznarowicz included texts with "historical, literary, religious" themes and "reprints of literary works, most of them deeply embedded in Polish culture". His analysis shows that texts in this category make up 4.2% of all the categories and 14.6% of all the material studied.[59] While their number is the lowest of the different topic categories (behind "Australia"), the actual space they take up in the corpus is second only to the categories of "Polonia" and "Advertisements".[60] A percentage of 26.4 of the material included in the category "cultural subject matter" was made up of novels, stories and book summaries, 20.3% of speeches, homilies and charitable appeals, 8% of poems and songs and 4.8% of reviews. The remaining texts are short biographies, memoirs and aphorisms.[61]

Lencznarowicz notes, however, that the incidence of texts of a cultural character diminishes over time, as reprints of classical and contemporary Polish literary works were no longer included in the press. The number of texts in the category of "cultural subject matter" fell from 22.2% of the material for 1953 to a mere 6.8% of the material for 1977.[62] Yet, despite the fact that cultural content in Polish-language media decreased over time, publications like *Wiadomości Polskie* continued to aspire to the role of a magazine of cultural and social affairs, addressed to intelligentsia readers dispersed across Australia.[63] Many periodicals published poems, short stories, fragments of novels, essays and book reviews, while some magazines were established solely to publish literary works, such as the monthly *Echo-Opowiadania* edited by Ludwik Tabaczyński in Perth (seven issues since 1952). Some commentators, as already mentioned, criticised such an attitude and such aspirations.

Lencznarowicz, however, highlights a very important role of the Polish-language press in popularising Polish literature, both classic and contemporary, as well as Polish émigré authors, among readers. He reports that:

> sometimes entire books as well as excerpts were reprinted. At first, particularly in *Tygodnik Katolicki*, the classics predominated: Henryk Sienkiewicz (*W pustyni i w puszczy* [In Desert and Wilderness], *Quo Vadis*, *Krzyżacy* [The Knights of the Cross]), Bolesław Prus (*Antek*, *Faraon* [Pharaoh]). *Wiadomości Polskie* published excerpts from contemporary Polish works (Karol Ludwik Koniński's *Straszny czwartek w domu pastora* [The Pastor's Terrible Thursday], Marek Hłasko's *Cmentarze* [Cemeteries]). *Nasza Droga*, and for a time also *Tygodnik Polski*, turned to authors likely to attract a wider range of potential readers: Maria Rodziewiczówna, Helena Mniszek. Another approach was to reprint works by Polish émigré authors dealing with immigrant life (Melchior Wańkowicz, Danuta Mostwin). It was easier, however, to resort to poetry than to long prose works. Usually patriotic poems were chosen, often by poets of the Romantic era. Poems by well-known Polish émigré poets also appeared.[64]

He also draws attention to other ways of popularising Polish literature and literary events:

> There were many reviews of new Polish books, mostly of those published outside of Poland. Particular authors were promoted, funds were raised towards the publication of books both in Australia and elsewhere, for example works by Kazimierz Wierzyński,[65] Andrzej Chciuk and Lech Paszkowski. Significant events in Polish émigré literary life were recorded. Bookshops placed advertisements in the [Polonia] media for publishers of Polish migrant literature and for Polish-language literary magazines.

> The promotion of Polish literature was not exclusive to larger-format media, but was also pursued by small-scale bulletins. For example in 1954 the Hobart 'Komunikat Informacyjny' (News Dispatch) reported that it had purchased books and was opening a library, for which it appealed for funds. [...] Readers of newsletters for various migrant associations would encounter advice on 'what to read' and 'how to read', as well as recommendations that they buy Polish books. They might also find accessibly written articles on the best-known Polish authors, and reports on local Polonia literary events.[66]

Among literary genres, satirical writing is one of the richest produced to date in Polish-language media in Australia, alongside lyric poetry, short fiction and memoir. A particularly important genre of Polish newspaper column is called *felieton* (from the French *feuilleton*). Addressing current issues, social and political concerns, and yet allowing for humorous and personal observations, and encouraging a literary style and form, the felieton became an indispensable tool of exiled Polish writers and journalists, aiming to express their nostalgia, anxiety, strong political views and literary ambitions. It shared the characteristics of its French counterpart that have not been adopted in the context of English-language newspapers, and often focused on, for example, "non-political news and gossip, literature and art criticism, a chronicle of the fashions, and epigrams, charades and other literary trifles".[67] In the Polish-language press in Australia this genre appeared regularly across various titles denoting their cultural, literary and arts sections. Felietons in *Kurier Zachodni* (Western Courier) indicate popular themes such as reflecting on the traditions and fashions Polish readers may refer to, lamenting cultural differences or misunderstandings, or satirising customs of Polish immigrants in Australia.[68] An example is *Życiorysy* (Life Stories) by Gawroński: this piece satirises the tendency of Polish immigrants in Australia to assume titles or rank they do not have, in the knowledge that the assumed identity cannot readily be disproven. Under the felieton column, politically and socially engaged poems were also published, such as "Psia Dola" (A Dog's Life) by Gawroński, written as a response to the unusual call of the Chief Council of Polish Organisations in Australia to boycott the first partly free elections in Poland in 1989.[69]

Some common themes of novels, short stories and poems published in the Polish-language press in Australia included the pain of longing for one's homeland, the need to maintain ties to Polish culture, but also reflections on landscapes, cities and people both in Poland and in Australia. There were also reflections on post-war Poland ("PRL" or the People's Republic of Poland), its subjugation by the Soviets, the country's anti-Communist opposition, ideals of freedom, ideas of what Poland could have been.[70] All of these themes were explored in the work of Andrzej Chciuk, Andrzej Gawroński, Zygmunt Przybyłkiewicz, Władysław Romanowski and Ludwik Tabaczyński. At the same time, contributors did speak of the need to engage more with Australian topics; for example, Chciuk's piece, "Write more about Australia" (*Forum* 5 April 1953).

Among Polish-language newspapers, *Wiadomości Polskie* features prominently as an ambitious Sydney periodical seeking to engage readers among the Polonia intelligentsia.[71] It was first published in 1942, as a monthly, 10–20 pages of which were in English to fulfil the government requirements. Its initial print-run of 150, then 200 copies, increased to 5000 copies in 1963–1965, thanks to the efforts of the publisher Dunin-Karwicki and co-editor Gronowski.[72] The official aim of *Wiadomości Polskie*, as defined in 1949, was: "to strive to reach the widest possible range of Australian readers of Polish heritage so as to (...) become a real hub of free Polish thought and expression". Although the weekly was not overtly political, it was decidedly addressed to those "for whom totalitarian ideologies, whether fascist or communist, are equally foreign".[73]

From 1954 onwards, the newspaper's publisher and editor Dunin-Karwicki declared additional goals for it: to help keep Polish culture alive in Australia and to actively *shape* that culture.[74] In one issue he states forcefully that a society's press "helps to constitute [its] culture".[75] Lencznarowicz explains that this comment needs to be understood in the context of the weekly's struggle to stay independent, specifically to "resist being coopted by a nationalist-Catholic viewpoint".[76] In the same issue, in an article titled "The Present Task", the former consul Sylwester Gruszka wrote that the need for "our people to take up professions similar to or better than the ones they worked in before the war" was, as he saw it, the most important problem facing the Polish community and that it provided a strong rationale for the continued publication of *Wiadomości Polskie*.[77]

This focus on talent and creativity and emphasis on the inclusion of cultural content suggests the role the weekly's publishers saw it playing in the local dissemination of Polish culture and tradition.[78] The most important contributors to *Wiadomości Polskie* included many intellectuals and literary figures. In the 1950s Fryderyk Goldschlag contributed literary and dramatic sketches, Adam Nasielski and Andrzej Chciuk wrote felietons as well as contributing excerpts of their novels, Alfred Poniński wrote historical articles and Edmund Jakubowski (Żagiell) edited a regular "Australian commentary" section. Andrzej Gawroński was renowned for his satirical pieces. Significant contributions were also made by Richard Krygier, Tadeusz Sariusz Bielski, Zbigniew Jasiński, Jerzy Malcharek, Lech Paszkowski, Władysław Polak, Zygmunt Przybyłkiewicz (Prawdzic), Father Wojciech Sojka, Jerzy Zubrzycki and many others.[79] *Wiadomości Polskie* published novels in instalments, such as Leszek Szymański's *Żywot codzienny Państwa Wiśniewskich w Australii* (The Daily Life of the Wiśniewski Family in Australia).

Tygodnik Polski (Polish Weekly), initially published under the name *Tygodnik Katolicki* (Catholic Weekly), also carried a good deal of literary work, particularly once it took on a more secular direction. Contributors included the satirist Andrzej Gawroński, Krystyna Jackiewicz, Maria Boniecka and, again, Andrzej Chciuk—who wrote a regular felieton for the weekly entitled "Szczypta soli" (A pinch of salt). An important contributor was Roman Gronowski, who became the paper's editor in 1960.

At the very end of 1950 the first edition of *Polski Tygodnik Niezależny—Echo* appeared in Perth, edited by Ludwik Tabaczyński (1950–15 June 1952), with a print-run of 3000 copies. It was a general weekly with community information but it also carried a significant proportion of literary content. Tabaczyński published his own poems, short stories, and articles in it under the pen names W.M. Tereński, Tyński and Obieżyświat (literally, "World-Rover").[80] Other contributors included Ludmiła Błotnicka, Marek M. Bułat, Henryk Jaworski, Jerzy Lechard, Janina Rejman, Józef Nilwen and Edmund Parnes.

The year 1952 saw the publication of the first issue of the literary-cultural magazine *Echo-Opowiadania. Polski Przegląd Literacko-Informacyjny* (Echo-Stories. Polish Literary Review & News Bulletin), also edited by Tabaczyński. This is an interesting example of a magazine which openly declared its cultural and literary aims, providing readers with a form of "cultural entertainment which gives them the opportunity to savour the beauty of their native language and to appreciate some works of foreign [world] literature" (1952, no 1). The editors promote *Echo-Opowiadania* by describing it (on the inside cover) as "the only magazine of its kind among Poles in exile".[81] The first text—a story—published in the issue number 3 begins by asserting that "*Echo-Opowiadania* carries pieces that are either true or invented, but always interesting".[82]

Andrzej Chciuk, Andrzej Gawroński, Mieczysław Grodzki, Andrzej Rawita and Lech Paszkowski, all published their work in *Echo-Opowiadania*. The main literary form published in the magazine was the short story, as one of the early issues—number 3 of 1952, indicates. There are also examples of travel writing and of cultural commentary. The editor Tabaczyński contributed several satirical pieces and felietons, using pen names. Some texts in English also appear, such as an English translation of a short story by Guy de Maupassant, and articles on Polish dance and on Polish immigrant culture (a library in Paris). These various texts are interspersed with jokes, in both Polish and English, and frequent advertisements; the issue concludes with a cycle of poems.

At first *Echo-Opowiadania* appeared as a fortnightly supplement to the weekly *Echo*, but later it became a monthly. Tabaczyński was clearly devoted to keeping a cultural and literary magazine going, since he continued to publish *Echo-Opowiadania* even after the weekly *Echo* stopped appearing (after its 50th issue). But after five issues, *Echo-Opowiadania* was replaced with an economic bulletin that no longer carried any literary content. The editor commented, in the final issue of *Echo-Opowiadania*, that "evidently a publication of this kind is not needed here", or else "economic circumstances are such that sales cannot be relied upon".[83]

Just as *Echo-Opowiadania* was being discontinued, a new independent magazine aimed at intelligentsia readers started appearing in Sydney, with an equally strong focus on culture and literature. This was the weekly *Forum. Polskie Pismo Niezależne w Australii* (Forum: Independent Polish Magazine in Australia), which appeared from January to July 1953, under the editorship of Bolesław Karpowski, a former editor of *Wiadomości Polskie*. Andrzej Chciuk and Zygmunt Przybyłkiewicz published their work in *Forum*. Another publication that lasted a good deal longer was *Nurt. Czasopismo społeczne* (Current: Social Magazine), published from

1963 until the end of 1968. This was a sociopolitical magazine by its own designation, but it also carried poetry, including the work of Zbigniew Jasiński, Maria Boniecka, and Jan Nordan-Schmit.[84]

Literary supplements to various newspapers were the most obvious venue for literary work to appear. Aiming to reach the widest possible audience and seeking to diversify the content of *Wiadomości Polskie*, Dunin-Karwicki published a large number of supplements with the paper: 24 supplements of varying frequency and 18 one-off supplements. Among them were supplements for children, for female readers, for sports enthusiasts and also a popular science supplement ("Wiek Wiedzy" [Age of Knowledge]), a historical supplement ("Ziemie Piastowskie" [The Piast Dynasty Territories]), and literary supplements such as "Widnokręgi" (Horizons) and "Iskry" (Sparks). The aim of "Widnokręgi" was "to acquaint Polish society in Australia and New Zealand with the original work of a handful of writers and artists living under the Southern Cross".[85] Attempting to revive "Widnokręgi" many years later, Andrzej Gawroński wrote that to attract Polish-Australian readers "we must be [...] as versatile as we can in our choice of material to ensure that we cater to as broad a range of interests as possible".[86] He conceded, however, that "Widnokręgi" could not attain the level of *Kultura* in Paris or *Wiadomości* in London.[87]

Although literary supplements were the most obvious vehicle for publishing literary work, they met with no popular support among either writers or readers, as Lencznarowicz notes. The supplement "Iskry" (Sparks), edited by Władysław Romanowski, appeared in the Christmas edition of *Wiadomości Polskie* in 1966[88] but was then discontinued. Andrzej Chciuk's "Margines" (Margin), a "literary-cultural" supplement to *Tygodnik Polski*, appeared from 1967 to 1972, in 15 four-page issues.

In the 1950s and 1960s, many texts in Polish by authors based in Australia also appeared in the well-known Polish émigré press in London or Paris. In the Parisian journal *Kultura* (Culture), from 1950 to 1956 and from 1973 to 2000, E. Żagiell (the pen-name of Edmund Jakubowski), Jerzy Dobrostański and Jerzy Grot-Kwaśniewski contributed an engaging overview of Polonia life in Australia. Roman Gronowski, Lech Paszkowski, Andrzej Chciuk and Adam Nasielski also wrote about the Australian Polonia for *Kultura*'s "Kronika australijska" (Australian Chronicles) section. Thematically, the Australian Chronicles did not differ much from other chronicles of this kind. Nevertheless, the care with which these authors portrayed a wide range of events, and the monthly appearances of the "Kronika", makes it a unique and remarkable document of Polish migrant experience in Australia, New Zealand and the United States.[89]

Other established Polish émigré writers residing in the UK, France or Germany published occasionally in Polish-language periodicals in Australia. Among them were Tymon Terlecki, a literary and theatre critic and doyen of Polish émigré literature, and Zygmunt Nowakowski, an actor, theatre director, Polish philologist and writer of felietons who published in *Wiadomości Polskie*. Flyers, reviews and appraisals of acclaimed Polish artists who started visiting Australia in the late 1950s, following the period of "thaw" in Poland, all helped to circulate news of cultural events via the Polish-language press. Among such visitors from Poland were singers (Mieczysław Fogg and Irena Santor), composers and artists (Krzysztof Penderecki and Konstanty Andrzej Kulka), travelling theatres and dance groups.

CONCLUSION

The intellectual and literary dimension of the Polish-language press in Australia is a significant aspect of these publications that has not really been explored to date. Approaching the foreign-language press in Australia through this lens can expand our understanding of it beyond its functions as a supplier of "culturally relevant and locally vital information to immigrants in the host society"[90] and its contribution "to the ethnic diversity of a multi-ethnic public sphere".[91] Investigation of the Polish-language press in Australia shows that it has also been a space for "a self-reflective discourse among migrants",[92] "a platform for self-expression",[93] and "the (re-)creation of alternative imaginative space alongside existing mappings".[94] The profusion of cultural and literary forms and themes in most of the periodicals created by professional and talented writers, in spite of decreasing readership and financial hardship, points to the press's role in the formation of *shared* identities as well as negotiating immigrants' personal spaces within a broader society.[95]

Approving of Kowalik's observation that "the most faithful companion of Polish migrant society is its press", Lencznarowicz draws attention to the cultural and literary dimensions of the Polish-language press in Australia. He also argues that the intellectual ambitions of the press did not mean that "most of the Polish [Australian] intelligentsia read Polish-language newspapers, but only that the style and fairly high standard of many of the papers was due to the number of representatives of that intelligentsia among both contributors and readers".[96]

The strongly literary and cultural character of the Polish-language press in Australia was particularly discernible in the 1950s and 1960s, and was gradually diluted as post-war migrants grew older and died. The second generation was not interested in this material or indeed in specifically Polish themes. Many would have been unable to read in Polish, even though they maintained some elements of Polish culture. In fact, the Polish-language press, as Lencznarowicz points out, never became a real diasporic press.[97] In other words, it was never developed by future generations as a platform for engaging with "matters Polish" or cultivating attachment to Polish culture and traditions.

In spite of its importance for the community in Australia and in a global context, the Polish-language press was often criticised for imposing opinions on readers, being too much focused on Poland (Andrzej Racieski), too political and yet ineffective in initiating a wider political debate, or even too snobbish. In 1972 Nasielski anticipated in an article on Australia for the Parisian Polish journal *Kultura* that historians of the post-Second World War Polish migration would undoubtedly report on a number of facts, among others "that the Polish press here was read by less than ten percent of Polish migrants and did not so much reflect public opinion as attempt to create it".[98]

Nevertheless, the literary ambitions of the Polish-language press form a small but very important element of the multi- and transcultural landscape of Australia. They help to define Polish culture in Australia and to characterise Polish émigré culture within a global context. They also illuminate some of the least known and most hidden histories of migration to Australia, and hence refine perspectives on Australia's migrant communities, past and present. Finally, they contribute to a broader understanding of migrant and diasporic cultures, and their extraordinary diversity.

Acknowledgement We would like to acknowledge the extensive research undertaken by Professor Jan Lencznarowicz (Jagiellonian University, Kraków) which we have drawn on throughout our chapter.

NOTES

1. Miriam Gilson and Jerzy Zubrzycki, *The Foreign Language Press in Australia 1847–1964* (Canberra: Australian National University Press, 1967), 17.
2. Gilson and Zubrzycki, *The Foreign*, 25.
3. *The Mercury* July 24, 1939, 6.
4. *The Mercury* July 24, 1939, 6.
5. *The Age* January 27, 1950, 3.
6. *The Age* January 27, 1950, 3.
7. Sir Richard Boyer, "The Australian Citizenship Convention, Canberra, 1961, official transcript, 95", cited in Gilson and Zubrzycki, *The Foreign*, 169.
8. M.D., *Le Courrier Australien* March 3, 1967, 7.
9. Jan Dunin-Karwicki, "Foreign Press has United Policy for Integration", *Good Neighbour*, March 1, 1967, p. 2.
10. Dunin-Karwicki, "Foreign Press", 2. However, the role of a foreign-language press during times of political mobilisation, such as national elections, cannot be underestimated. For example, during the Federal elections of 1974, the biggest foreign-language newspaper in Australia at that time, the Italian paper *Il Globo* (ed. XX, circulation 45,000) took a neutral stand, the second largest, Greek *Neos Kosmos* (ed. Gogos, circulation 20000) supported Labor, while the third largest, *Tygodnik Polski* (ed. Gronowski)— the Liberals (David Balderstone, "What the migrant papers say", *The Bulletin* 096 (4905) May 11, 1974, 18).
11. Marian Kałuski, "Prasa Polska w Australii 1928–1988", *Studia polonijne*, 13 (1989), 231.
12. Kałuski, "Prasa Polska", 229.
13. Polish migrant newspapers were never set up as joint-stock companies, nor financed by banks, they had to support themselves. (Kałuski, "Prasa Polska", 233).
14. Kałuski, "Prasa Polska", 221–235.
15. See Jon Bekken, "Negotiating Class and Ethnicity: The Polish-Language Press in Chicago", *Polish American Studies*, 57, no. 2 (2000), 5.
16. See Myria Georgiou, *Diaspora, Identity and the Media* (New Jersey: Hampton Press, 2006).
17. Joanna Kujawa, *Migration, Belonging, Alienation: The narratives of Polish adventurers, artists and intellectuals in Australia* (Saarbrucken Germany: VDM Verlag Dr. Muller, 2010).
18. Stefan Markowski, Katarzyna Kwapisz Williams, "Australian Polonia: A Diaspora on the Wane?" *Central and Eastern European Migration Review*, 2, no. 1 (2013), 13.

19. Markowski, Kwapisz Williams, "Australian Polonia", 14.
20. For an extensive review of works on the diasporic Polish-language press, see Jan Lenczarowicz, *Prasa i społeczność polska w Australii 1928–1980* (Kraków: Księgarnie Akademickie, 1994), 5–7.
21. Kałuski, "Prasa Polska", 221.
22. Katarzyna Kwapisz Williams, "Between Utopia and Autobiography: Migrant Narratives in Australia", in *Migrant Nation: Australian Culture, Society and Identity*, ed. Paul Longley Arthur (London & New York: Anthem Press, 2018), 179.
23. Egon Kunz, *Displaced Persons. Calwell's New Australians* (Sydney: Australian National University Press, 1988); Kwapisz Williams, "Between Utopia", 179.
24. Lenczarowicz, *Prasa i społeczność*, 88.
25. Lenczarowicz, *Prasa i społeczność*, 89, 91.
26. Mary Besemeres, "Evoking a Displaced Homeland: The 'Poetic Memoir' of Andrzej Chciuk", *Transnational Literature* 10.1 (2017), http://fhrc.flinders.edu.au/transnational/home.html.
27. Adam Nasielski, "Początek końca", *Kultura* 5 (320) (1974): 104.
28. Adam Nasielski, "Australia", *Kultura* 4 (295) (1972): 124.
29. Nasielski, "Początek", 103–104.
30. Kałuski, "Prasa Polska", 232.
31. Lenczarowicz, *Prasa i społeczność*, 119.
32. Lenczarowicz, *Prasa i społeczność*, 105.
33. Trzeciak, cited in Lenczarowicz, *Prasa i społeczność*, 63.
34. Nasielski, "Początek", 103.
35. Nasielski, "Początek", 103.
36. Jan Lenczarowicz, "Wiadomości Polskie w Sydney", *Kwartalnik Historii Prasy Polskiej*, 31.2 (1992): 39.
37. *Polonia Australijska,* February 1931, 45.
38. Cited in Kujawa, *Migration, Belonging*, 128.
39. Lenczarowicz, *Prasa i społeczność*, 105.
40. Lenczarowicz, "Wiadomości Polskie", 43.
41. Cited in Kujawa, *Migration, Belonging*, 122.
42. Kujawa, *Migration, Belonging*, 128.
43. Kujawa, *Migration, Belonging*.
44. Kujawa, *Migration, Belonging*, 111.
45. Jan Paszkowski, cited in Kujawa, *Migration, Belonging*, 121.
46. See Cigdem Bozdag, Andreas Hepp and Laura Suna, "Diasporic Media as the 'Focus' of Communicative Networking Among Migrants", *Mediating Cultural Diversity in a Globalized Public Space*, ed. Isabelle Rigoni, Eugenie Saitta (London: Palgrave Macmillan, 2012): 96–115.

47. Jerzy Smolicz, "Personal Cultural Systems in a Plural Society", *The Polish Sociological Bulletin* 50, no. 2 (1980): 21.
48. Kujawa, *Migration, Belonging.*
49. *Tygodnik Katolicki,* November 13, 1954.
50. Ludwik Tabaczyński, *Echo* February 10, 1951; cited in Lencznarowicz, *Prasa i społeczność,* 93.
51. Lenczarowicz, "Wiadomości Polskie", 39.
52. Gilson and Zubrzycki, *The Foreign.*
53. Lenczarowicz, *Prasa i społeczność,* 190.
54. Lenczarowicz, *Prasa i społeczność,* 189.
55. *Forum,* July 5, 1953.
56. *Wiadomości Polskie,* March 12, 1955.
57. Markowski, Kwapisz Williams, "Australian Polonia", 13–36.
58. Kałuski, "Prasa Polska", 221–235.
59. These thematic categories are not clearly defined. Lencznarowicz uses a different system from Gilson and Zubrzycki. The latter define "culture and education" more broadly (e.g. they include childrearing and keeping up national customs, and state that 'culture and education' in this sense take up 12.5% of the material and 5.9% of responses).
60. Lenczarowicz, *Prasa i społeczność,* 191–192.
61. Lenczarowicz, *Prasa i społeczność,* 198.
62. Lenczarowicz, *Prasa i społeczność,* 194.
63. Lenczarowicz, "Wiadomości Polskie", 40.
64. Lenczarowicz, *Prasa i społeczność,* 198.
65. A celebrated Polish poet who lived in New York from 1941 until 1964.
66. Lenczarowicz, *Prasa i społeczność,* 198–199.
67. Chisholm Hugh, ed. "Feuilleton", *Encyclopædia Britannica* 10, 11th edn. (Cambridge: Cambridge University Press, 1911), 305.
68. *Kurier Zachodni,* January 1990; *Kurier Zachodni,* May 1991; *Kurier Zachodni,* March 1989.
69. *Kurier Zachodni,* June 1989, 28. See also Andrzej Gawroński, *Mój punkt widzenia: Felietony australijskie,* ed. Bogumiła Żongołłowicz (Toruń: Uniwersytet Mikołaja Kopernika, 1999), 27–28.
70. For example, Chciuk's poem "Modlitwa" (Prayer) proclaims: "wierzył będę/aż do śmierci/w polski kanon i legendę:/w wolność pieśni" [I will believe/till my death/in the Polish canon and legend:/in the freedom of song].
71. Lenczarowicz, "Wiadomości Polskie", 45.
72. Lenczarowicz, "Wiadomości Polskie", 26.
73. Editorial, *Wiadomości Polskie,* March 1949, 40.
74. Lenczarowicz, "Wiadomości Polskie", 36. *Wiadomości Polskie* was to "1. Inform readers of world events, from a Polish perspective anchored in the

idea of a free and independent Poland. 2. Impartially report on Polish migrant life. 3. Safeguard Polish interests in Australia and New Zealand. 4. Represent Polish life in Australia and New Zealand and social issues in a way that will consolidate the Polish community. 5. Preserve an attachment to Polishness among the migrant community; 6. Nurture the use of an undiluted Polish language. 7. Work towards greater closeness between Poles and Australians". "Nowy etap", *Wiadomości Polskie* February 7, 1954.

75. *Wiadomości Polskie* 10 October 1965.
76. Lenczarowicz, "Wiadomości Polskie", 37.
77. Lenczarowicz, "Wiadomości Polskie", 41.
78. Lenczarowicz, "Wiadomości Polskie", 39.
79. See Lenczarowicz, *Prasa i społeczność*, 60; Lenczarowicz, "Wiadomości Polskie". In the 1960s "particularly active contributors not yet mentioned included: Eugeniusz Bajkowski, who wrote mainly on economics for many Australian newspapers, the Adelaide historian Marian Szczepanowski, Jerzy Steinmetz who had recently arrived from Poland, and Jerzy J. Działak (J. Flemming) who was temporarily in Australia. Others were Gabriela Barton-Bartkowska, Zygmunt Konrad Bernaś, General Juliusz Kleeberg, Leopold Muszkat, Tomasz W. Ostrowski, Władysław Romanowski, Roman Rossleigh, Aleksander Sienkiewicz, Tadeusz Sobolewski and Janusz H. Wróblewski."
80. Lenczarowicz, *Prasa i społeczność*, 69.
81. *Echo-Opowiadania*, 3, 1952.
82. *Echo Opowiadania*, 3, 1952, 3.
83. *Echo-Opowiadania*, 5, 1953, cited in Lencznarowicz, *Prasa i społeczność*, 70.
84. Lenczarowicz, *Prasa i społeczność*, 72–73.
85. *Wiadomości Polskie*, 1 April 1956; Lenczarowicz, *Prasa i społeczność*, 198.
86. *Tygodnik Polski*, 28 October 1978.
87. Lenczarowicz, *Prasa i społeczność*, 198.
88. Lencznarowicz, Prasa i społeczność, 198; Lenczarowicz, "Wiadomości Polskie", 31.
89. Iwona Hofman, "Kroniki emigracyjne paryskiej *Kultury*, Rekonesans badawczy", *Annales Universitatis Mariae Curie-Skłodowska, Lublin - Polonia* 9 (2002): 87–99.
90. Hang Yin, "Chinese-Language Cyberspace, Homeland Media and Ethnic Media: A Contested Space for Being Chinese", *New Media and Society*, 17, no. 4 (2013): 558.
91. Charles Husband, "Media and the Public Sphere in Multi-Ethnic Societies," In *Ethnic Minorities and the Media*, ed. Simon Cottle (Buckingham: Open University Press, 2000), 206.
92. See Bozdag, Hepp and Suna, "Diasporic Media".

93. Bekken, "Negotiating Class", 5.
94. H. Karim Karim, "Mapping the Diasporic Mediascape," in *The Media of Diaspora*, ed. Karim H. Karim (London: Routledge. Karim, 2003), 1–18.
95. Bekken, "Negotiating Class", 5.
96. Lenczarowicz, *Prasa i społeczność*, 105.
97. Lenczarowicz, *Prasa i społeczność*, 119.
98. Nasielski, "Australia", 124.

CHAPTER 8

Exploring the Migrant Experience Through an Examination of Letters to *The New Australian*

Karen Agutter

In September 1946, an estimated 14 million civilians, 12 million *Volksdeutsche* (ethnic Germans), and the survivors of the Reich's 500 concentration and work camps were uprooted and mobile across Europe and beyond.[1] From this mass of people, the United Nations Relief and Rehabilitation Administration (UNRRA), which was responsible for administering aid to the victims of war, officially labelled eight million as Displaced Persons (DPs).[2] While the majority of these DPs were, sometimes forcibly, repatriated to their countries of origin, over 1.2 million, from a number of ethnic and national origins, remained stateless, housed in the over 700 makeshift camps which extended from northern Germany to Southern Italy.[3]

K. Agutter (✉)
University of Adelaide, Adelaide, SA, Australia
e-mail: karen.agutter@adelaide.edu.au

© The Author(s) 2020
C. Dewhirst, R. Scully (eds.), *The Transnational Voices of Australia's Migrant and Minority Press*, Palgrave Studies in the History of the Media,
https://doi.org/10.1007/978-3-030-43639-1_8

As the International Refugee Organisation (IRO) replaced UNRRA as the responsible agency, the emphasis on finding homes for the displaced shifted from repatriation to resettlement. The wait for a new start in a new homeland was long, with some DPs spending years in one or more of the camps. Eventually, between 1947 and 1954, over one million DPs were resettled globally, including in Britain and within Europe, in the Americas and Canada, and in Australia and New Zealand.[4] Scholars continue to debate the humanitarian nature of this global response with many concluding, as Ruth Balint argues, that for the majority of nations the acceptance of these refugees was primarily motivated by the need to provide a labour supply to fuel post-war economies.[5] In Australia, this was certainly the case, as the need for post-war economic and population expansion drove the acceptance of over 170,000 DPs (second only to the United States) between 1947 and 1953.[6]

In contrast to the majority of receiving nations, Australia exerted considerable control over the DPs from the time of their arrival, and for the early months and years of their settlement. These European refugees represented the first mass intake of non-English-speaking migrants in a nation, which had been deeply committed to an immigration policy (*Immigration Restriction Act* 1901), which not only ensured "whiteness" but also supported the Britishness of its population and the hard-fought protection of its workers. Therefore, it was essential to the success of the scheme that the DPs quickly and seamlessly assimilated into the Australian way of life[7] and did not compete with Australians for housing or employment.

This need to appease the general Australian population, to condition them towards the acceptance of large numbers of non-British, non-English-speaking migrants, resulted in a range of unique conditions. First and foremost was the requirement for DPs to work for a period of two years in allocated employment, the men generally as labourers, the women as domestics.[8] Secondly, all DPs (and later other assisted European migrants) were housed on arrival in government-run accommodation, beginning with the Reception and Training Centres. Once allocated to employment, breadwinners were housed in workers camps while dependent women and children were sent to Holding Centres.[9] Aside from the very basic facilities and unaccustomed food, the most significant and often long-term consequence of the combination of the accommodation centres and the work contract was the terrible separation of family units, often across thousands of miles. Finally, the expectation of rapid assimilation exposed DPs (and later European migrants) to a variety of methods to achieve this aim, including English language and Australian history and civics lessons, interaction with the specifically established *Good Neighbour Council*, and exposure to a dedicated monthly newspaper, *The New Australian*.[10] This newspaper aided assimilation through regular features, including lessons in English and information about the Australian way of life.

This chapter, after a brief description of *The New Australian,* examines the previously unstudied letters written by new arrivals to the monthly "Write to us" column within this publication. Through an exploration of these letters, held in their original form in the National Archives of Australia, this chapter demonstrates that this correspondence not only contributes to our knowledge of the post-war European refugee and migrant experience in Australia, but also offers a rare opportunity to explore the historical migrant voice.

A NEWSPAPER FOR NEWCOMERS: *THE NEW AUSTRALIAN*

In December 1947, the Department of Immigration's publicity officer, Hugh Murphy, drew up plans for a monthly newspaper, tentatively entitled *Advancing Australia*, with the explicit aim of conditioning the Australian public towards the acceptance of large numbers of non-English-speaking migrants.[11] The first edition, under the banner *Tomorrow's Australians,* was distributed in April 1948 amongst the wider press, radio, Good Neighbour Councils, churches, and social welfare organisations, unions, employers, and other interested parties.[12] The perceived success of this publication led the Department of Immigration to establish a second monthly newspaper, *The New Australian* (January 1949–December 1953). This second publication was specifically aimed at European migrants, and DPs in particular.

Heavily illustrated, and written in simple English, the primary aim of *The New Australian* was to educate new-arrivals in the Australian way of life, to begin the process of assimilation, and to help them to become, in the words of Hugh Murphy, "good Australian citizens".[13] Accordingly, each month the newspaper published articles about the nation, on topics such as Australian sport, and explanations of public holidays and customs. These feature articles ran alongside regular columns including "Easy English" and "What's in the newspapers", which summarised mainstream news items in simple language.[14] The newspaper also informed new arrivals on the requirements of alien registration and citizenship, provided news from the DP camps in Europe and on the arrival of DP ships, and regularly featured stories about the industries in which DPs were working; again in the words of Hugh Murphy, in order "to impress on them the importance of their work".[15]

The first issue ran to 17,000 copies. However, production quickly expanded to 40,000 copies per month, and then significantly more, though exact numbers are difficult to ascertain. Initially production costs were carefully monitored and debated, but as the success of the newspaper grew, more and more were printed, including the reprinting of back issues and 2000 extra copies per month for distribution overseas.[16]

One copy of *The New Australian* was given to each DP on arrival in Australia, as a way of introducing them to the publication and in the hope of encouraging future readership. The newspaper was also available at the Reception and Training and other accommodation centres, and the content was extensively used within the English and civics lessons. Once placed in employment, issues were sent to the migrants' places of work on the basis of one copy to each migrant employed separately, and one copy among three for migrants employed in groups.[17] Lists of DPs and workplaces were provided, and regularly updated by the Department of Labour and National Service, which was responsible for the allocation of employment. This ongoing contact with migrants after they had left the Reception and Training Centres was seen as particularly important and interaction between the European migrants and the immigration publicity office was encouraged through two regular columns, "My Australia" and "Write to us".[18]

The aim of the "My Australia" column was to provide an account, usually positive and successful, of the experiences of individual migrants in their early weeks and months in the country. To encourage submissions, "New Australians" were offered a prize of 10/6 for the best article received and five shillings for "runner up articles" each month. According to the newspaper itself, the response was "splendid" and they received so many articles that it was "hard to decide which ones should be published".[19] Although cross-checking of the contributors' names within the archives indicates that the featured migrants and the general content (such as place of abode or employment) were accurate, the perfect English and the general positivity of the content of this column suggest editorial manipulation. Therefore, as the original submissions are not locatable in the archives, and there is some question as to the authenticity of the migrant voice within the content of this column, they are not considered here.

By contrast, the letters written to the newspaper for the "Write to us" column are available in their original form, in the migrants' own hand, in the files of the National Archives of Australia. Furthermore, each letter was answered either in person by the staff of the Department or, especially if the question was one of potential interest and/or relevance to many, within the newspaper itself. Therefore, an exploration of these letters provides useful insight into migrant life in Australia in this period and to the social interaction between the new arrivals and the receiving society.

From the very first edition, readers were encouraged to write to *The New Australian*; to ask questions, discuss problems, make suggestions about the content of the newspaper, and generally have their say on their new homeland. This invitation continued to be issued in all subsequent editions, and readers were further encouraged to write, even if they did not know much English, as it would be good practice for them.[20] It is important to note, however, that letters written in other languages were translated into English, and that the paper was apparently open to all comments, as they noted: "a few of you have criticised us. We do not mind that. Some of you have made suggestions. We like that".[21]

So what do these migrant letters say? The subjects of the letters are varied, however by far the most common are those requesting copies of *The New Australian*, or notifying the Department of any change of address in order to continue to receive the publication. The sheer scale of these letters indicates a genuine level of support for the publication, an overwhelming sense of gratitude on behalf of many of the correspondents. In fact, there are a number of quite effusive letters of praise for the publication including one from Lithuanian, Romualdas Maziliauskas of Adelaide, who wrote that he was surprised with the first copy of the *New Australian* "a paper published special" to help them start a new life. He went on that he wanted to see it grow bigger and perhaps weekly.[22] Similarly, Ina Kirstuks who worked at the District Hospital in Cowra commented: "It is rather a very nice Paper and we could spend quite a lot of Time with it [*sic*]".[23]

Another DP, H. R. Saraph, an Estonian who worked and lived at Warragamba Dam, commented that *The New Australian* created "a feeling of security among us - the feeling that we are not forgotten, but taken care of".[24] This sentiment was echoed by Lithuanian Linda Grebliauskas who wrote that the newspaper was a "very good idea ... It gives us a good information and keeps us in contact with the other migrants. Some of the migrants are working in very lonely place [*sic*], and we often think, we are forgotten".[25]

However, there were some contrasting voices including that of Estonian Elvira Karmik, of the Mulwala Hostel in Canberra, who was insulted to have received *The New Australian*. She wrote:

> I have been sent "The New Australian" without having asked for it ... Being a university graduate, I am able to read and understand Australian newspapers and literature of higher intellectual standard.[26]

In his reply, Hugh Murphy stated that:

> The majority of the new settlers reaching our country from Europe find the newspaper most informative, and they are particularly pleased with the simple English that is used for their convenience.[27]

Three months later, Elvira wrote again:

> I regret to inform you that I still receive the New Australian at the Bureau of Census & Statistics ... where I work. I want to point out once more that in a democratic country I feel and want to be free to read what I like.[28]

Elvira had arrived on the first DP transport, the *General Heintzelman*, and, with a small number of other women, was specifically selected for her standard of education and her language skills to work as a typist in a government department.

In another letter, Latvian Ilse Simon wrote expressing more general grievances, stating that there were many good reasons to complain as migrants did not know the truth of the living and working conditions in Australia. Ilse's letter went on to compare the Australian camps and the food provided unfavourably to those in Germany. As she explained, she had left a job as a dentist in a US army hospital to come to Australia; however, she was now employed as a domestic in a hospital, as she was unable to work as trained, and unable to register as a dentist without studying for a further four years. In her words:

> I feel very bitter about it all and can truly say that I was brought here on false pretences ... my opinion is shared by dozens of migrants ... we can not [*sic*] be expected to feel enormously thankful ... a great part of us come from

countries with high culture. We discern the truth but as we have choice we have to make the best of a bad bargain … many of us will leave Australia when the 2 years are over.[29]

Ilse is not alone in her anger and disappointment: the second-most common theme within the letters is about work, specifically the problems of the required work contracts and the associated issues of pay and taxes.

As already stated, after arrival DPs were required to work under contract for two years in allocated positions, generally in jobs which were very physical in nature and in industries which were considered essential to the post-war recovery and advancement of Australia. Male DPs were employed as general labourers in sugar and other harvesting, in infrastructure projects, including road, rail, and hydro-electricity, and in the manufacture of essential materials, such as building bricks and fertiliser, with no consideration given to any previous experience or qualifications. Women, with very few exceptions, were employed in domestic service in private homes, and in institutions such as hospitals.

This homogenous allocation as labourer or domestic was understandably difficult for many DPs, especially the large numbers of highly educated and professionally qualified arrivals. Many migrant letters asked why their qualifications were not accepted, why they could not choose their employment, and if they could refuse the allocated positions. Just one of many examples is that of Lithuanian Viktoras Sniuksta, who on 3 May 1949, asked, "Has the Employment Officer at the Reception Centre an obligation to respect the profession and desire of the new settler", and can a migrant refuse to accept a specific job?[30] Letters such as Viktoras' prompted regular columns in *The New Australian*, as the Department of Immigration reminded the DPs of their obligations under the IRO agreement they had signed in Europe, outlined the rare reasons for change of employment, such as severe ill health, and repeated the threat that they would be subject to deportation if they did not comply.[31]

For some DPs the situation was untenable, and in January 1949 a DP from Sydney who signed himself, simply and anonymously, "R. R." asked what he called an "unpleasant question"—"How is it possible to leave Australia?".[32] R. R. was deeply unhappy and unsettled, and believed he would never be happy in Australia. He sought a legal means of departure, however he also hinted at deliberately leaving his job, so that he might be deported to Germany.[33]

Rarer are the examples of the other side of the argument as expressed by Ukrainian Wasyl Miroschnyk, who was working for the Railways on the Broken Hill Line. He wrote:

> In the last edition of "The New Australian" I read through the article "MINISTER'S STERN WARNING TO THOSE WHO LEAVE JOBS" – about four displaced persons who had left their job without permission. I cannot image [sic] that among D.P.'s are people who can do so ... They should not forget that they were brought to Australia without any charge 13.000 miles; they were given the job and the same wages as Australian workers. I am shy that among D.P.'s such kind of people are to found. If these four men are not satisfied with conditions and the living standard in Australia, they won't find satisfaction nowhere on our Planet. Let them go to the DREAMLAND, where the people do not work, where the rivers are full of vine, where the fried pigs and hens are running around. But I think they will not be content there too [sic].[34]

REUNIFICATION OF FAMILIES

The separation of families and loved ones in the post-war period was particularly acute. DP families sometimes found themselves separated across continents, either as relatives' whereabouts were unknown or as a result of resettlement on different sides of the world. The reunification of families and friends is another dominant theme in the letters to *The New Australian*. For example, a letter from Latvian Heinrich Kukkit asked how he and his friend could get their wives and children to Australia as they were "stuck in the Russian Zone".[35] The advice in the letter of reply was to the point and not hopeful as it explained that the families must cross into the British or US zones to be eligible as nothing could be done from the Russian zone.[36] Questions about the European zones of occupation or about the other countries that DPs had been sent to by the IRO were common, and as a reply to Estonian-born Alfreds Krievins, whose mother and sister had been settled in England, stated: "Unfortunately, if the IRO has settled people in other countries, it is most unlikely that it will resettle them in another land".[37]

The situation was also complicated by status, as this correspondence between Polish-born Stanislaw Rybak and the Department indicates. Stanislaw, or Stanley as he called himself, wrote that he had now been in Australia for three months and he, like many others, had left women and children in Germany who are not DPs. He asked, how could they get them to Australia? In response, the Department of Information stated:

> You do not say whether you are married to these women. For example they might be widows whom you and your friends wish to marry. That is a very important point. If they are the wives of you and your friends, there will not be much trouble in bringing them out. If they are your fiancés there will be a lot of trouble in bringing them from Germany. The best thing you can do is to write to the Commonwealth Migration Officer ... In your letter make it clear what relation these women and children in Germany are to you and your friends. Also tell him that you would like them to obtain D.P. status, but if that is not possible, that you would like a landing permit for them to come to Australia.[38]

This level of helpfulness and advice was not uncommon and some effort was made by the employees of the Department to help in the reunification of families, especially where separation had occurred due to IRO resettlement. For example, Elmer Johanson, who was living in Canada, wrote that he was looking for his brother Endel who he thought had been sent to Australia. In response, the Department established that he was in Australia and passed on the Canadian address of his brother so that he might contact him if he wished.[39] In response to enquiries of a more general nature, such as the letter from Maria Sihver-wiegand of Sweden, a paragraph was published in *The New Australian* asking European migrants if they knew anything of her missing son, Dimitri.[40]

Letters seeking reunification were not confined to those with loved ones overseas and there are many examples of letters from within Australia of DPs seeking information about other DPs, both friends and relatives, and of the Department passing on addresses or the names of the accommodation centres in which they had been placed so that contact could be made.[41] In fact one DP, J. B. Wolny, suggested that *The New Australian* would be of better service if instead of sports columns they had a find a friend section where migrants could have their name and address printed alongside the name of the person they are trying to locate,[42] however the Department continued to conduct most of these enquiries outside of the publication.

PROBLEMS: GENERAL AND PERSONAL

There are many other interesting and varied letters which give insight into the life of DPs and migrants in Australia in this period. Some of these raise awareness of unexpected issues, such as the letter signed by a group of DPs who were housed at the Graylands centre in Western Australia. For reasons unknown, these refugees were very unhappy and believed that they had missed out on something that other DPs had experienced as they demanded to know why they "never saw the eastern states" and why they were not sent to the Reception Centres in Victoria and New South Wales, as others were.[43]

In quite a different tone, a letter from a Polish ex-serviceman explained that he was about to finish his contract at the Tasmanian Hydro-Electric Scheme and would like to drive to Sydney (some 1500 km and across the sea), and he requested that the Department send him maps and give him advice on the places he should see along the way.[44] He was obviously excited by the prospect of the freedom to travel and the opportunity to see more of his new homeland.

Again, on a very different subject, Polish-born Alfred Fiala, who had been an agriculturalist before the war, wrote that he had:

> a small problem which I hope your department can help me solve. A new type of garden hoe which I have designed should be of benefit to every gardener, but I feel that this idea should be protected for me to ensure that I am not exploited, before plans can be made for its manufacture. Could you therefore advise me of what steps I can take to take out a patent and what would be the cost of this procedure.[45]

Displaced Person, Pawel Lubimowski, who had arrived with his wife and child on the *Wooster Victory* in 1949, wanted to know where he could access Russian language newspapers. In his letter he also apologised for his English and stated that this was the first letter he had written in his new language. In reply he was given a Sydney address to write to for access to Russian newspapers but, not missing an opportunity for assimilation, the reply also suggested that he had "lessons in English either from your nearest school or by correspondence" and encouraged him saying that "[s]ince the letter you sent us was the first one in English you are to be congratulated. It was very good and easy to understand. Perhaps you will write to us again some time".[46]

Other DPs sent in long written pieces based on their experiences, written as either fact and/or fiction.[47] There are many letters which offer comment on Australia, including a long correspondence (January 1949) from a migrant, Wilhelm von Pfieffer, who was working at Cheetham Salt in Victoria. Wilhelm was obviously struggling to understand Australian customs around entertainment and licencing laws. He stated that he and his friends had arrived a few months ago and had learned a great deal about their new country but could not understand why the cinemas were closed on Sundays and why the pubs closed at six o'clock. He wrote:

> This is wrong. In Europe the bars are opened all evening and Sundays too. If it would be the same way here everybody would go home after work, clean up, have a meal and if he then still felt he wanted some beer, he could go. We are sure that many wifes [*sic*] would also like a cool drink in the company of their husbands. We are of the opinion that there are only so many drunks on the streets because everybody has to drink in a rush and the main thing, on an empty stomach.[48]

The contrast to past lives and customs is obvious, and understandably challenging.

For others, their wartime experiences and fears are evident as they expressed their concerns about the other migrants with whom they lived and worked. An example is Yugoslavian-born Luigi Cobanov's five-page letter in which he expressed his worries about a number of issues primarily around nationality and wartime activities. Luigi was particularly concerned about the status of babies born in Australia, to German women who had married DPs, and most of all about his fear that many Germans who had served in the *Waffen SS* had entered Australia. "Some of them", he wrote, "have still the "blood group sign" under their arms and one of them, showing proudly those signs, had provocated [*sic*] German born wives of Poles, Yugoslavs and Czechs".[49]

These letters, although varied in subject, give enormous insight into the mix of emotions that European migrants and refugees experienced as they tried to negotiate their new lives in Australia, from trying to look positively to the future, to trying to escape the past.

The hardest letters to read are those which give us very personal insights into the issues of loneliness and depression that these migrants faced, and the problems which stemmed from the separation of families as male DPs were sent to work camps and wives and children to Holding Centres. A

DP who signed himself "Mr Treide" wrote: "After the ex-DPs will have finished the contract … The husbands and wifes [*sic*], would not like to be separated any longer, the young people would like to get married".[50]

On a more personal level, S. Panic wrote:

> I landed on 17th November last year at Melbourne with my family (mother-in-law, wife and two boys) coming from Egypt where I was as a soldier since 1941 and my family lived in the I.R.O. camps. Now, I work in the Forest, my mother-in-law in the Lewisham General Hospital at Sydney and my wife with children in the H. Centre at Uranquinty, until I am able to find accommodation for them.[51]

This situation was certainly not uncommon, however, as Mr Panic so emotionally wrote, he had been separated for "too many years" from his family, first as a soldier, and again now in Australia, and he begged for family reunion.

For men sent to work in remote areas, the loneliness and hopelessness of the situation were acute. Forestry worker, Polish-born Hejwosz Antoni complained that he was cut off from Australian people because he was in the bush 12 miles from the nearest town of Mt Gambier (South Australia). He wrote:

> I hate a solitary life, about six years in concentration camps in Germany it is enough for me. I long also for a human life with wife and children as another people. Now I am thirty seven years old and after two years I shall be finish. I will work and I shall work, but my new life must be worth living.[52]

The isolation and remoteness of many workplaces recalled the horrendous wartime conditions that many of these DPs had already suffered. For many, there seemed no escape. As Andrew (Andreas) of Burnie in Tasmania asked:

> [how] to solve the personal solitude which oppresses my life since I lose my family in the war-time … Australian-born girls and women have not much matrimonial interests of us and, what is worse, don't understand us as human beings tired out by the wicked fate. There are also the questions of language and religion which make the marriage of a newcomer to a new comer more desirable. But whom can I marry in the case the nearest place where my female compatriots are settled is 300 mile away? I assure you that sad thoughts bother and worry many of us.[53]

For some, such as the author of this translated letter, the despair was unbearable:

> I am working now for 5 month in the wood ... I am getting crazy, the woods and only woods round me are choking me ... I can not eat. I can not sleep. [*sic*] My nerves are so bad, that is it difficult for me to control them, and I am not far from committing suicide. Please help me.[54]

CONCLUSION

This chapter has presented a small sample of extracts from the hundreds of letters written to *The New Australian* by European refugees and migrants who arrived in Australia following the Second World War. For these new arrivals the opportunity to write to the newspaper provided an outlet for their questions, their comments, and most importantly their pain and grievance as they tried to make a new life for themselves and, in some instances, seek much-needed help.

For the Department of Immigration, *The New Australian* provided an opportunity to extend the process of assimilation beyond the accommodation centres and into the wider migrant community, and to continue the Australianisation of the new arrivals. Certainly, many letters highlighted issues which the authorities addressed through specific and repeated articles within the publication. While there is no direct evidence that the totality of these letters had any influence on overall departmental policies, it is clear from individual written responses that there was a degree of humanity and, for some individuals, positive resolutions for some issues. For historians, these letters provide a valuable and underutilised source. They give access to a migrant voice which is all but lost due to the passage of time and offer insight into both the pain and the relief these European refugees and migrants felt as they tried to negotiate their new lives in Australia.

NOTES

1. Mark Wyman, *DPs Europe's Displaced Persons, 1945–1951* (London: Cornell University Press, 1998), 1–21.
2. Daniel G. Cohen, *In War's Wake: Europe's Displaced Persons in the Postwar Order* (Oxford: Oxford University Press, 2012), 5.

3. It should also be noted that many others would appear in other areas of Europe, across the Middle East and into Asia between 1947 and 1950. See Cohen, *In War's Wake*, 5, 7, 66–70.
4. See United Nations, *The Refugee in the Post-War World: Preliminary Report of a Survey of the Refugee Problem* (Geneva: United Nations, 1951).
5. Ruth Balint, "Industry and Sunshine," *History Australia* 11, no. 1 (2014): 106.
6. There is a considerable and growing literature on the DPs in Australia. Specialist studies include my own work on DP women and children and migrant assimilation more generally. See for example: Karen Agutter, "Fated to Be Orphans: The Consequences of Australia's Post-War Resettlement Policy on Refugee Children," *Children Australia* 41, no. 3 (2016): 224–231; Karen Agutter and Catherine Kevin, "The 'Unwanteds' and 'Non-Compliants': 'Unsupported Mothers' as 'Failures' and Agents in Australia's Migrant Holding Centres," *The History of the Family* 22, no. 4 (2017): 554–574; Karen Agutter, "Her Majesty's Newest Subjects: Official Attempts to Assimilate Non-English Speaking Migrants in Post-War Australia," *History Australia* 16, no. 3 (2019): 480–495. For a more general discussion on the current state of DP and migrant scholarship in Australia today see Ruth Balint and Zora Simic, "Histories of Migrants and Refugees in Australia", *Australian Historical Studies* 49, no. 3 (2018): 378–409.
7. The phrase "the Australian way of life" came into regular use in the 1950s across official, public and advertising vernacular and represented an imagined, quintessentially Australian character and lifestyle which revolved around the traditional nuclear family and ill-defined character traits. See: Richard White, *Inventing Australia: Images and Identity 1688–1980* (Sydney: Allen & Unwin, 1981).
8. The Australian Government had negotiated this requirement with the IRO as part of the agreement to accept DPs. For more on the work contracts see: Alexandra Dellios, "Displaced Persons, Family Separation and the Work Contract in Postwar Australia," *Journal of Australian Studies* 40, no. 4 (2016): 418–32; Karen Agutter, "Displaced Persons and the 'Continuum of Mobility' in the South Australian Hostel System", in *On the Wing: Mobility Before and After Emigration to Australia*, eds. Margrette A. Kleinig and Eric Richards (Spit Junction, NSW: Anchor Books Australia, 2013), 136–52.
9. There was a structured system of government-operated accommodation centres across Australia which, during the early 1950s, at the peak of the post-war migration scheme, totalled approximately 100 centres and many hundreds of workplace camps.

10. Good Neighbour Councils were formed and partially funded by the Australian Government. They had two official tasks: to assist new arrivals to assimilate into the norms and expectations of the host society, and to educate the Australian public about the benefits of the mass migration scheme towards a level of acceptance of new arrivals. See for example Gwenda Tavan, "'Good Neighbours': Community Organisations, Migrant Assimilation and Australian Society and Culture, 1950–1961", *Australian Historical Studies* 27, no. 109 (1997): 77–89.

11. Murphy to Secretary Department of Immigration 30 December 1947 in Immigration—'Tomorrow's Australia'—Part 1, National Archives Australia (NAA): CP815/1, 021.153 Part 1.

12. NAA: CP815/1, 021.153 Part 1.

13. Department of Information to W. Funnell (Secretary of the Commonwealth Department of Labour and National Service) October 28, 1948, in NAA: Displaced Persons Publicity, B550, 1948/23/5454. The Department of Immigration determined that the newspaper would be produced in English as they believed that they "would be laying ourselves open to charges that we were encouraging the migrants to continue using their native tongues" rather than learn English. Furthermore, as there was no common language among DPs, they believed that choosing one, even German, would lead to complaints of unfairness. See undated Memorandum from Department of Immigration Publicity Section in NAA: B550, 1948/23/5454.

14. Mr Ewers (Department of Education) advised the Department of Immigration that as migrants came to the newspaper at different issues, it would be best if the newspaper emphasised the acquisition of vocabulary, for example in the form labelled pictures and short, independent dialogues. Murphy to Marsh (Commonwealth Employment Service) November 12, 1948 in NAA: B550, 1948/23/5454.

15. Between 1939 and 1971 the Australian Government required all "aliens" (i.e. non-British subjects/foreign nationals living in Australia) to register with local authorities. For Murphy see Murphy to Funnell 28 October 1948 in NAA: B550, 1948/23/5454.

16. Murphy to Marsh 12 November 1948 in NAA: B550, 1948/23/5454.

17. Details of Monthly Immigration Publications in NAA: Publication—"The Good Neighbour", A445, 261/6/5.

18. NAA: B550, 1948/23/5454.

19. In the late 1940s the Minister for Immigration, Arthur Calwell, introduced the term "New Australian" as he believed it to be a more positive term, more in keeping with the assimilationist ideals of the day, to the commonly used derogatory terms "reffo" and "Balt". However, over time the term itself became derogatory.

20. NAA: Immigration—'The New Australian'—Letters from readers—Part 3, CP815/1, 021.192 Part 3.
21. NAA: CP815/1, 021.192 Part 3.
22. NAA: Immigration—'The New Australian'—Letters from readers—Part 1, CP815/1, 021.192 Part 1.
23. NAA: Immigration—'The New Australian'—Letters from readers—Part 2, CP815/1, 021.192 Part 2.
24. NAA: CP815/1, 021.192 Part 1.
25. Ms. Grebliauskas goes on to request an extra copy to send to her sister in Germany. NAA: CP815/1, 021.192 Part 1.
26. NAA: CP815/1, 021.192 Part 2.
27. NAA: CP815/1, 021.192 Part 2.
28. NAA: CP815/1, 021.192 Part 2.
29. NAA: CP815/1, 021.192 Part 2.
30. NAA: CP815/1, 021.192 Part 3.
31. O'Heare to Director of Employment February 16, 1949 in NAA: B550; 1948/23/5454.
32. NAA: CP815/1, 021.192 Part 1.
33. NAA: CP815/1, 021.192 Part 1.
34. NAA: CP815/1, 021.192 Part 3.
35. NAA: CP815/1, 021.192 Part 1.
36. NAA: CP815/1, 021.192 Part 1.
37. NAA: CP815/1, 021.192 Part 2.
38. NAA: Immigration—"The New Australian"—Letters from readers—Part 4, CP815/1, 021.192 Part 4.
39. NAA: CP815/1, 021.192 Part 3. Endel had come to Australia as a DP on the *Svalbard* which departed Genoa December 11, 1948.
40. NAA: CP815/1, 021.192 Part 2.
41. For example, there were letters asking about whether relatives had arrived. For example, a Mr. Murnicks (8 July 1949) asked after the whereabouts of his relatives, Anna and Otto Kleinberg. The reply indicated that they "had not yet landed … [but] it should not be long" and reassured him that he would be notified. Similarly, in July 1949, Otto Uhlberg of the Nelson's Bay Hostel Port Stephens enquired after his brother in law and his wife and was told they were due in to South Australia on the *General Stuart* and would proceed to Woodside Migrant Centre where he could write to them. See NAA: CP815/1, 021.192 Part 4.
42. NAA: CP815/1, 021.192 Part 3.
43. NAA: CP815/1, 021.192 Part 1.
44. NAA: CP815/1, 021.192 Part 3.
45. NAA: CP815/1, 021.192 Part 3.
46. NAA: CP815/1, 021.192 Part 4.

47. For example, Gerzik, Anatole [Anatoly] writes a three-page piece entitled Extract from a Diary. This is a story about Nikolas, a refugee from Europe who finds peace, and love, in the Blue Mountains. NAA: CP815/1, 021.192 Part 3.
48. NAA: CP815/1, 021.192 Part 1.
49. NAA: CP815/1, 021.192 Part 3.
50. NAA: Immigration—The New Australian [newspaper], CP815/1, 021.188.
51. NAA: CP815/1, 021.192 Part 2.
52. NAA: CP815/1, 021.192 Part 2.
53. NAA: CP815/1, 021.192 Part 4.
54. NAA: Immigration—"The New Australian" [newspaper for new migrants]—Part 3, CP815/1, 021.188 Part 3.

.

CHAPTER 9

Crónicas in Australia's Spanish-Language Press: The Case of *El Expreso*

Michael Jacklin

In *Wanderwords: Language Migration in American Literature* (2014)—a study of bilingualism and multilingualism in the literary work of second- and third-generation immigrants to the United States—Maria Lauret makes the point (following multilingual literature scholar Marc Shell) that literary criticism of ethnic and migrant literature in the United States has focused predominantly on works written in English.[1] The result is that the literature of migrant communities written and published in their language(s) of origin goes unremarked by those researching the relationship between migrant writing and the national or transnational imaginary.[2]

Nicolás Kanellos, scholar of Hispanic literature in the United States, makes a similar claim in the opening pages of his *Hispanic Immigrant Literature: El Sueño del Retorno* (2011): a study focusing on "literature written by immigrants in their native language".[3] He is at pains to differentiate the substantial body of work, written in Spanish in the United States, from works in English, written by the descendants of migrants, and

M. Jacklin (✉)
University of Wollongong, Wollongong, NSW, Australia

© The Author(s) 2020
C. Dewhirst, R. Scully (eds.), *The Transnational Voices of Australia's Migrant and Minority Press*, Palgrave Studies in the History of the Media,
https://doi.org/10.1007/978-3-030-43639-1_9

169

he argues that most academic work on American migrant writing either dismisses or neglects non-English literary production. He quotes the editors of a major anthology on immigrant experiences portrayed in American literature, who assert that "first-generation, non-English speakers of any nationality seldom produce much literature".[4] Finding a similar bias in three other scholarly studies of migrant writing, he asks:

> How can so many scholars be so confused? … And in the case of Hispanic or Latino literature, why is practically the entire corpus of works written in Spanish by immigrants ignored and, instead, works about immigrants by native Hispanic authors emphasized? Is it that the majority of critics who treat Hispanic immigrant literature do not speak or read Spanish?[5]

Kanellos maintains that to ignore Spanish-language writing produced in the United States—as he insists the majority of literary scholars have done—"is to condemn that language and its speakers to perpetual foreignness and estrangement from the American nation".[6] One factor, he argues, that may have contributed to this mainstream neglect is that much of this writing in Spanish was produced by working-class immigrant writers and intellectuals often publishing in newspapers and magazines produced for, and only circulating within, the Spanish-reading communities.

In Australia, Spanish-language writing remains practically unknown for similar reasons. Despite half a century of literary production in Spanish from migrants from Spain and Latin America—in newspapers, magazines, books of poetry, novels and plays—English-reading Australians know almost nothing of its existence. There is, in fact, very little general awareness in Australia of any aspect of Spanish-speaking migrant lives and, with a few exceptions, scholarship in this field is quite recent. One of the first investigations of Spanish migration was *Operación Canguro: The Spanish Migration Scheme, 1958–1963* (2002) by Ignacio García, who was also the first to begin documenting the literary production of this community with his studies of the Spanish Club of Sydney and its literary competitions from the 1960s to the 1990s. Catalan migration has been the focus of several studies by Robert Mason and his book *The Spanish Anarchists in Northern Australia* (2018) draws attention to a forgotten group of migrants from the early 1900s. Latin American migration to Australia, which began in the 1970s, is the subject of three recent edited volumes: Barry Carr and John Minns' *Australia and Latin America: Challenges and Opportunities in the New Millennium* (2014); Elizabeth Kath's

Australian-Latin American Relations: New Links in a Changing Global Landscape (2016); and Fernanda Peñaloza and Sarah Walsh's *Mapping South-South Connections: Australia and Latin America* (2019). One of the most significant differences between Spanish-speaking migrants and those from other linguistic backgrounds is their national diversity, with nearly twenty countries of origin contributing to the approximately 100,000 Spanish speakers in Australia. Yet in spite of political, cultural and historical differences, their common language has meant that since the 1960s there has been a substantial newspaper and magazine culture in Spanish in Australia, one that grew in the 1980s and 1990s into a literary culture. García initiated research in this direction with his two volumes: *Spanish Fiction Writing in Australia* (1997) and *Concurso literario Club Español de Sydney 1969–1996* (1997). I have continued investigations into Spanish-language writing in Australia, and this chapter aims to bring a portion of that writing to the attention of not only readers and scholars in the fields of Australian migrant or multicultural literature but also scholars engaged in the transnational dimensions of Latin American writing.

Among the most vital of this Australian writing in Spanish is the genre known as the *crónica*—a literary form common throughout Spanish-speaking America, appearing in newspapers and magazines often in the form of "short meditative pieces, autobiographical in scope, and characterized by a combination of personal confession, everyday observation, and a memorializing drive".[7] In Australia, there have been many hundreds, and possibly thousands, of *crónicas* published and now found only on microfilm or in the hard copies of newspapers in state and national libraries, or, in some cases, in rare and crumbling copies of community periodicals. This chapter offers an analysis of just one of the many Spanish-language newspapers publishing *crónicas* in Australia: *El Expreso*, a dynamic but short-lived newspaper, published weekly in Sydney between July and November 1979. Reading a selection of these Australian *crónicas* from *El Expreso* provides an opportunity to investigate the role of this unique genre, its place in the migrant press, and consider the intersections of local and global factors contributing to the negotiation and formation of Spanish-language Australian identities. One of the first scholars to theorise the *crónica*, Aníbal González, describes it as "a hybrid genre that combines literary with journalistic elements in a variety of ways, resulting in brief texts that often focus on contemporary topics and issues addressed in a self-consciously literary style".[8] Highlighting its incorporation of seemingly incongruous characteristics, Mexican novelist and *cronista* Juan

Villoro describes the *crónica* as "the platypus of prose".[9] Villoro suggests that its hybrid form results from the challenge of translating the incredible or near-incomprehensible events of daily experience in Mexico to its readers in ways that will "make it true to life".[10] Emerging across Latin America in the late nineteenth century at a point in time when modernisation was having tremendous impact on urban expansion, economic development and the rapid growth and consolidation of the newspaper industry, *crónicas* became a popular component in periodicals from Mexico City to Buenos Aires. Julio Ramos argues:

> The chronicle, like the newspaper itself, is a space rooted in cities on the road to modernization at the turn of the century: first of all, because the authority (and value) of the correspondent's word is based on his or her representation of urban life in some developed society for a designated audience desiring – although at times fearful of – this modernity.[11]

Cronistas—those who write *crónicas*—interpreted modernity for their readership, commenting on all aspects of modern life, bringing into focus incidents, places or people whose circumstances illustrated the challenges and dilemmas of urbanisation and swiftly changing social realities in Latin America.

At the same time as this process of urbanisation was occurring in Latin America, social transformation was taking place in the United States, with mass Hispanic migration in the first decades of the twentieth century. Commenting on *crónicas* published in the American Spanish-language press, Kanellos describes the chronicle as "a short weekly column that often humorously and satirically commented on current topics and social customs in the local community".[12] In the American context, *cronistas* often became "community moralists",[13] whose columns criticised migrants eager to assimilate at the expense of their language, culture and religion. Others focused on the deplorable living conditions and the exploitation of migrant workers. In both Latin America and the United States, *crónicas* differed from journalistic reporting in their use of the stylistic devices of fiction: dialogue, narrative, characterisation, figurative language, pathos, wit and humour. *Cronistas* often wrote under a pseudonym and, over time, not only developed a recognisable voice and persona but also attracted dedicated readerships that turned to their weekly columns for both entertainment and argument.

In her study of early twentieth-century *cronistas*, *Urban Chroniclers in Modern Latin America* (2011), Viviane Mahieux claims that throughout Latin America in the 1920s and 1930s, *crónicas* "became necessary reading".[14] She argues that chroniclers became "spokespeople of modernizing communities [who] guided their publics through a constantly changing cityscape and advised on matters of cultural taste, playing an instrumental role in shaping the identity and collective memory of their cities".[15] In terms similar to those used by Kanellos, Mahieux describes *crónicas* as "short articles that commented on various aspects of city life in a light and anecdotal tone. They were written with a self-conscious literary style, often in the first person, and were framed by a signature, if not also a caricature or photograph of the chronicler who penned it".[16] Although maintaining that these *crónicas* helped shape the collective memories of Latin American cities, Mahieux also acknowledges the ephemeral nature of *crónica* writing and points out that "the works of many chroniclers who were widely read in their day remain forgotten in yellowing newspaper archives. Relatively few articles from this early period have been collected and reissued in book form".[17] Despite, then, claims of their contribution to the construction of collective memory, *crónicas*, for the most part, have been fragile, ephemeral texts whose narratives, humour and critique were produced for the consumption of the day, to be read and discussed and argued over, but ultimately to be discarded along with yesterday's sports pages, news and classified advertisements.

Their ephemeral quality and their quotidian concerns, combined with their literary style and their commitment to representations of and for the specifics of locality, and the vast quantity in which *crónicas* were produced across the Spanish-speaking world for over a century by literary authors as well as career journalists, have turned the genre from an object of neglect to one of contemporary critical fascination. The first to draw attention to the significance of *crónicas* was Mexican author Carlos Monsiváis, himself a well-known *cronista*, with his anthology, *A ustedes les consta: antología de la crónica en México* (1980). This was followed by Aníbal González's critical study, *La crónica modernista hispanoamericana* (1983), Julio Ramos's *Divergent Modernities* (1989) and Susana Rotker's *La invención de la crónica* (1989). An explosion of interest dates from 2001 with Linda Egan's *Carlos Monsiváis: Culture and Chronicle in Contemporary Mexico*, followed by Ignacio Corona and Beth Jörgensen's edited collection, *The Contemporary Mexican Chronicle: Theoretical Perspectives on a Liminal Genre* (2002), and Anadeli Bencomo's *Voces y voceros de la megalópolis: la crónica periodístico-literaria en México* (2002). Numerous critical studies have since been published, including Esperança Bielsa's *The Latin American Urban Chronicle* (2006), Viviane Mahieux's *Urban Chroniclers in Modern Latin America* (2011) and Andrew Reynold's *The Spanish American Crónica Modernista, Temporality, and Material Culture: Modernismo's Unstoppable Presses* (2012). Despite this substantial documentation and analysis of *crónica* writing overseas, Australian *crónicas* are only beginning to receive critical attention. In 2014, Louis Di Paolo completed a master's thesis on the Australian *crónicas* of Luis Abarca. More recently, Catherine Seaton's 2018 doctoral thesis analyses the work of four Australian *cronistas*: Salvador Torrents, Clara Espinosa Noriega, Luis Abarca and Guillermo Hertz. Research conducted by this author, stemming from investigations of Spanish-language Australian writing for the AustLit database, has resulted thus far in three publications dealing with Australian *crónicas* (Jacklin 2010, 2016, 2019); this current chapter continues this work.

THE AUSTRALIAN SPANISH-LANGUAGE PRESS AND *CRÓNICAS*

Crónicas have been an important component in almost every Spanish-language newspaper in Australia, beginning in the 1960s with *La Crónica* published in Melbourne from 1964 to 1966. Ignacio Garcia, the first scholar to document Australian writing in Spanish, has written on the significance of *La Crónica* to the Spanish migrant community of the 1960s. Australia's first newspaper in Spanish featured a weekly column, titled "Ripios de la semana", which translates as "Scraps of the week" or perhaps "Doggerel of the week". Such weekly instalments of poetry are rarely considered in discussions of *crónicas*; however, the themes, tone and function of "Ripios de la semana", in which the editor of the newspaper Manuel Varela offered commentary in verse on issues that impacted on the Spanish migrant community, are exactly those of the genre. Some of Varela's verse columns are light-hearted: the instalment appearing on 27 May 1965 is a complaint in rhyme that to get a driver's licence in Australia one needs to speak English with all its commas and full stops in the right places. Others, such as that appearing on 4 August 1965 describe the economic hardships facing working-class migrants, who after paying bills do not have enough left over for even the bus fare [*Pues cuando pagas la renta, /los plazos, el gas, la luz… / no te queda de la cuenta /ni el gasto del autobus*].[18]

Although *La Crónica* lasted only two years, it was succeeded by *El Español en Australia* in Sydney (the two newspapers overlapped for a brief period, and the competition was a likely factor in *La Crónica*'s demise). By the 1970s, *El Español en Australia* was joined by two more Spanish-language weekly newspapers—*The Spanish Herald* (1971–to date and *Noticias y Deportes* (1975–2012)—and by the end of the decade, Australia's first Spanish-language magazine, *Vistazo* (1978–1981), was up and running. Writing across several of these papers, at different times through 1978 and 1979, was Luis Abarca, or Lucho Abarca as he was, and still is, known. He was also known as Bladi Woggi (later Bladi Woggie, then Blady Woggie), the pseudonym under which Abarca published a series of *crónicas*, commenting satirically on the lives of Spanish-speaking migrants in Sydney. Bladi Woggi is a phonetic rendering of "bloody woggy", the derogatory term for migrants that was commonly heard in Australia in the 1970s. Abarca had studied journalism in Santiago and had gained experience writing a column for the youth magazine *Ramona* (1971–1973). His columns proved popular with Chilean readers and a selection of these was published as *Viaje por la juventud* [Journey through Youth] (1972). However, following the coup that overthrew the socialist government of Salvador Allende, Abarca was expelled from university and, fearing continued oppression in his home country, he migrated to Australia in 1974.

Despite his experience as a writer in Chile, it took Abarca several years to re-establish himself in the Sydney Spanish-language press. In August 1978, his first Australian *crónica* appeared in the weekly newspaper *El Español en Australia*. Titled *Bienaventurados los aconsejadores!* ["Blessed are those who give advice"], the piece recounts the narrator's first morning at a migrant hostel in western Sydney and the advice he received from other migrants round the breakfast table. The first speaker tells him: *Ten mucho cuidado. … Te van a llover los tipos que vengan a darte consejos sin que los pidas. Te van a acosejar tonterias, por eso cúidadte, y no les hagas caso* [Be very careful. You'll be inundated with advice you never asked for. They're going to tell you nonsense, so watch out, and don't listen to them].[19] The irony of this first piece of advice being not to listen to any advice—that all the advice will be *tonterias* [foolishness]—is typical of Bladi Woggi's narratives. His *crónicas* are always in the first-person; they include dialogue, often in Chilean slang, and are frequently marked by irony and hyperbole. Each *crónica* is devoted to some aspect of migrant life, whether that be employment, rental accommodation, child care, driving lessons, language acquisition or discrimination. His *crónicas* are narratives of the everyday, of the present circumstances of the migrant community. They are humorous, at times outrageous, and frequently risk offending some portion of the readership.

By late September of 1978, after only seven instalments, Bladi Woggi left *El Español en Australia*, following a column in which he criticised the quality of Spanish-language radio programming in Sydney and singled out a female announcer whose programme he found particularly inane. Reader response to this *crónica* was polarised, with the newspaper publishing two representative letters titled *Pero qué bien, Bladi Woggi* [Good on you, Bladi Woggi] and *Pero qué mal, Bladi Woggi* [Shame on you, Bladi Woggi]. The negative letter took exception to the harshness of Bladi Woggi's criticism, pointing out that the announcer was one of many who have been working hard and giving so much to the Spanish-speaking community [*personas que durante más que tres años trabajando tan duramente y hacienda tantísimo por nuestra comunidad de habla hispana*].[20] The correspondent also objected to the anonymity of these *crónicas*, pointing out that all other contributions to the paper were attributed to named authors, to which the editor responded by identifying Luis Abarca as Bladi Woggi and assuring the reader that Abarca was contrite and repentant [*En todo caso, su carta plena de profundus y contundentes argumentos, lo dejó contrito y arrepentido*].[21] The appreciative reader, on the other hand, defended Bladi Woggi, remarking that he simply writes of his adventures and what he makes of them in a humorous and uninhibited manner, and that his adventures are actually the adventures of us all [*nos relata sus aventuras (que al final son las aventuras de todos nosotros) y sus conclusiones, todo contado de una manera muy divertida y sin inhibiciones*].[22]

In January of 1979, Blady Woggie (with i changed to y and a final e added to his name) appeared in the new magazine *Vistazo*, with the headline, "El Blady Woggie Strikes Again". His third column in *Vistazo*, titled *El periodismo de la tijera y el engrudo* or "The journalism of cut and paste", criticised the poor quality of Australia's Hispanic press, which relied, he claimed, on recycling articles from overseas Spanish publications, usually without acknowledgement. At the end of this article, he called for the appearance of a new newspaper with fresh ideas and original reporting, to provide Spanish-language readers with the quality of journalism they deserved. This was in March 1979. By July of that year, *El Expreso* began publishing and Abarca was at first a columnist, and by the second issue its editor as well as one of its several *cronistas*. The emphasis and column space given to *crónica*-style writing was a deliberate strategy, aimed at distinguishing *El Expreso* from what it saw as its cut-and-paste rivals. In the editorial *Un desafío y una esperanza* [A challenge and a hope] introducing its first issue, the paper promised: We will always avoid the practice of publishing mere newspaper clippings from other latitudes, a practice that is at odds with quality and professional ethics [*Evitaremos siempre la practica de publicar meros recortes de diarios de otras latitudes por considerarlo una practica reñida con la calidad y la etica professional*].[23] Instead, *El Expreso* promised to bring its readers reporting and commentary that was original, responsible, serious and accurate as well as entertaining, cultured and fun [*Es decir, en el de entregar noticias de una manera seria, documentada, responsable y veraz ... y por supuesto, en al no menos importante función de hacer llegar al lector entretenimiento, agrado y cultura*].[24] In its proposed delivery of this combination of serious journalism and entertaining reading, *crónicas* would play a major role.

EL EXPRESO AND A FLOURISHING OF AUSTRALIAN *CRÓNICAS*

The masthead of *El Expreso*'s Issue 0, dated Tuesday, 31 July 1979, identifies Daniel Bascur as Director, Patricia Boero as Editor, and Xavier de Bárcenas as Editor-in-Chief. Journalists included María Ibañez, María del Carmen Rose, Luis A. Abarca, Alejandro Arellano, Dr John Brotherton and Luis F. Escudero, while those identified as columnists were Dra Elsa Cabrera, Alberto Dominguez, Fernando Portilla, Dr Jose Manuel Rey and Dr Luis Vargas Saavedra. The five doctorates among the above are indicative of the involvement of staff from the University of New South Wales and particularly Dr John Brotherton, who at the time was a member of the Spanish department there. This is not to suggest that *El Expreso* was a university or a student newspaper. For its short life-span, it achieved significant distribution, with a circulation of 6000 copies, and advertising from a wide range of businesses and organisations seeking to attract customers and clients from the Spanish-speaking migrant communities. *El Expreso* aimed to compete with the longer-established Spanish-language weekly papers; its news coverage was international (drawing on United Press International for Latin American and Spanish-related articles) and national, with Australian content provided by its own journalists. However, it was the paper's *crónica*-style columns that comprised a substantial portion of its content and set it apart. Although the contributions of several of the journalists and columnists listed could be considered, this chapter will focus on those of Brotherton, Abarca and Dominguez.

Brotherton introduces himself to readers through a dialogue between two unnamed staff on *El Expreso*, who begin by wondering what kind of name John Brotherton is for a journalist with a Spanish-language newspaper [*¿Y qué tipo de nombre es ése para un periódico en español?*].[25] Brotherton explains himself, in the third person: "they say he's an Englishman, and a Spanish-speaker, a professor at the university of I-don't-know-where" [*Dicen que es un típo inglés, que se las da de hispanohablante, profesor en la universidad de Nosedonde*].[26] The fictional dialogue is maintained throughout the column, as the two debate the possible contribution of an Englishman to issues relating to Australian Spanish-speakers, with the first speaker highly doubtful, and the second offering explanations and defence, starting with the suggestion that as almost the entire staff consists of Chileans, Argentinians, Uruguayans and, worse [*para peor*], Spaniards, Brotherton might act as an impartial arbiter, stepping between quarrelling parties, like a referee at a soccer match. The first is unconvinced, suggesting that, rather than referee, this Brotherton may be some form of spy, insinuating himself amongst Spanish-speakers like a CIA or KGB agent. The second replies not to worry, that English migrants are almost "as woggie as us" [*son casi tan woggies como nosotros*]. He explains that just like Spanish-speakers, English migrants cannot understand what Australians are saying half the time, and moreover they do not have someone like Al Grassby (then Minister for Immigration and a proponent of Australia's new policy of multiculturalism) looking out for them. He speculates that Brotherton had to learn Spanish so as to have someone to talk to in his new country. Sensing his interlocutor's objections wavering, he adds: "think of it this way, in a certain sense, we get two Blady Woggies for the price of one!" [*en cierto sentido tendremos a dos Blady Woggies por el precio de uno*]. "Alright, you've convinced me", the first speaker relents. "I'll give him three weeks to prove himself".[27]

Over the ensuing weeks and months (*El Expreso* folded in November of 1979, after thirteen issues), Brotherton's contributions evolved into a form of cultural mediation. Much in the sense of the early twentieth-century Latin American *cronistas* who translated the often-confusing experiences of urbanisation and modernity to their readers, Brotherton discusses issues that new migrants from Chile or Uruguay might find strange or inexplicable. In his first few columns he explains to his Spanish-speaking readers the differences between England and Australia in terms of language and accent and the way this relates to perceptions of class; he also discusses racism and the conditions of disadvantage and prejudice faced by Aboriginal Australians.[28] In later columns he begins to draw attention to contrasts in Australian ways of thinking in comparison to that of Spanish-speakers, with Brotherton positioning himself as sharing the world-views of his Spanish-speaking colleagues and readers. In a pair of columns appearing over two issues (11 and 18 September 1979), Brotherton takes this to extremes as he explains what he sees as Australians' lack of seriousness, which results in a perception that Australians are permanently on vacation. This has nothing to do with working or not working, he clarifies, but more to do with Australians' state of mind [*no tiene nada que ver con el hecho de trabajar o no trabjar. Es más bien un estado de conciencia*].[29] He makes the extraordinary claim that there are many concepts which we [and here he means Spanish-speakers] consider fundamental which simply do not exist in Australia: concepts including free will, sacrifice and a tragic sense of life as defined by Miguel de Unamuno, which are all part of the collective conscience of people from the "old world", as he puts it [*Hay tantos conceptos que nosotros consideramos fundamentals que simplemente no existen aqui. Hablo de conceptos de libre albedrío, de sacrificio, del sentimiento trágico de la vida, tan precisamente definido por Unamuno, entre miles de otras nociones que no todo individuo en el viejo mundo podría vocalizar pero, sin embargo, están bien arraigadas en su conciencia colectiva*].[30] Spanish-speaking migrants encountering the "She'll be right, mate" attitude to life that was perhaps still common in Australia in the decade in which Brotherton was writing, might understand it as resulting from Australia's bountiful resources and natural beauty, as well as its economic prosperity and abundant work and business opportunities. Brotherton acknowledged these factors but stressed that it was more a matter of world-view, and that his readers should realise that their old-world values, perspectives and culture, including literary culture, would most often not be shared or understood by Anglo-Australians, few of whom, it was certain, had read or even heard of Unamuno, Spanish-Basque novelist, poet, playwright, philosopher and *cronista*.

If Brotherton's columns were exercises in thinking through cultural differences aimed at assisting Spanish-speaking migrants make sense of Australian life, those of Lucho Abarca, or El Blady Woggie, were zanier and more unpredictable. His first *crónica* in *El Expreso*, under the main title of *Comentarios de un Blady Woggie* (which remained constant through *El Expreso*'s entire run), was subtitled *Comentarista deportivo* or 'Sports commentator' and, like Brotherton's initial column, took the form of a conversation. "Blady Woggie, we want to make you an offer so good that you won't be able to refuse it", his colleagues tell him [*Blady Woggie, que-remos hacerte una oferta tan buena que no podrás rechazarla*].[31] For Blady Woggie, this brings to mind the voice of Don Corleone, from the 1970s' *Godfather* films, and soon he is imagining the horrors that await him: a horse's head in his bed, maybe his body found dismembered in Glebe, or perhaps returning to work as editor for *El Español en Australia* [*Como encontrarme de madrugada con un cabeza de caballo cortada entre las sabinas. O aparecer descuartizado en los escampos Glebe el día menos pensando. O volver a trabajar como editor en 'El Español en Australia', cosas así, escalofriantes*]. No, they tell him. "We're going to start a new newspaper!" They tell him this will be a real newspaper and that, if he joins, he is not even to think about his "famous columns" [*en primero lugar, tus ya famosos comentarios, eso ni que hablar*].[32] Instead, they want Blady Woggie to be the sports columnist. The rest of the column then becomes a headlong ramble of sports names, facts and figures, as Blady Woggie demonstrates beyond argument that he has the necessary knowledge for the position. The entire column is, of course, a joke, as his colleagues and his readers know that Blady Woggie writes *crónicas* on all manner of issues relating to migrant life, except, that is, for sport and, not surprisingly, sport gets no further mention in any of his *El Expreso* columns.

Readers familiar with Blady Woggie from his publications previous to those in *El Expreso* would have expected humour to feature significantly in his new *crónicas* and they were not kept waiting. El Blady Woggie's contribution to the second issue of the paper is titled *¿De qual qual chancho me hablan?* [What pig are they talking to me about?], a diatribe on personal hygiene, advertising, movies and the American way of life that can be read as an extended metaphor for migrant acclimatisation. It ends with the recounting of a joke about two friends, one telling the other that he has just bought a pig and it is going to live with him in his flat. "But, compadre, what about the smell?" the first one asks. "Not to worry", says the other, "the pig is going to get used to it" [*Pero compadré, y el olorcito…— Bueno… el chancho va se va a ir acostumbrando*].[33] The reader is left to draw conclusions regarding who the pig may be and who it is that smells.

In the following issues, Blady Waggie tackles topics facing migrant families including day-to-day concerns such as child care and accommodation rental. In an instalment titled *Señora Africana pastorea niños* [African lady caring for children], he comments on the trend of earning extra income by providing child care in private homes. He assures readers that he takes up this theme only because of repeated requests to do so, and because of the stories he has been told about the awful things that can happen. He says that when he asks whether he should write about it in seriousness or in jest [*Escribirlo en serio on en broma?*], they tell him to write like he always does, fifty-fifty [*Como caiga… así como lo hacís tú… Fifti-fifti*].[34] In one of the cases he recounts, a woman has ten or twelve children in her care and one day Blady Woggie's friend arrived unexpectedly to pick up her child early, only to find all the children sound asleep, at eleven o'clock in the morning, as if they had been drugged. Blady Woggie writes that this friend could not wake his daughter until three in the afternoon. He assures readers that he is not joking, that this is a serious issue, but as hyperbole is a trademark of Blady Woggie's *crónicas*, it is difficult to know whether to believe this anecdote or not. Another of his *crónicas* titled *no children, plis…* describes his efforts in trying to rent a flat in Sydney, an impossibility it seems with the size of his family. When the real estate agent asks if he and his wife have any children and Blady Woggie answers, "yes, five", the real estate agent is aghast: "*CINCO*!!!! Jesuschrist! You're kidding!!" … "You must be kidding".[35] This column ends with Blady Woggie conceding defeat, but revelling in being defeated by admitting they had dogs as well as children; a lot of dogs: "one Saint Bernard, five Dobermans (mansitos eso sí) [tame, yes], seven German Shepherds, four collies, a Great Dane and a couple of dozens of Chihuahuas". "Are you crazy?" the real estate agent asks. "Y un león y dos dinosaurios" [And a lion and two dinosaurs], Blady Woggie replies. He ends by advising his readers that when they go to see a real estate agent they would do well to enter with their hands in the air, in complete surrender, in order to save time, because in the end, they are going to rob you the same [*Siempre que uno entre con las manos arriba. Para ir ganando tiempo, digo yo. Porque al final, lo van a cogotear igual*].[36] The two dozen chihuahuas, the lion and the dinosaurs at the end of this *crónica* are typical of the exuberance of Blady Woggie's narratives. The absurdity, however, effectively conveys the frustrations likely familiar to some of his readers in their own experiences of seeking rental accommodation with limited English.

Although exaggeration, absurdity and humour featured in many of Blady Woggie's *crónicas*, there were exceptions. In the issue of *El Expreso* on 11 September 1979, his column is titled *Recuerdo en gris menor* [Memory in grey minor] and is devoted to the anniversary of the coup d'état in Chile in 1973. Not all Chileans living in Australia came after the 1973 coup, but many, like Abarca, did and for them the pain of their exile and the memories of comrades who did not survive the events of six years previous were more painful than ever [*Y aunque han pasado seis años, parece que duele e importa, cada día más*].[37] In the penultimate issue of *El Expreso* published on 6 November 1979, Blady Woggie's *crónica* titled *de los discriminados sea el reino de los cielos*... [to the discriminated shall belong the kingdom of heaven] began with the question "Does discrimination exist in this country?" [*¿Existe la discriminación en este país?*].[38] The *cronista* makes the obvious point that prejudice and intolerance are human failings and discrimination, therefore, exists in every country on earth, with Australia being no exception. His column outlines circumstances of racial discrimination and class discrimination in Australia. The latter, he points out, would hardly be noticed by anyone in the Spanish-speaking community, though—whether they work in a factory or as white-collar, English-speaking professionals—because their wages or salaries are such an infinitesimal proportion of those earned by directors or corporate bosses that their worlds never touch. "We never see these people, or even know they exist", he says, "nor do the ordinary Australians" [*Pero a esa gente nunca la vemos, ni siquiera sabemos que existe, nosotros ni tampoco el australiano común y corriente*].[39] On the other hand, he claims, cultural discrimination is something everyone in his community has experienced. The epithet "wog" is so commonly used for new migrants that soccer was called "Wog-Ball" by school children. The prevalence of cultural discrimination in Australia, he writes, is strongly related to the monolingual world-view of Anglo-Australians. He explains that Europeans are not bothered when at a first attempt to communicate with someone, they are met with incomprehension; they will try in a second language. Blady Woggie says that out of frustration the first thing he learned how to say in English in Australia was "OK, I don't speak English, but how many languages do you speak?" [*OK... Yo no hablo inglés... ¿Y cuantos idiomas hablas tú?*].[40] Although the sarcasm may have been lost on those Anglo-Australians whom Blady Woggie says he addressed in this manner, his readers would have no difficulty appreciating it.

A third *cronista* writing in *El Expreso* was the Uruguayan-born Alberto "Pocho" Domínguez, who was a tremendously important figure amongst the Spanish-speaking community not only because of his newspaper columns, but also due to his many years as an announcer and host for Sydney's Spanish-language community radio. His radio-voice was well known to every migrant from South America who settled in Sydney in the 1970s and 1980s, and his programme, "Folklore, Tangos y Rosas", provided not only music but also news, social announcements and essential information for new arrivals. His column in each issue was simply titled "Comentarios". Whereas those of Brotherton attempted to provide a form of cultural mediation, introducing or explaining aspects of Australian life possibly new or strange to migrants from Spanish-speaking countries, and the *crónicas* of Luis Abarca writing as Blady Woggie offered a mirror to migrant readers in which they could see much of the absurdity, humour and frustration of their daily lives, the *crónicas* of Domínguez would sometimes move between the present in Australia and the past of the migrant's home country, in a way that acknowledged both the sense of rupture and the continuities.

His *crónica*, titled "A los hijos" [To the children], which appeared in the second issue of *El Expreso*, is an example of these shifting time frames that Domínguez frequently employed. He begins with the present, with life in Sydney, where an incident evoked memories of his life in Uruguay prior to migration, to which a substantial portion of the *crónica* is then devoted, before returning to the present in Australia. In the opening, the *cronista* pays a visit to Prince Henry Hospital in Sydney to see a friend who is gravely ill. The sight of the cables and tubes and the sounds of the medical apparatus to which his friend is attached [*aparatos eléctricos, cables, agujas, plásticos, espadrapos en la cabeza recién operada. Y ruidos, ruidos muy conocidos para mí*] take the narrator back to a hospital in Montevideo where, in his memory, he sees his father attached to similar tubes and apparatus following a heart operation.[41] In the same instant, the narrator recalls another hospital—and here it is not stated whether it is in Uruguay or Australia—in which his infant son struggles between life and death amidst the incessant noise of medical equipment and hospital procedures. This superimposition of times is a trope that appears often in migrant writing, with the places, friends and family one will never see again breaking into the present moment, asserting themselves into the ordinary, or at times extraordinary, occurrences of the migrant's new life. The memories evoked in this *crónica* of witnessing both a father and a son struggling for life in hospital are attached to the narrator's present, and to the present of his readers, through his description of the Prince Henry Hospital, a centre at the time for oncology and brain surgery. In the final section of this *crónica*, Domínguez writes sincerely, perhaps sentimentally, of the need for communication between parents and children, not only to express one's love but also to talk through challenges and overcome isolation. It is a theme which would strike a chord with his readers, many of whom would have been raising children in a country which does not speak their language, does not know their culture and cares little for their memories, or their stories. Their own experiences of Australian hospitals and possibly associated memories of hospitalisation in their home countries would be similarly activated by their reading this *crónica*.

The narrative becomes even more poignant when we know—as we do now—that by a strange twist of fate, Alberto "Pocho" Domínguez was a passenger on American Airlines Flight 11 when it was flown into the northern tower of the World Trade Centre in 2001, and as such he was the first Australian to die in the terrorist attacks of 11 September.[42] After his death, a literary competition bearing his name was established and the "Concurso Literario Alberto (Pocho) Domínguez" has awarded numerous prizes in the years since for short stories and poetry, so the community's memory of this *cronista* lives on.[43] Yet his *crónicas* have not been collected. They remain scattered through the pages of Sydney's Spanish-language press, published over a twenty-five-year period, in which those appearing in *El Expreso* are only a small portion, and certainly they have never been translated.

Most of the *crónicas* written in Australia have not been collected. There are a few exceptions—Luis Abarca is one who has published some of his *crónicas* in book form, as *Las historias de un Blady Woggie* (1992). However, the majority of this writing remains hidden in rolls of microfilm or in the crumbling pages of newsletters. The thirteen issues of *El Expreso* are held by only one library, the State Library of New South Wales, which has both microfilm and hard copy of the newspaper. In the future these may be digitised but for the present the only way to read *El Expreso* is to visit the library, load the microfilm, and scroll through to find the *crónicas* reported on here. In one of the critical works cited earlier, Andrew Reynolds comments on precisely this issue in the context of Latin American writing: that of inaccessibility of a wealth of literary work that remains, for all practical purposes, lost. Reynolds cites Rubén Darío who refers to a selection of his *crónicas* which appeared in the 1896 book, *Los Raros* [The Eccentrics], as having been pulled out of "the thick forest of *La Nación*", the Buenos Aires newspaper in which they were first published a few years before [*los habéis ido á sacar del bosque espeso de La Nación*].[44] Reynolds writes: "Literary texts published in newspaper format … are lost until someone performs the necessary labor to find them and bring them into their permanent existence in book form".[45] However, once incorporated in book form, "the *crónica*'s status as a journalistic text is erased".[46] This double-bind is a challenge, especially in an English-speaking nation like

Australia where literary production in other languages within that nation is barely recognised.

The *crónicas* that appear in the thirteen issues of *El Expreso*, along with the newspaper's other content, including reviews of theatre and music, interviews, and commentary on issues of the day, offer unique insight into the lives and perspectives of a migrant community striving to establish a place for itself in Australia's multicultural society. They are not only journalistic; they are also of significant literary and historical value. As Kanellos has remarked, too often scholarship on migrant writing relies exclusively on that which is available in English, the language of the host society. The *crónicas* examined here were not intended for the eyes of Anglo-Australians; they were written by migrants for a migrant readership, exclusively. They are written with the understanding that their humour, their cultural assumptions, their concerns and conceits will be shared by their readership. They are also written with the recognition that although Spanish-speaking Australians have come from many different nations and have migrated for a range of reasons, their experience of migration and their efforts to fit into Australian society provide the common ground upon which these *crónicas* and their narratives unfold. And today, with the children and grandchildren of Spanish-speaking migrants having grown up in Australia, having studied and worked and lived their lives here, these *crónicas* are now as much Australian stories as they are Chilean ones, or Uruguayan, or Spanish. They are a part of Australian literature that deserve to be recognised and they should be acknowledged as a part of our shared history.

NOTES

1. Maria Lauret, *Wanderwords: Language Migration in American Literature* (New York & London: Bloomsbury Academic, 2014), 4.
2. This chapter is part of the ARC Discovery project "New Transnationalisms: Australia's Multilingual Literary Heritage". The author wishes to thank the Australia Research Council and the University of Wollongong for financial assistance.
3. Nicolás Kanellos, *Hispanic Immigrant Literature: El Sueño del Retorno* (Austin, TX: University of Texas Press, 2011), 9.
4. Katherine B. Payant and Toby Rose, in Kanellos, *Hispanic Immigrant Literature*, 11.
5. Kanellos, *Hispanic Immigrant Literature*, 13.

6. Kanellos, *Hispanic Immigrant Literature*.
7. Paul Allatson, "Foreword", in *Killer Crónicas: Bilingual Memories*, ed. Susana Chávez-Silverman. Albany: State University of New York Press, 2011, ix.
8. Aníbal González, *Companion to Spanish American Modernismo* (Woodbridge: Tamesis, 2007), 24.
9. José Joaquin Blanco, Vincente Leñero and Juan Villoro, "Questioning the Chronicle," in *The Contemporary Mexican Chronicle: Theoretical Perspectives on the Liminal Genre*, ed. Ignacio Corona and Beth E. Jörgensen (Albany: State University of New York Press, 2002), 66.
10. Blanco, Leñero and Villoro, "Questioning the Chronicle", 67.
11. Julio Ramos, *Divergent Modernities: Culture and Politics in Nineteenth-Century Latin America*, trans. John D. Blanco (Durham, NC: Duke University Press, 200), 113.
12. Kanellos, *Hispanic Immigrant Literature*, 48.
13. Kanellos, *Hispanic Immigrant Literature*.
14. Viviane Mahieux, *Urban Chroniclers in Modern Latin America: The Shared Intimacy of Everyday Life* (Austin: University of Texas Press, 2011), 5.
15. Mahieux, *Urban Chroniclers in Modern Latin America*, 6.
16. Mahieux, *Urban Chroniclers in Modern Latin America*.
17. Mahieux, *Urban Chroniclers in Modern Latin America*, 6-7.
18. Varela, "Ripios de la semana", *La Crónica*, Miercoles, Agosto 4, 1965, 3. All translations from Spanish to English, either direct or paraphrase, are by the author unless otherwise noted.
19. Luis Abarca, "Crónicas de un Bladi Woggi: Bienaventurados los aconsejadores!", *El Español en Australia*, Agosto 15, 1978, p. 6.
20. A. Mora, "Pero qué mal, Bladi Woggi!", *El Español en Australia*, Septiembre 26, 1978, p. 22.
21. Mora, "Pero qué mal, Bladi Woggi!".
22. Jofre Mioche, "Pero qué bien, Bladi Woggi!", *El Español en Australia*, Septiembre 26, 1978, p. 22.
23. "Un desafio y una esperanza", *El Expreso*, Martes, Julio 31, 1979, p. 3.
24. "Un desafio y una esperanza".
25. John Brotherton, "Comentarios", *El Expreso*, Martes, Julio 31, 1979, p. 3.
26. Brotherton, "Comentarios".
27. Brotherton, "Comentarios".
28. John Brotherton, "Comentarios", *El Expreso*, Martes, Agosto 28, 1979, p. 3.
29. John Brotherton, "Comentarios", *El Expreso*, Martes, Septiembre 18, 1979, p. 3.
30. Brotherton, "Comentarios".

31. Luis Abarca, "Comentarios de un Blady Woggie: Comentarista Deportivo", *El Expreso*, Martes, Julio 31, 1979, p. 9.
32. Abarca, "Comentarios de un Blady Woggie: Comentarista Deportivo".
33. Luis Abarca, "Comentarios de un Blady Woggie: ¿De cual cual chancho me hablan?", *El Expreso*, Martes Agosto 14, 1979, p. 21.
34. Luis Abarca, "Comentarios de un Blady Woggie: Señora africana pastorea niños", *El Expreso*, Martes Agosto 21, 1979, p. 21.
35. Luis Abarca, "Comentarios de un Blady Woggie: no children, plis...", *El Expreso*, Martes, Octubre 2, 1979, p. 19.
36. Abarca, "Comentarios de un Blady Woggie: no children, plis...".
37. Luis Abarca, "Comentarios de un Blady Woggie: Recuerdos en gris menor", *El Expreso*, Martes, Septiembre 11, 1979, p. 21.
38. Luis Abarca, "Comentarios de un Blady Woggie: de los discriminados sea el reino de los cielos", *El Expreso*, Martes, Noviembre 6, 1979, p. 19.
39. Abarca, "Comentarios de un Blady Woggie: de los discriminados sea el reino de los cielos".
40. Abarca, "Comentarios de un Blady Woggie: de los discriminados sea el reino de los cielos".
41. Alberto Pocho Dominguez, "A los hijos", *El Expreso*, Agosto 14, 1979, p. 20.
42. Bel Vidal, "The First Australian", in *Culture Is...: Australian Stories across Cultures*, ed. Anne-Marie Smith (Kent Town, SA: Wakefield Press, 2008), 1–13.
43. Comité organizador concurso literario "Concurso literario Alberto (Pocho) Dominguez", *Noticias y Deportes*, Marzo 25, 2004, p. 5.
44. Andrew Reynolds, *The Spanish American Crónica Modernista, Temporality, and Material Culture*, (Lewisburg, PA: Bucknell University Press, 2012), 154. Translation by Reynolds.
45. Reynolds, *The Spanish American Crónica Modernista*, 154.
46. Reynolds, *The Spanish American Crónica Modernista*, 156.

CHAPTER 10

News Reporting of Italian Organised Crime in Australia: Examining *Il Globo's* Editorial Commentary

Clare Johansson and Simone Battiston

The association between immigration and criminality—and its exploitation by the media—is as powerful, and damaging, today as it was in the past.[1] Despite emerging scholarship challenging the nexus between immigration and crime, sensationalistic media coverage of crimes committed by immigrants and racial minorities tend to have a strong impact on public opinion.[2] The degree to which the media has impacted public opinion is evident in research, which indicates that in many Western

C. Johansson (✉)
Department of Management and Marketing, Faculty of Business and Law,
Swinburne University of Technology, Hawthorn, VIC, Australia
e-mail: cjohansson@swin.edu.au

S. Battiston
Department of Social Sciences, Faculty of Health, Arts and Design,
Swinburne University of Technology, Hawthorn, VIC, Australia

© The Author(s) 2020
C. Dewhirst, R. Scully (eds.), *The Transnational Voices of Australia's Migrant and Minority Press*, Palgrave Studies in the History of the Media,
https://doi.org/10.1007/978-3-030-43639-1_10

nations—Australia included—a high proportion of the general public believe that immigrants commit more crime than the native-born.[3]

In fact, David Hollinsworth found that, within the Journalist Union guidelines, racial stereotyping remains routine in much media coverage.[4] Racial stereotyping is even necessary for a story to survive the editorial culling process before publication. This mainstream media practice can not only misguide the general public's perceptions of immigration and crime, but it can also silence minorities by denying them the opportunity to "talk back" to the mainstream media's about their portrayal.[5]

So, how do immigrant communities and minorities "talk back", if and when they do, to the depictions of them in mainstream media sources in relation to crime? What about organised crime? One way to understand how ethnic groups cope with, and react to, alleged racial stereotyping in mainstream media is to assess, through their editorial commentary, the ethnic press's responses to damaging media reporting of immigration and criminality. By analysing selected editorials in the Melbourne-based, Italian-language newspaper, *Il Globo* (founded in 1959), in the period 1979–1989, this chapter offers a case study that would allow us to expand our knowledge on the ethnic press's reaction to mainstream media reporting of organised crime, specifically the Calabrian 'Ndrangheta.[6]

Recent scholarship on news coverage of migrant communities, organised crime and racialisation of gang violence in Australia has focused by and large on mainstream media.[7] This chapter's contribution to the literature, instead, is to focus on ethnic and minority media representation of organised crime. If one bears in mind that media in migrant receiving countries like Australia "serve as key mechanisms through which discourses around multiculturalism are produced and circulated",[8] yesterday as well as today's concerns about diasporic identities and discourses of exclusion and inclusion can be better understood if ethnic and minority media editorialising of organised crime and racialisation of violence is also analysed.

The selected period is crucial for different reasons. Firstly, the exposed criminal activity of syndicates operating in rural and metropolitan areas in association with the 'Ndrangheta had made headlines in the national press, triggering an editorial response by *Il Globo*. Secondly, the composition of the Italian community in Australia was shifting. The rapid increase of the Australian-born component of the Italian-Australian and the simultaneous decline of the first generation made the need for a discourse counter-reacting to the damaging association of immigration-organised criminality, but also ethnic community-criminality, even more urgent. Thirdly, renewed efforts by law enforcement authorities to uproot the illegal activities and interests of the 'Ndrangheta in Australia exposed as never before the tentacular presence of Italian organised crime in the country, making the editorial response of the ethnic press worth exploring.[9]

This chapter begins by providing a précis of the literature on representations of immigration, ethnicity and criminality in the mainstream media of migrant-receiving countries, above all Australia. The literature strongly suggests that insofar as criminality committed by immigrants is concerned there is a persistent dichotomy between empirical evidence, on the one hand, and media-fuelled perception, on the other hand. Namely, data indicate that immigrants commit less crimes than non-immigrants. Yet, reporting practices in mainstream media that cover immigrant-related crime sensationalistically lead to misguided perceptions of immigration and ethnicities among the general public. The next section introduces *Il Globo*'s editorial commentary, penned by its editor-in-chief Antonino ("Nino") Randazzo (1932–2019). The most relevant of the organised crime-themed editorials comprised within the years of 1979–1989 are translated and analysed in the sections below.

So difficult to separate:
THE IMMIGRATION-CRIMINALITY NEXUS

In many migrant-receiving nations, including the United States, Canada, Australia, and New Zealand, the imagined link between immigration and crime has been thoroughly examined.[10] Immigrants in Australia, particularly non-British immigrants, have historically been associated with an increase in crime.[11] Given the importance of immigration to the growth of the country, the nexus of immigration-criminality has led to a number of post-war inquires, the results of which were published in the so-called Dovey Committee Reports.[12] During the 1950s, the Immigration Advisory Council commissioned three reports, which comprehensively disproved the link between immigration and criminality.[13]

Contrary to widely held opinions that see a direct correlation between immigration and crime, little empirical evidence has shown this to be true.[14] Recent studies have reiterated this point and demonstrated that immigration rates are largely un-associated with crime rates.[15] Compared with the native-born cohort, immigrant crime rates are lower. Immigration does not increase crime; in fact, it can reduce it.[16] Research suggests, instead, that the link between the second-generation migrants and crime is actually stronger, as second-generation migrants catch up to native-born crime rates.[17] Both generations are vulnerable to being associated with crime activity. Yet, the first is statistically less prone to offend than the second- and the native-born cohorts.

How the media portrays immigrants—the way in which they integrate and how narratives of immigration-crime news stories are constructed—has a direct influence on how the host society views the new arrivals, their settlement patterns and offending trajectory.[18] In host societies, immigrants are not only featured disproportionately in news coverage compared with non-immigrants, but they also are subjected to negative stereotyping, which can negatively influence public opinion regarding immigrants and minority groups.[19] This perceived bias is not confined to the perpetrators of crime, but extends to the victims too, with the literature suggesting that media reporting on the criminality of immigrants is much greater than its reporting on the victims of crime in the same immigrant minorities.[20] These reporting practices in mainstream media can misguide perceptions of immigration and crime among the general public.[21]

Sensationalistic media coverage of crimes committed by immigrants and racial minorities appears to have a strong impact on public opinion, in spite of Australia having become a modern multicultural society. Illegal boat arrivals and the Tampa incident in 2001; the Cronulla Beach riots in 2005; Sudanese gangs in Melbourne in 2007; the attacks on Indian foreign students in Melbourne in 2008–2009; the Lindt terrorist attack in Sydney in 2014: all have perpetuated the stereotype and instilled the perception that asylum seekers, foreign-born residents and citizens are more likely to commit crimes than native-born citizens and pose a threat to the Australian way of life.[22] This threat links the fear of the stranger or "Other" with ethnic, minority crime in such a way that it is racialised and constructed as being worse than other crime, particularly when compared to non-immigrant crime.[23] This type of media coverage has contributed to the establishment of a "hierarchy of whiteness".[24]

ITALIAN ORGANISED CRIME: *IL GLOBO*'S EDITORIAL COMMENTARY

Recent scholarship on Italian organised crime in Australia has painstakingly reconstructed the presence, evolution, and international connections of the 'Ndrangheta; from its initial manifestation in the sugarcane plantation sector in 1920s rural Queensland to the complex organisation of today, devoted to drug trafficking and various other criminal activities.[25] Scholars have, for instance, examined the transnational and global dimensions of the Australian 'Ndrangheta, investigated both the histories of Calabrian migration and Calabrian crime; or bridged Italian scholarship with Australian journalist and archival sources, and in so doing provided an holistic view of the phenomenon.[26]

For its long-standing and proactive role within the Italian-Australian community,[27] *Il Globo* can be viewed as an ideal prism through which one can gauge how the ethnic print press has been coping with, and reacting to, instances of racial stereotyping in the mainstream media when reporting about crime, including organised crime originating from the community. The 1980s represent a period worthy of research attention in relation to Italian organised crime history and Italian community history in Australia. During this period, evidence of the presence of—and law enforcement operations against—Italian background-organised crime in Australia had made headline news nationally and also generated wider (often negative) commentary on immigration and ethnic communities in the media, which triggered a robust response by *Il Globo*.

Dozens of Italians in country towns, such as Griffith, were subject to criminal investigations relating to organised crime and drug trafficking. These investigations were conducted throughout the 1980s, into the 1990s, and beyond. In the late 1970s, the New South Wales government promoted the Royal Commission into Drug Trafficking (1977–1979)—also known as the Woodward Royal Commission (after the commissioner, Justice Philip Morgan Woodward)—in order to investigate drug trafficking in the state, with special reference to the links between the Mafia and New South Wales Police, and the disappearance and murder of the Griffith anti-marijuana campaigner, Donald Mackay.[28] The Royal Commission concluded that 'Ndrangheta was likely to have been behind Mackay's murder, the latter having exposed the illegal activities of the syndicate in New South Wales's Riverina region.[29]

How did *Il Globo* editorialise these events? How did it react to the often-sensationalistic tone of mainstream media reporting of Italian organised crime? The source primarily used for this study was the newspaper's editorial articles, published between 1 January 1979 and 31 December 1989. Purposely, we zeroed-in on the editorials dealing with "organised crime". In order to select the most appropriate pieces, an initial data sample of 464 editorials covering the 10-year period was collected.[30] The content of each editorial was analysed and subsequently coded by theme. A theme that emerged, and was prevalent throughout the period, was indeed that of "organised crime". Thirty editorials devoted to organised crime and/or migrant issues relating to organised crime, such as discrimination, were found. For this study, we then selected, and translated into English, the most relevant (about half) of the organised crime editorials.

Il Globo's editorials during the selected period were penned by Nino Randazzo, its editor-in-chief. Randazzo was a pivotal figure at the newspaper and its most public face. Born in the Aeolian Islands (Italy), at the age of 20, he emigrated from Italy to Australia. In 1957, he became an Australian citizen and helped establish *Il Globo* in 1959. Starting as deputy editor, he became editor-in-chief in 1978 and held this position until 2006. He was also a many-sided character with a versatile personality: journalist and editor, but also playwright, essayist, translator, historian and—later in life—politician (in 2006, he successfully contested for the centre-left coalition, *L'Unione*, the newly created senatorial seat of Africa–Asia–Oceania–Antarctica in the Italian Parliament).[31] As stressed elsewhere, the newspaper did not shy away from lobbying "relevant authorities and Australian governments alike on issues that mattered most to the Italian community, especially those related to domestic politics, migrant settlement and immigration".[32]

Randazzo himself had in fact "gained a considerable following of readers for his lively and often controversial writing style, and for his campaigns against attacks on the Italian community"; notable was the newspaper's uncovering in 1962 of a fabricated story of prostitution by national broadcaster Channel 7's *Meet the Press*, whose objective was to deliberately question the morality of Italian immigrants.[33]

Mindful of the damaging public effects of immigration-crime nexus, Randazzo's editorials on Italian organised crime downplayed the dangers of the presence of an Australian 'Ndrangheta from 1979 to 1989, whilst emphasising, at the same time, the risks of sensationally finger-pointing one regional group (immigrants from Calabria) and unfairly criminalising an entire ethnic community (Italian-Australians). When reporting about organised crime, Randazzo adopted a narrative that leading Mafia scholar Salvatore Lupo would term revisionist.[34] As recently underlined by Stephen Bennetts, who cites Lupo, a "liberal progressivist" variation on the negationist theme of the Mafia developed in Australia too in the post-war period, not only among Italian-American scholars and community leaders.[35] Liberal progressivism downplays or denies the role or existence of organised crime, whilst the damaging public effects of an immigration-organised crime nexus and ethnic/racial stereotyping are emphasised. *Il Globo*'s editorial commentary appears to have espoused a liberal progressive "negationism" of the 'Ndrangheta whose notion could have destabilised "the conventionally heroic narratives of Australia's multicultural history".[36]

One case in point is the three-week community campaign launched by *Il Globo* in 1977. In the wake of Donald Mackay's murder, articles published in the Melbourne-based *Herald,* and ensuing nation-wide TV reports by Channel 9, alluded to Mafia links in Griffith.[37] In the mainstream media reporting, *Il Globo* saw "ridiculous generalisations" mixed with elements of racial hostility and counter-reacted by inviting Italians to send a prefilled complaint letter (published in the newspaper) to Channel 9. The mounting community campaign paid off and weeks later the TV network apologised.[38]

Upon release, in 1979, the media published the key findings of the Woodward Royal Commission report, including the identities of 'Ndrangheta members. Similar to what had occurred two years before, *Il Globo* expressed anxiety about the mainstream media commentary of Mafia-related stories and its often-used sensationalistic tones. It found that news items offered "systematic misrepresentations" and "[… a] heap of free and scandalistic speculations, exaggerations, generalisations on the reality and on the tendencies of the Calabrese community in Australia".[39] Worse still, there were "regurgitations of an ill-concealed racism" in the media that were to poison society no less than drugs.[40]

Il Globo published further editorials targeting the Australian mainstream press for its alleged unbalanced and poor reporting. In one editorial, "irresponsible" journalists and newspaper owners were put on the same level of criminals and corrupt police:

the Australian press as a whole deserves the most open condemnation for its incapacity for balance and analysis, for its rancorous racism. And confirmed by the services of the last days in the Australian press about a raid by the Mafiosi in Calabria, as well as by previous misrepresentations and inventions of declarations by the "police spokesman" in anti-Italian function: of some Australian colleagues, ignorant colleagues, only to shame us. At least they deserve the moral condemnation of honest people, since they seem incredibly protected against a more than deserved dismissal. […] The Australian press has once again become an open wound in the body of our multicultural society. In Australia today we have—and we are not too surprised—

criminals of Italian origin and of any other national extraction, we have corrupt cops, but we also have, above all, irresponsible journalists and news-paper owners who tolerate and even seem to encourage so much irresponsi-bility. It is very sad to have to observe and document this uncivil phenomenon just from the columns of a newspaper![41]

In another editorial, *Il Globo* criticised the media for not understanding the issue of "Italian Mafia" in their reporting, thereby creating misrepre-sentations and misconceptions of the Italian community in the eyes of the Australian public.[42]

Leading media outlets thus became the focal targets for the Italian newspaper. *Il Globo* alleged a defamation campaign against the Italian eth-nic community and singled out *The Sun* (published from Melbourne, but available throughout the Riverina and beyond) and John Silvester, its crime reporter. Randazzo made much of the fact that John Silvester was the son of the head of the Bureau of Criminal Intelligence and the then newly appointed Chief of the Australian Bureau of Criminal Intelligence in Canberra, Detective Superintendent Fred Silvester; accusing him of tak-ing advantage of his family connection in the bureau.[43] Through its col-umns, and an editorial's headline partly published in English, *Il Globo* called on the Minister of Police Services in Victoria to silence Fred Silvester from making further accusations about the Italian-Australian community to the mainstream press, particularly *The Sun*, where he had particular influence over his son.[44]

Then-Federal Commissioner for Community Relations, Al Grassby, responded to Randazzo's message and intervened by writing a letter to the Victorian Police Commission regarding the allegations that Silvester had made. The Victorian Chief Commissioner of Police, Sinclair Imrie "Mick" Miller's response to Al Grassby was published in *Il Globo*, in which he stated:

I must confess to you that in the article [published in *Il Globo*], I found a certain excessive sensitivity, together with an incorrect interpretation or a misrepresentation of the facts. Indeed, I believe that misrepresentation is a consequence of the erroneous translations. However, it is understandable, given the circumstances, to verify this. Even I have often been accused by some media in this state of reacting in the same way when the police (even if it is a minority group) are attacked for reasons that I consider invalid. I certainly think it superfluous to reiterate that I will never tolerate any dis-crimination against any ethnic group in my area of competence. I can categorically assure you that there are no police departments "with the specific task of investigating and prosecuting individuals of a particular racial or ethnic group". This does not mean that individuals of any racial or ethnic group, suspected of criminal activity, will not be investigated.[45]

Miller stated he had had an editorial from *Il Globo* translated. While Miller's response to Al Grassby shows empathy towards the Italian-Australian community, Miller was unapologetic for the investigation into organised crime and clearly thought *Il Globo's* response was excessively sensitive and had misinterpreted the facts, demonstrating the lack of understanding between the two parties on the issue. Randazzo commented in response:

> the effort of S. I. Miller is unacceptable, to cover for, and to justify, his small responsibility for his ex-employee, Fred Silvester, that until now has not added a single word of clarity or apology to the Italian community's "misrepresentation" provoked by the rubbish on the mafia which he propagated or raised within the Australian public opinion.[46]

The "rubbish on the mafia" was picked up by at least another local newspaper (the *Sunraysia Daily*) which questioned the activity of Italian growers now in Mildura. In 1983, the editor of the *Sunraysia Daily* signed off on an editorial article in which he accused the Italian farmers of "producing drugs instead of grapes".[47] *Il Globo* responded directly to the *Sunraysia Daily* by publishing numerous letters to the editor sent by Italians and Australians that condemned the *Sunraysia Daily* article. Randazzo also wrote:

> It is useless to dramatise, we need to look at the roots of this new racial explosion. That the editor of a newspaper, a person who is supposed to have some responsibility and mental and cultural stature, [would] write and sign an offensive piece as published by the *Sunraysia Daily* of 10 January 1983 [is] scandalous, but should not be surprising. This is just the tip of an iceberg, or if we want the consequence of a vague xenophobic hysteria that winds across the country and is fed, often also by omission, from Canberra. It is not an isolated fact; it is the consequence of culpable and obtuse attitudes at the top. The speech should be broadened, the faults are upstream, the incautious provincial journalist of Mildura is just an element of the antiethnicity that sweeps Australia.[48]

The Italian community did receive some support from the mainstream press in Mildura. The *Mildura Independent* published an article titled "A State of Shock", which *Il Globo* re-printed within the English-language section. Pressured by *Il Globo*, a series of Letters-to-the-Editor from Italian Australians and Australians condemning the article were eventually published by the *Sunraysia Daily*, upon which Randazzo articulated:

> The reaction, the phone calls, and the letters to the newspaper, the protest reunions were immediate and the 12th edition of the *Sunraysia Daily* published a series of letters from Italian and Australian readers, all condemning the editorial of Tiley, including one front page, even on the headline, entitled "an ethnic group protests" and signed by Steve Panuccio, Jim Murenue Giuseppe Roccisano, respectively president, secretary and treasurer of the "Leonardo Da Vinci circle" and respected local businessmen.[49]

Randazzo felt that an "anti-ethnic wind" was sweeping Australia.[50] It is notable that, given there was also a strong anti-Asian mentality (later on ignited by historian Geoffrey Blainey's views of Asian immigration and increasing Asianisation of Australia), in order to prevent the same shame being brought upon the Asian community, a statement was issued by the Italian Ambassador in Canberra, Sergio Angeletti, urging the Italian community to fight anti-Asian racism, in which he stated "to defame the Italians with the myth of the mafia in Australia is also racism".[51]

"To defame the Italians with the myth of the Mafia in Australia is also racism"

On 6 May 1984, two bodies were found weighted down in the Murrumbidgee River near Griffith. The bodies were those of Rocco Medici and Giuseppe Furina. Their murders were thought to be a part of the struggle for control over the Queen Victoria Market in Melbourne and a revenge for the attempted assassination of Liborio Benvenuti. A year earlier, Benvenuti's car was blown up at the market. The murders of Medici and Furina are believed to have been a payback for the car bomb. One of the men had his ear sliced off, a supposed mafia warning to others that the victim had heard too much.

The reporting of the 1984 mafia murders brought the issue of Italian organised crime back to the frontline, to which *Il Globo* responded by publishing an editorial titled, "To defame the Italians with the myth of the mafia in Australia is also racism".[52] Whilst not denying the involvement of local Italians in criminal activities and illegal drug trafficking, *Il Globo* denied the existence of a connection—for which it blamed the Silvester— between the Italian community and the mafia. This was articulated as follows:

> There is no denying the presence of Italian elements—few in relation to the emigrant mass—involved in the world of drugs and crime. But there is no evidence of the mafia "connection". Only the novelists of journalism speak of "evidence" acquired always relying on anonymous police spokespersons [...]. It is significant that the former police officer Fred Silvester came back to life, to mumble his discredited theses and to feed his own son, John Silvester, the crime reporter of the Melbourne newspaper *The Sun* who this time, as in the past, distinguished himself for imaginative findings on the "honourable society". We would like to remind you that exactly three years ago this newspaper requested Fred Silvester to backtrack and publicly apologise to the Italian community for similar foolishness he pronounced at the time.[53]

Randazzo was adamant to stress, again and again, that news reporting of Italian organised crime by the mainstream press was based on misunderstandings and misinterpretations of the criminal phenomenon, a practice from which he sought to disengage:

> when—from an Australian press that no longer knows the basics of irresponsibility and indecency—one arrives at the insulting and unbelievable absurdity of "twenty thousand belonging to the honoured society in Victoria only". [...] At this point we do not debate, we no longer reason, and it is impossible to communicate with a person that writes and allows the spread of monstrous fantasies of that kind. With former fixated and neurotic police officials, with ignorant and prejudiced journalists, with police officers in charge who maintain their anonymity by use of "a police spokesman" to feed the filthiest of lies to a superficial and impressionable public opinion of the type of those described in the article to which this note makes comment, one must inevitably give up direct and open dialogue.[54]

Instead, Randazzo framed it as "a battle that concerned all ethnic groups, not just Italians, and their civil liberties in the host country's society".[55]

By the late 1980s, the police were homing in on their investigation into the death of Donald Mackay. Mackay was a Liberal Party candidate who unsuccessfully contested the state seat of Murrumbidgee in 1973 and 1976. In the Federal election in 1974, he stood for Riverina. His preferences helped to unseat Labor minister for immigration, A. J. Grassby. During his time campaigning in the Riverina, Mackay became aware of the drug problem at Griffith and actively began to campaign against drugs. Mackay passed on information to the Drug Squad in Sydney which led to a drug raid in the Riverina during which the police found the largest single crop of marijuana yet discovered in Australia. Court hearings for the case began on 7 March 1977 during which Mackay's covert role may have been revealed and shortly following this on 15 July 1977 he vanished. Mackay's car was found bloodstained with three spent .22 cartridges laying nearby. The Woodward Royal Commission reported in 1979 that Mackay was murdered by a "hit man" on behalf of the Griffith cell of 'Ndrangheta.[56] Although no one was ever charged with Mackay's murder, three men—James Bazley, Gianfranco Tizzoni and George Joseph—were charged with conspiracy to murder Mackay and received jail sentences. One of them, Bazley, was said to be the alleged hitman. He, however, denied being the killer and blamed instead Krahe, an allegedly corrupt ex-detective from Sydney.

By 1987, the final reports of developments into the Mackay's death appear to have minimalised the role of the 'Ndrangheta, even de-ethnicised events, upon which *Il Globo* reiterated its views on past events:

> It was to be bet on. A bit of waiting, a little patience, and the hoax of the "Italian mafia in Australia", "responsible" for the assassination of the anti-drug activist in Griffith Don Mackay on 15 July 1977, of a vast chain of other crimes and of a vast circle of drugs and corruption, would also fall, not only that, but it would turn against those institutional frameworks—of the press, of the politics [and] above all, of the police forces—which had built it, and sold it "with relative success to influence public opinion". As always in the past. As for the fable of the "black hand" of the 1920s in the sugarcane plantations of North Queensland, where "etched into the memory" of the members of the old Anglo-Australian establishment [was] the fact that Sicilian, Calabrian and Venetian farmers had secured a near monopoly of sugar production. As in 1964, at the time of the notorious shootings at Victoria Market in Melbourne, when two other Victoria Police officers, chief inspectors Matthews and Ford, reinvented the mafia to cover the abortion racket for which they ended up in gaol a few years later.[57]

Further, *Il Globo* made much of the fact that Melbourne newspapers, particularly *The Sun*, chose to focus on the Mafia ties in the murder of Mackay rather than the fact that the ex-head of the Crime Investigation Bureau of Sydney, Fred Krahe, was named as being instrumental in the killing of Mackay.

> Here and now, a journalist "veteran of the events of 1964 at Victoria Market", an Australian professional of rare courage, Tom Prior, of the Melbourne newspaper *The Sun*, is rattling some skeletons in the cupboard. Prior gathered not only the revelations of James Bazley, who is serving a long sentence in the prisons of Melbourne for Mackay's murder on the alleged commission of the mafia boss Bob Trimbole, according to information from the Victoria police of a "missing person", Gianfranco Tizzoni, but also from statements from authoritative people above suspicion in the Griffith's area at the time of the tragedy. Revelations and declarations that concur to indicate the ex-head of the Crime Investigation Bureau of Sydney Fred Krahe as being the material executor in the killing of Mackay. Such is the number of new clues to be evaluated on the basis of the journalistic services of Prior, that the current New South Wales Police Chief, John Avery, is negotiating with the president of the anti-crime federal body National Crime Authority, Judge Donald Stewart, for the reopening of investigations into Mackay's disappearance. What does the aggressive newshound of a journalist Tom Prior bring to light today? So many disturbing facts, buried for too long together with the never-found cadaver of Mackay.[58]

On 10 January 1989, the Assistant Commissioner of the Australian Federal Police, Colin Winchester, was shot dead as he stepped from his car in Canberra. Speculations that the killing of Winchester was a Mafia "hit", due to covert anti-drugs operations, was widely reported (or rather misreported for *Il Globo*) in the press in Italy:

> We sincerely hope that the Italian press of Italy is [usually] more accurate, responsible, credible, informed and informative in giving its readers a framework of organised crime from north to south of the peninsula, than it has been regarding the killing of the deputy chief of the Federal Police, Colin Winchester, in Canberra a couple of weeks ago. What some Italian newspapers have written is mind boggling and puts to shame the most fanciful fantasies of the Australian journalists. [...] So, what have the Italians read in Italy is the ever-abundant newspaper crime stories? For *La Repubblica* the order to liquidate Winchester would have originated from Platì, where the bulk of the proceeds from the Australian operations of the 'Ndrangheta

would flow. *La Stampa* writes that "Mackay, a Labor Party supporter (sic!), had been targeted by the 'Ndrangheta for some time", that since the 'Ndrangheta had become the most powerful organisation in Australia, superior to the mafia crime novel, and that "Trimboli died two years ago in England under a false name". […] *Il Messaggero* of Rome recalls "the crime of the Australian politician (Mackay was a candidate for the Parliament for Labor)". Long ago, the weekly *Europeo* had even written that Mackay was a member of parliament. In another edition of the *Messaggero* we learn, through the pen of a special correspondent, that the killing of Winchester is undoubtedly "a crime of the mafia, an Italian-style crime".[59]

The extracts from the Italian press showed a disconnect, not only between the narrative of the mainstream press in Australian and *Il Globo*, but also between the mainstream press in Italy and *Il Globo*.[60] *Il Globo* picked up on some of the plain inaccuracies attributed to Mackay's life (Mackay was a Liberal Party candidate who unsuccessfully contested the state seat of Murrumbidgee in the elections of 1973 and 1976) but most importantly rejected the thesis that the killing was carried out by the 'Ndrangheta. For mafia scholars, the Winchester killing—although not proven by law that it was indeed an organised crime murder—was somehow a turning point against Italian organised crime, which sparked in the coming years several police operations that unearthed significant illegal activities in the triangulation Australia-Italy-South America.[61]

In the final editorial commentary on this topic, Randazzo's line did not diverge from the past and painted a grim picture for the Italian community, one that was being discriminated against, marginalised, even forgotten by the federal government:

With its political delusion of greatness, the National Crime Authority has, among other things, put into place the strategy of aiming not at single criminals, but entire ethnic groups (they are in turn the Italians and the Chinese, and at times the Greeks), criminalising them in the eyes of a biased and misinformed public opinion. At times the Federal Police and the State Police protest because the National Crime Authority negates them the access to a notable volume of information. The links between the various police only exist in "pro-forma"; there is an uncoordinated national fight against crime bound by the trafficking of narcotics that would be all smiles if it wasn't for the tragic and the felonious bitter bloody fruits that are born from it. And the federal government rests mute, it is almost victim of blackmail unknown to most. It seems almost gagged, powerless, left to run, not intervening with an attempt to reform nor a word of balancing. Not even when the most honest ethnic group of Australia, the most respectful of the law, comes covered in the mud of the accused "mafia" launched often by entities and police with men, in uniform and without, from the hands and the conscience as much dirty as those from the authentic mafia of every nationality.[62]

By the late 1980s, *Il Globo* still saw itself as a powerful tool to counteract the "anti-ethnic wind" narrative circulating in the media and a staunch defender of the honour of migrant communities.

Il Globo's editorial commentary on organised crime in the 1979–1989 period on the one hand sought to downplay the presence and role of the mafia in Australia, namely of the Calabrian 'Ndrangheta. On the other hand, it mounted a campaign denouncing what it thought to be racial stereotyping and criminalisation of the Italian community in the mainstream news reporting of organised crime. Randazzo was instrumental in *Il Globo*'s campaign. *Il Globo*, through the editorials penned by Randazzo, opposed "sensationalism" with "negationism", or rather through the liberal progressive variation of negationism, separating the trajectory of hardworking and law-abiding Australia's Italians (the overwhelmingly majority) from the handful of criminals within the ethnic community.

Moreover, through its editorials, *Il Globo* accused the Australian press, its crime reporters and authorities at large of sensationalising the myth of the mafia in Australia, singling out immigrants from Calabria and unfairly criminalising the Italian-Australian community. The need to protect the public honour of the community and defend innocent Calabrian migrants from being incorrectly labelled as criminals took precedent over any other considerations on organised crime, a *modus operandi* that recalls certain Italian press in the United States and in Italy at the beginning of the twentieth century.[63] *Il Globo* was successful in getting the government's attention and a response from the Police Commissioner in Victoria, but did not deviate from its tirade against the press and the authorities.

This chapter sought to contribute to the literature by analysing how one ethnic and minority media outlet (*Il Globo*) represented organised crime ('Ndrangheta), often in reaction to Australian mainstream media reporting. In the 1980s, *Il Globo* constructed a counter-narrative through its editor-in-chief that boldly pursued the defence of the diasporic identity and legacy whilst downplaying the rising menace of organised crime. In opposing "sensationalism" with "negationism", *Il Globo* sought to move the debate to anti-racist discourses at the time when multiculturalism, as government policy and societal model, was beginning to be questioned. To examine how today's ethnic and minority media editorialise organised crime and the racialisation of violence is thus to understand how discourses of diasporic identities, exclusion and inclusion, and not only crime-related, are being produced and circulated.

NOTES

1. Scott Poynting, "Ethnicising criminality and criminalising ethnicity", in *The other Sydney: Communities, identities and inequalities in Western Sydney*, ed. Jock Collins and Scott Poynting (Melbourne: Common Ground, 2000), 63–78.
2. On immigration and crime, see: John Hagan, Ron Levi and Ronit Dinovitzer, "The symbolic violence of the crime-immigration nexus: Migrant mythologies in the Americas," *Criminology & Public Policy* 7, no. 1 (2008), 95–112; Graham C. Ousey, and Charis E. Kubrin, "Exploring the connection between immigration and violent crime rates in US cities, 1980–2000," *Social Problems* 56, no. 3 (2009): 447–473. On the media coverage and its impact, see: Jennifer K. Fitzgerald, K. Amber Curtis and Catherine L. Corliss, "Anxious publics: Worries about crime and immigration," *Comparative Political Studies* 45, no. 4 (2012): 477–506.
3. Rita J. Simon and Keri W. Sikich, "Public attitudes toward immigrants and immigration policies across seven nations," *International Migration Review* 41, no. 4 (2007): 956–962.
4. David Hollinsworth, "My island home": Riot and resistance in media representations of Aboriginality," *Social Alternatives* 24, no. 1 (2005): 16–20.
5. Kerry McCallum and Kate Holland, "Indigenous and multicultural discourses in Australian news media reporting," *Australian Journalism Review* 32, no. 2 (2010): 5.
6. The Calabrian 'Ndrangheta is a well-structured mafia grouping that has been operating in Calabria since the late nineteenth century and later expanded internationally with cells located in Germany, Netherlands, France, the United States, Canada and Australia. See Letizia Paoli, *Mafia brotherhoods: Organized crime, Italian style* (Oxford and New York, Oxford University Press, 2003).
7. David Nolan, Karen Farquharson, Violeta Politoff and Timothy Marjoribanks, "Mediated multiculturalism: newspaper representations of Sudanese migrants in Australia," *Journal of Intercultural Studies* 32, no. 6 (2011): 655–671; Adrian Leiva and David A. Bright, ""The usual suspects": Media representation of ethnicity," *Trends in Organized Crime* 18 (2015): 311–325; John Budarick, "Why the media are to blame for racial-

ising Melbourne's 'African gang' problem", *The Conversation*, 1 August 2018 https://theconversation.com/why-the-media-are-to-blame-for-racialising-melbournes-african-gang-problem-100761 (accessed November 29, 2019).

8. Nolan, Farquharson, Politoff and Marjoribanks, "Mediated multicultural-ism", 659.

9. Pierluigi Spagnolo. "L'ascesa della 'Ndrangheta in Australia," *Altreitalie* 40 (2010).

10. See, for instance, Darnell F. Hawkins, *Ethnicity, race, and crime: Perspectives across time and place* (Albany, NY: SUNY Press, 1995); Michael Tonry, "Ethnicity, crime, and immigration," *Crime and Justice* 21 (1997), 1–29; Benjamin Bowling and Coretta Phillips, *Racism, crime and justice* (Harlow, UK: Pearson Education, 2002); Daniel P. Mears, "Immigration and crime: What's the connection?," *Federal Sentencing Reporter* 14, no. 5 (2002): 284–288.

11. Andy Kaladelfos and Mark Finnane, "Immigration and criminality: Australia's post-war inquiries," *Australian Journal of Politics and History* 64, no. 1 (2018): 48–64.

12. Since the post-Second World War period, Australia has seen a steady increase in the percentage of its population born overseas. See, Australian Bureau of Statistics 2018.

13. Kaladelfos and Finnane, "Immigration and criminality".

14. Kaladelfos and Finnane, "Immigration and criminality".

15. Mears, "Immigration and crime:," *Federal Sentencing Reporter*, 284; Jock Collins and Carol Reid, "Minority youth, crime, conflict, and belonging in Australia," *Journal of International Migration and Integration/Revue de l'integration et de la migration internationale* 10, no. 4 (2009): 377–391.

16. On immigration not increasing crime, see: Jörg L. Spenkuch, "Understanding the impact of immigration on crime," *American Law and Economics Review* 16, no. 1 (2014): 177–219; On immigration reducing crime see: Matthew T. Lee and Ramiro Martinez Jr., "Immigration reduces crime: An emerging scholarly consensus," in *Immigration, Crime and Justice (Sociology of Crime, Law and Deviance, Vol. 13)*, ed. William F. Mcdonald (Bingley, UK: Emerald Group Publishing Limited, 2009), 3–16.

17. Bianca E. Bersani, "An examination of first and second generation immigrant offending trajectories," *Justice Quarterly* 31, no. 2 (2014): 315–343.

18. Trine M. Struer-Tranberg and John M. Innes, "Media influence on host society responsibility in the integration of immigrants," *Journal of Psychological Sciences* 3, no. 1 (2017): 50–68; Casey T. Harris, and Jeff Gruenewald, "News media trends in the framing of immigration and crime, 1990–2013," *Social Problems* 67, no. 3 (2020): 452–470.

19. Franklin D. Gilliam Jr., Shanto Iyengar, Adam Simon and Oliver Wright, "Crime in black and white: The violent, scary world of local news," *Harvard International Journal of Press/Politics* 1, no. 3 (1996): 6–23.

20. Collins and Reid, "Minority youth, crime, conflict, and belonging in Australia"; Scot Wortley, "Misrepresentation or reality? The depiction of race and crime in the Toronto print media," in *Marginality and condemnation: An introduction to critical criminology*, ed. Bernard Schissel and Carolyn Brooks (Halifax, NS: Fernwood Publishing, 2002), 55–82.

21. McCallum and Holland, "Indigenous and multicultural discourses".

22. Data from the 2016 Australian census show that nearly half (49%) of all Australians were either born overseas, the so-called first generation, or had at least one parent born overseas, the so-called second generation (Australian Bureau of Statistics 2017). The percentage of "first" and "second" generation migrants has increased over time and this shift reveals that the Australian population may have approached a tipping point. There are now nearly as many first- or second-generation migrants as people who are at least third-generation Australians. See, Katherine Betts, "Boat people and public opinion in Australia," *People and Place* 9, no. 4 (2001): 34–48; Peter Gale, "The refugee crisis and fear: Populist politics and media discourse," *Journal of Sociology* 40, no. 4 (2004): 321–340; Scot Wortley, "Introduction. The immigration-crime connection: Competing theoretical perspectives," *Journal of International Migration and Integration/Revue de l'integration et de la migration internationale* 10, no. 4 (2009): 349–358; Joel Windle, "The racialisation of African youth in Australia," *Social Identities* 14, no. 5 (2008): 553–566; Gregory Noble, *Lines in the sand: The Cronulla riots, multiculturalism and national belonging* (Sydney: Institute of Criminology Press, 2009); Simon Marginson, Christopher Nyland, Erlenawati Sawir and Helen Forbes-Mewett. *International student security* (New York: Cambridge University Press, 2010); Val Colic-Peisker, Maša Mikola and Karien Dekker, "A multicultural nation and its (Muslim) other? Political leadership and media reporting in the wake of the 'Sydney Siege'", *Journal of Intercultural Studies* 37, no. 4 (2016): 373–389.

23. Collins and Reid, "Minority youth, crime, conflict, and belonging in Australia".

24. Suvendrini Perera, "Whiteness and its discontents: notes on politics, gender, sex and food in the year of Hanson," *Journal of Intercultural Studies* 20, no. 2 (1999): 185.

25. Spagnolo, "L'ascesa della 'Ndrangheta in Australia"; Anna Sergi, "The evolution of the Australian 'Ndrangheta. An historical perspective," *Australian & New Zealand Journal of Criminology* 48, no. 2 (2015): 155–174; Stephen Bennetts, "'Undesiderable Italians': prolegomena for a

history of the Calabrian 'Ndrangheta in Australia," *Modern Italy* 21, no. 1 (2016): 83–89.

26. Spagnolo, "L'ascesa della 'Ndrangheta in Australia"; Sergi, "The evolution of the Australian 'Ndrangheta", 155–174; Bennetts, "'Undesiderable Italians'".

27. Clare Johansson and Simone Battiston, "Ethnic print media in Australia: *Il Globo* in the 1980s," *Media History* 20, no. 4 (2014): 416–430.

28. The Royal Commission was originally appointed for a period of six months, but was extended twice, with the final report being submitted to the Governor on 31 October 1979.

29. *Canberra Times*, "Mackay 'murdered by organisation'," *Canberra Times*, November 7, 1979, p. 19.

30. A full list of articles is available in Clare Johansson, "The editorial commentary of the Italian-language newspaper *Il Globo* from 1979 to 1989: A critical analysis", Honours dissertation (Swinburne University of Technology, 2011).

31. Riccardo Schirru and Laura Egan, "The Italian community in Australia bids farewell to Nino Randazzo," *Il Globo*, July 16, 2019, https://ilglobo.com.au/news/44189/the-italian-community-in-australia-bids-farewell-to-nino-randazzo/ (accessed July 16, 2019); Johansson and Battiston, "Ethnic print media in Australia".

32. Johansson and Battiston, "Ethnic print media in Australia".

33. Schirru and Egan, "The Italian community in Australia."

34. See: Salvatore Lupo, *Quando la mafia trovò l'America* [When the Mafia found America] (Torino: Einaudi, 2008).

35. Lupo, *Quando la mafia trovò l'America*; Bennetts, "'Undesiderable Italians'".

36. Lupo, *Quando la mafia trovò l'America*; Bennetts, "'Undesiderable Italians'".

37. Schirru and Egan, "The Italian community in Australia".

38. Schirru and Egan, "The Italian community in Australia".

39. Nino Randazzo, "Gli italiani d'Australia di nuovo al centro d'una campagna diffamatoria," *Il Globo*, November 12, 1979, p. 1; 34.

40. Randazzo, "Gli italiani d'Australia di nuovo al centro d'una campagna diffamatoria."

41. Nino Randazzo, "Una stampa australiana senza senso di misura," *Il Globo*, June 1, 1981, p. 1; 37.

42. Nino Randazzo, "E parlano di 'Mafia italiana'!," *Il Globo*, June 22, 1981, p. 1; 16.

43. Nino Randazzo, "Droga in Australia: diffamati gli italiani," *Il Globo*, April 13, 1981, p. 1; 32.

44. Nino Randazzo, "Adesso basta con la campagna di diffamazione degli italiani! (Fred Silvester should put up or shut up)," *Il Globo*, April 27, 1981, p. 1.
45. Nino Randazzo, Untitled, *Il Globo*, May 25, 1981, p. 38.
46. Randazzo, Untitled.
47. Nino Randazzo, "Grave tensione razziale anti-italiana a Mildura," *Il Globo*, January 17, 1983, p. 1; 24.
48. Randazzo, "Grave tensione razziale anti-italiana a Mildura."
49. Randazzo, "Grave tensione razziale anti-italiana a Mildura."
50. Nino Randazzo, "Razzismo: la nuova ondata," *Il Globo*, January 17, 1983, p.1; 24.
51. For anti-Asian mentality, see: James Jupp, *From White Australia to Woomera: The Story of Australian Immigration* (Port Melbourne, Victoria: Cambridge University Press, 2007), 124. For *Il Globo* quotation, see: Nino Randazzo, "Italo-australiani contro la recrudescenza del razzismo anti-asiatico," *Il Globo*, March 5, 1984, p. 1; 25.
52. Nino Randazzo, "Diffamare gli italiani col mito della mafia in Australia è anche razzismo," *Il Globo*, May 14, 1984, p. 1; 22.
53. Randazzo, "Diffamare gli italiani col mito della mafia."
54. Nino Randazzo, "Occorre reagire con coraggio e dignità," *Il Globo*, May 21, 1984, p. 1; 12.
55. Randazzo, "Occorre reagire con coraggio e dignità."
56. See, http://adb.anu.edu.au/biography/mackay-donald-bruce-don-10976; John Flood Nagle, *Report of the Special Commission of Inquiry into the Police Investigation of the Death of Donald Bruce Mackay* (Sydney: Government Printer, 1987).
57. Nino Randazzo, "Forse adesso si può cominciare a far luce sui fatti di Griffith. Don Mackay fu ucciso dalla mafia italiana o da un ex ufficiale della polizia di Sydney?," *Il Globo*, November 23, 1987, p. 1; 35.
58. Randazzo, "Forse adesso si può cominciare a far luce sui fatti di Griffith."
59. Nino Randazzo, "Dall'Italia un pessimo esempio," *Il Globo*, January 23, 1989, p. 1; 10.
60. Randazzo, "Dall'Italia un pessimo esempio."
61. Spagnolo, "L'ascesa della 'Ndrangheta in Australia" ; Sergi, "The evolution of the Australian 'Ndrangheta" , 165; Bennetts, "'Undesiderable Italians'", 92.
62. Nino Randazzo, "Dietro la maschera della 'mafia in Australia'," *Il Globo*, March 6, 1989, p. 1; 23.
63. See: Lupo, *Quando la mafia trovò l'America*, 22–23.

CHAPTER 11

A Treasure Trove of Community Language Newspapers

Hilary Berthon

While digitisation and the emergence of digital libraries in the 1990s are a relatively recent phenomenon, the collaborative underpinnings of the National Library of Australia's Trove service have a much longer history. The Australian Newspaper Plan (ANPlan), a cooperation established in 1992 between the national and state libraries in Australia to collect, to provide access and to preserve Australian newspapers, provided the foundation for a national collaborative approach to Australian newspaper digitisation.[1] In 2011, ANPlan libraries conducted an audit which found that an estimated total of 7700 newspapers (including pre-Federation newspapers) had been published within Austbvralia. Trove also has its origins in the aggregation of descriptions of items in Australian libraries' collections undertaken for decades by the National Library to assist users to find these items. The focus of this activity changed in the late 1990s with multiple services for different formats—for example, Picture Australia—being developed by the Library to assist researchers and the general public to

H. Berthon (✉)
National Library of Australia, Canberra, ACT, Australia
e-mail: hberthon@nla.gov.au

© The Author(s) 2020
C. Dewhirst, R. Scully (eds.), *The Transnational Voices of Australia's Migrant and Minority Press*, Palgrave Studies in the History of the Media,
https://doi.org/10.1007/978-3-030-43639-1_11

discover Australia's collections. These were ultimately combined in the single discovery platform, Trove, which enabled the National Library to provide direct access to collections held in research, cultural heritage and community organisations across Australia. These range from the collections of small local volunteer-run cultural and historical groups to large institutions such as state libraries and universities; from schools and public libraries to research organisations and data repositories.

The birth of Trove in 2009 followed the release of a beta version of the Australian Newspapers service the previous year with Trove providing a platform for a global audience to access and engage with the National Library's then small but rapidly growing collection of digitised Australian newspapers. Since then, the National Library's newspaper digitisation programme has grown into a mass digitisation programme with digital capture being primarily from microfilm. The importance of a collaborative and coordinated approach to digitisation projects has been identified as critical to their success.[2] Trove provides a national infrastructure for digitising, delivering and achieving long-term access to a significant body of Australian content.[3]

From Trove's inception, building a digitised collection that reflects the diversity of the Australian community and its documentary output has been fundamental. Over the last decade, this has been achieved through close cooperation between the National Library of Australia and the state libraries; an online facility enabling suggestions from the public of newspapers for digitisation; and an increasingly popular contributor programme. Through Trove's digitisation contributors' programme, over 150 organisations, big and small, have nominated and supported the digitisation of newspaper and journal content. In this programme, the National Library of Australia provides end-to-end support for digital capture of content, for processing this content so that it is easily discoverable and for delivering the content on Trove. All digital content is managed for access in the long term within the National Library of Australia's digital repository. Access was provided to the first digitised non-English-language Australian newspapers in 2012 and in 2019. Trove's newspaper collection included non-English-language titles in over 15 languages. While most renowned for its digitised newspapers, Trove also hosts a collection of Australian government gazettes and a rapidly growing collection of digitised journals. Other formats delivered through Trove include still images, maps, posters, manuscripts, ephemera and sheet music, sound and audiovisual recordings including oral histories, and a vast and growing collection of born-digital content such as archived websites and electronic journals.

As Trove has expanded, there has been the need to upgrade the back-end systems that support it and to update and refresh Trove's user interface. The National Library of Australia's Digital Library Infrastructure Replacement project, completed in June 2017, upgraded much of the back-end systems and a modernisation programme, running from 2016 to mid-2020, has focused on positioning Trove to meet the needs of its diverse contemporary audience and providing a welcoming place for all Australians to discover and explore their stories.

Migrant Community Australian Newspapers

Digitised historic newspapers provide a rich resource for uncovering hidden histories and stories of our past. Historian, archivist and researcher Helen Morgan has described Trove's digitised newspapers as Australia's "historical curb."[4] This terminology is derived from Jennifer Sinor's book *The Extraordinary Work of Ordinary Writing: Annie Ray's Diary* in which she writes:

> In determining the values of a society, you need only investigate what gets discarded. Our literal and cultural detritus tell us as much about who we are as do our museums and libraries. Dumpster loads from our past would indicate that, in general, we value the new, the aesthetic, the whole, the extraordinary, the masculine, the Anglo, and the fast—not because our dumpsters are filled with these but rather because our textbooks are. On the historical curb rest the domestic, the broken, the consumable, the useful, the female, and the ordinary.[5]

Morgan observes that much of Australia's history, which would otherwise be forgotten or left without acknowledgement, can be uncovered within Trove's digitised newspapers.

It is not difficult to find evidence of the "historical curb" occurring with migrant stories. The *Chinese Fortunes* exhibition, from the Museum of Australian Democracy at Eureka in Ballarat, told the stories of the Chinese migrants who came to pre-Federation Australia in search of gold and new opportunities. It drew upon Trove's digitised newspaper collection with newspapers such as the *Australasian Sketcher*, and government gazettes, providing both evidence and context. Exhibition curator, Cash Brown, used these sources to examine the language and the agency of the media to persuade and influence enabling "an essentially positive story that dispels stereotypes and busts myths that have endured for 150 years" to be uncovered. Noting the "biased filters" through which we have received the stories of Chinese on the goldfields, she describes the Chinese migrants as a varied and vibrant group who, despite experiencing disadvantage, made extraordinary, rich and complex contributions to society.[6]

The Chinese Australian Family Historians of Victoria (CAFHOV) has embraced the wealth of information and stories to be found in Trove. CAFHOV has partnered with the National Library to digitise and make accessible on Trove the *Maryborough and Dunolly Advertiser* (Vic.). This newspaper, which began in 1854, provides information on the business and social relationships of the gold seekers, including thousands of Chinese, who moved into the various mining sites around Maryborough after gold was discovered in 1854. It complements those of other goldfields towns also on Trove such as the *Ballarat Star*, the *Bendigo Advertiser*, the *Mount Alexander Mail* and the *Ovens and Murray Advertiser*. According to CAFHOV, having the *Maryborough and Dunolly Advertiser* available on Trove is not only a way of uncovering the family history of many Australians with Chinese heritage, but also a fruitful way of making discoveries pertinent to broader Australian history—the labour movement, the franchise, the role of women in running businesses, church history, agriculture, the tobacco and opium trades, the construction of railroads, the timber industry, viticulture, the expansion of education, sports participation, military service, and of course cultural clashes and exclusion.[7]

CAFHOV member, historian and editor of *Journeys into Chinese Australian Family History* Sophie Couchman writes that Trove "has opened up not only Australia's historical newspapers (including Chinese-language newspapers) and journals, but also photographic collections, published books and other resources from public collections around Australia."[8] CAFHOV member Wayne Brown has described finding reports and photographs of his great grandfather and his sons in digitised newspaper articles about agriculture and in sports reports as well as rich context through the reports on floods, bushfires, local sports picnics and race days, dances, concerts, harvests, festivals and other local events.[9] Sally Keam has explored details about the difficult conditions encountered by Chinese working in the laundry industry in the early twentieth century.[10]

Historian Kate Bagnall has also used Trove's digitised newspapers and gazettes collection to uncover the histories of Chinese-Australian migrants. For example, she draws on pieces published in the *NSW Government Gazette*, *Mount Alexander Mail*, *Weekly Times* (Melbourne), the *Sydney Morning Herald*, *Goulburn Herald and Chronicle*, *Evening News* (Sydney), *Newcastle Morning Herald* and the *Telegraph* (Brisbane) to uncover the history of a missionary named George Graham Mackie Ah Len from the Victorian goldfields of the late 1860s through to his death in Sydney in 1889.[11]

Stephen Nova, a researcher and artist at the University of South Australia, has used Trove's digital collection of archived newspaper articles, photographs and oral recordings to "retrieve and re-present" the Maltese migrant experience during the Great Depression.[12] At this time, many single unemployed men camped on the south bank of the Torrens River constructing makeshift huts from a variety of recycled materials and establishing gardens until, in 1938, they were finally forced to vacate the land. The articles and illustrations in Trove's digitised newspapers provide the colour and detail that enabled Nova to reflect on and imaginatively explore the narratives, material culture and social life of these migrants. He draws on pieces from Adelaide's *News* and *Mail*, describing the appearance of these residents' dwellings, both inside and out, and a resident's attitude to being evicted: "I like it here…I cannot pay rent, and here I do not have to pay rent. And I do not starve."[13] Photographs from these newspapers and descriptions, for example of "an ornate garden with terraced steps, bright flowers, and a healthy looking vegetable plots," provide further detail.[14]

While English-language newspapers have provided rich source material for uncovering stories about our history, many migrant community newspapers, including those in non-English languages digitised and available in Trove have the capacity to help researchers tell interesting stories about our past. Migrant community newspapers form a significant component (approximately nine per cent) of the total number of titles published. An analysis of the number of titles associated with particular migrant communities (see Fig. 11.1) shows that the Chinese-languages communities account for the most Australian migrant community newspaper titles.[15] However, other languages well-represented amongst the just-over-fifty language groups in Australia's migrant community press output include Greek, German, Italian, Arabic, Turkish, Croatian and Vietnamese. Newspapers catalogued as being "English language" represent migrant

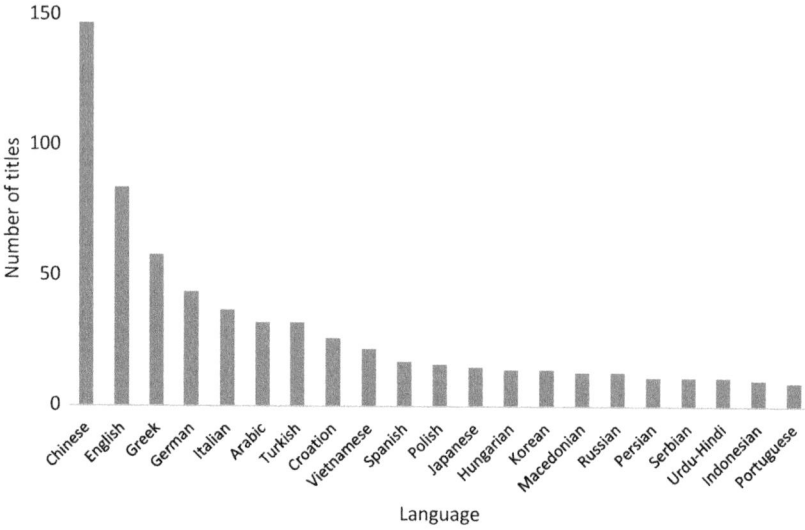

Fig. 11.1   Australian migrant community newspaper titles

communities with a diverse spread of ethnolinguistic and ethnoreligious groups, including Urdu-Hindi, Filipino, Greek, Irish and Jewish.

Data about the existence and longevity of newspaper titles can tell a story about the locations, growth or decline of the communities that produced and supported them. For example, the much later arrival of people of Vietnamese origin compared with German-speaking migrants can be seen at a glance by plotting life spans of newspapers catering for each of these migrant communities (see Fig. 11.2).[16]

Migrant community newspaper editors' conceptions of the requirements of their readers were many and varied. They included informing readers of their rights and responsibilities, the services they were entitled to, as well as local current affairs. Some newspapers attempted to provide a bridge to the "home country," keeping their readers abreast of news from abroad, keeping alive language and cultural identity, or promoting social cohesion within the community. Newspapers played a central role in the migrant community and family experience. According to one new Australian newspaper reader, interviewed as part of a study conducted for the Australian government in 1991:

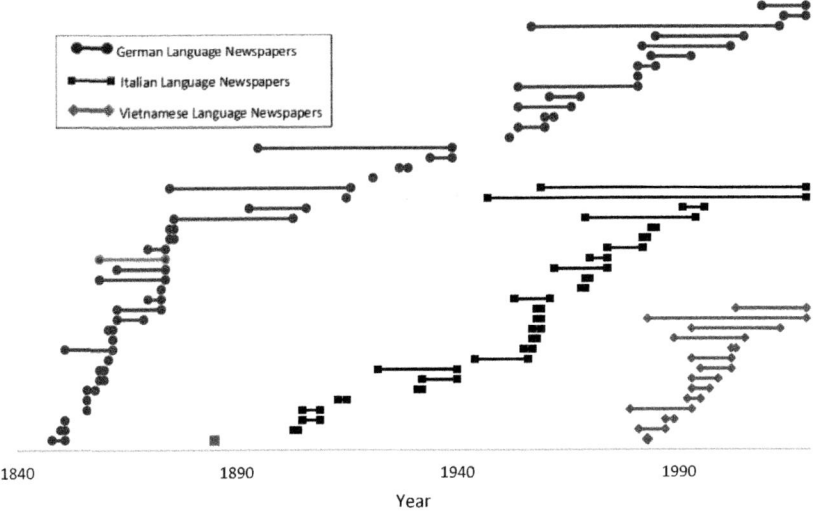

Fig. 11.2   Lifespans of some Australian community newspapers

> It is part of our lives. Every Monday, I go to the club to get the newspaper, we talk about the latest news at the club and then I take it home and it does the rounds of my family.[17]

Involvement in the production of migrant community newspapers was motivated by a desire to document a group's history in Australia and the newspapers played a role both in reflecting and in leading community sentiment. The same study reported:

> All of the editors who were interviewed could see their newspapers as contributing in a significant way to the written history of their communities in Australia... Two editors commented that the ethnic press is more than a record of the history of the community in Australia. The press itself can be an instrument of change.[18]

Over 150 Chinese-language newspapers have been published in Australia and Trove includes *The Chinese Advertiser*, the earliest bilingual Chinese-English newspaper in Australia, which was published weekly in Ballarat from May 1856.[19] This newspaper changed name to the *English and Chinese Advertiser* in 1856 as more of its content was in English.[20]

The fragile source copies were brought together for the first time in Trove through a digitisation project involving source copy from Ballarat Library, the Gold Museum at Sovereign Hill, the State Library Victoria and the State Library of NSW. This significant newspaper includes archaic Chinese script printed from hand-carved blocks.[21]

Trove also includes digitised versions of other (later) Chinese-language newspapers such as the first major Chinese newspaper in Australia, *Guang yi hua bao—The Chinese Australian Herald* (Sydney) which had a wide distribution in Australia, New Zealand and the Pacific and Melbourne's first major Chinese newspaper, the *Chinese Times* (Melbourne).[22] The *Chinese Republic News* (Sydney), established in Sydney in 1914 by 23 Chinese Republicans sympathetic to the nationalist cause, the *Tung Wah News* (Sydney), funded through shares held mostly by Chinese merchants and the official newspaper of the Chinese Chambers of Commerce of New South Wales, and its successor, the *Tung Wah Times* (Sydney) are also available in Trove.[23] Bagnall highlights the "editorials, news articles (both local and international), shipping timetables and advertisements" as being particularly valuable for researchers.[24]

A German-language newspaper, the bi-lingual *Die Deutsche Post fuer die Australischen Kolonien,* was the first non-English-language newspaper to be published in Australia.[25] Many German-speaking immigrants settled in South Australia which is where most of the German-language newspapers which have been digitised to Trove were published. These include *Suedaustralische Zeitung, Süd Australische Zeitung,* the *Adelaider Deutsche Zeitung* and *Australische Zeitung.*[26] The very first issues of the *Suedaustralische Zeitung* were in Roman type, not the traditional Gothic type, and it has been suggested that this was to do with indicating its rejection of tradition—it was considered to be progressive and radical in its outlook.[27] After 1862, circulation of the *Süd-Australische Zeitung* soared from 400 to 1500, and it was distributed in 25 South Australian towns, as well as nine Victorian towns, four in New South Wales, and five in Queensland.[28] These newspapers focussed heavily on news from Germany. Other-world news—with a focus on Europe—was reported as well as news from "our neighbour colonies"—Victoria, New South Wales and the Northern Territory and from South Australian settlements. Announcements range from market prices, news about fundraising activities and church services to animal impoundings and advertisements for pills and ointments.

The first issue of the Polish-language newspaper, *Nasza Droga*, published on Wednesday 24 December 1952, carried a piece placed by the Good Neighbour Council: "After our arrival in Australia we have met many difficulties. We did not know either the language or any of the customs of this country. It was rather difficult to find a decent job, to deal with authorities, to arrange any social contacts."[29] As with other migrant community newspapers, helping its readers to adjust to life in Australia, including learning the language and understanding their entitlements was a key objective. The same issue of *Nasza Droga* carried a message from the South Australian Education Department letting readers know about free English lessons, correspondence courses and listening lessons on the radio, saying that "To become an Australian citizen and to succeed in your new life in this country, you must learn the English language."

In response to the thousands of Italian workers who migrated to Australia, and the support of the Fascist regime in Italy for Italian-language newspapers in foreign countries, *Il Giornale Italiano* ("The Italian Journal") commenced publication on 19 March 1932.[30] Although published in Sydney it included news from throughout Australia. *Il Giornale Italiano* had a wide circulation with 8000 copies sold each week.[31] Published weekly, from June 1938, it included an English Section with its own separate masthead. The style of language used in *Il Giornale Italiano* was "officious and uncompromisingly 'pure'...Dialects were...dismissed as obsolescent by the Mussolini government, so an insistence of Standard Italian in a stilted form was part of the purpose of such a newspaper."[32] From March 1940, *Il Giornale Italiano* included a "Women's Section" supplement, *La donna, la casa, il bambino* which included recipes, advice for mothers, fashion news and baby photographs. *Stampa Italiano* = *The Italian Press* (Perth), *Eco Italiano* (Perth), *Il Canguro* = *The Kangaroo* (Perth), a weekly publication dealing mainly with sport and *La Rondine* (Perth), which commenced publication in 1969, are also available in Trove.[33]

Meie Kodu (or "Our Home") began in 1949 as a weekly publication for the Estonian community and continues to be published to this day.[34] In the first issue, the newspaper acknowledges that the establishment of an Estonian newspaper in Australia might be an ambitious venture in a country where the total number of Estonians is only in the vicinity of three thousand, but notes the steadily increasing number of Estonians migrating to Australia. Newspaper editions from this era include cartoons, advertisements, reports from the Estonian Relief Committee, ecclesiastical posts, sporting news, family notices including news of Displaced Persons and death notices. The digitisation of this newspaper was supported by the Estonian Archives in Australia.

Other European-language titles in Trove include the *Dutch Australian Weekly* (Sydney), which was followed by the *Dutch Weekly* (Sydney).[35] A portion of *Le Courrier Australien* (Sydney), first published in 1892, ceasing in 2011 and revived in 2016 in a digital version, is also in Trove.[36] Due to its founder's links with Poland, it included a column devoted to Polish affairs. During World War II, the paper became the official organ in the Pacific of the Free French.[37]

Of the "over 140 (Jewish) newspapers and periodicals since the 19th century," Trove includes in its digitised newspapers collection *The Hebrew Standard of Australasia* (Sydney) which was later continued by the *Australian Jewish Times*, the *Jewish Herald* (Vic.) which also had a Sydney edition and included an insert, *Yiddisheh Post*, and the earlier publication, *The Voice of Jacob. or, the Hebrews' Monthly Miscellany* (Sydney, 1842) of which there are only three issues.[38]

The Tasmanian paper, *The Irish Exile and Freedom's Advocate* (Hobart Town) includes glimpses of daily life in Hobart, including sport and entertainment in the 1850s, as well as information about what was being imported at the time and from where.[39] It was first published by Patrick O'Donohue, who was transported for his part in the failed uprising in 1848 in Ireland. The paper was closed down the following year by Governor Denison. The *Irish Exile* used some Irish language (Gaeilge) and was highly political.[40] *The Irish Harp and Farmers' Herald*, published in Adelaide between 1869 and 1873, included news from Ireland as well as commentary on local ecclesiastical issues.[41]

Western Australian migrant newspapers included in Trove through the support of the Government of Western Australia include the Greek-language newspapers, *The Hellenic Echo* (Perth, WA) and *The Voice of Freedom = Elefthera Phoni* (Perth), the Macedonian newspaper, *Vesnick* (Perth) and the *Mediterranean Voice* (Perth), whose text in the first five issues includes Greek, French, Italian, Spanish, Portuguese, Turkish, Maltese, Yugoslav and English with Issue 4 including text in Arabic and Serbo-Croatian.[42] Its stated purpose was "to provide newcomers to Australia with the initial guidance and information which will enable them to establish themselves in the Australian Community...to alleviate the inevitable nostalgia at first experienced by everyone entering a new way of life" and to strengthen "understanding between "old" and "new" Australians."[43]

COLLABORATIVE ENRICHMENT OF CONTENT

Trove offers a place for drawing communities together around collection material and supporting conversations around Australia's history. Trove's audience actively works to build and enrich Trove. The National Library's digitised Australian newspapers service, and most particularly its newspaper correction features arose in the context of an environment of experimenting with ways to engage with users.[44] The development of Trove as a platform for the community to interact reflects an understanding of libraries as facilitators of conversations.[45] Emphasising the collection at the expense of the community that uses the collection has been highlighted as a potential risk for digital libraries for which engagement with the communities they serve is a key challenge.[46]

From the outset, the ability of the community to enrich Trove through its own contributions—particularly through correcting the computer-generated text imperfectly generated by Optical Character Recognition (OCR) software—has been enthusiastically embraced and has contributed to an enhanced sense of community ownership of digitised newspapers on Trove. To date, over 300 million lines of OCR-generated newspaper text have been corrected through crowd-sourcing, estimated to be equivalent to 781 working years.[47] Using some basic tools in Trove's interface, Trove's community can share their knowledge about Trove content online and this additional information becomes available to everyone, supporting collaborative understandings of our history. Researchers can create public lists connecting content from disparate sources enriching Trove for everyone. In terms of understanding our migrant history, there is potential for the communities whose histories are represented in Trove to guide their interpretation.

Trove's Application Programming Interfaces (APIs) which make Trove's data freely available in machine-readable format enable a wide range of research questions—including those about migrant Australians—to be explored. For example, QueryPic, developed by digital humanities researcher, Tim Sherratt, provides a way of seeing, searching and understanding digitised newspapers made available by Trove and New Zealand's Papers Past.[48] Using Trove's large corpus of digitised historic newspapers, Sherratt has investigated the frequency and occurrence of words that appear around terms such as "naturalisation," "aliens" and "immigrants" across time and related these to the national context.[49] Importantly, researchers who have developed databases using Trove's resources can make this enriched content available through Trove, sharing the results of their research.[50]

Trove's vast and growing corpus of text-searchable resources makes it an ideal platform for surfacing hidden stories and for enabling people to make connections and discover new meaning. It also provides a location for communities and researchers to engage in conversations around particular collection material, to enrich resources with their own knowledge and to interpret migrant histories. Trove is exposing more and more migrant language newspapers to a global audience, enabling the Australian migrant experience to be preserved, shared and told by an increasing number of voices.

Notes

1. Hilary Berthon and Wan Wong, "Facing the future of Australian newspapers", Paper presented at: ILFA WLIC 2013—Singapore, 2013. http://library.ifla.org/234/1/153-berthon-en.pdf (accessed November 22, 2019).
2. Margaret Coutts, *Stepping Away from the Silos: Strategic Collaboration in Digitisation* (Cambridge, MA: Elsevier, 2017), 5. Katherine Howard, "International Comparators: How does Australia compare internationally?: A research report contributing to the Digital Access to Collections initiative," GLAM Peak Report, http://www.digitalcollections.org.au/sites/default/files/GLAM-Peak-International-comparators-research-report.pdf (accessed November 21, 2019).
3. Marie-Louise Ayres, "Digging deep in Trove: Success, challenge and uncertainty", (National Library of Australia, 2012), https://www.nla.gov.au/our-publications/staff-papers/digging-deep-in-trove-success-challenge-and-uncertainty (accessed November 22, 2019).
4. Helen Morgan, "Discovering history at scale through Trove: The Australian Women's Register", Paper presented at: Australian Historical Association Annual Conference, 2018. https://help.nla.gov.au/sites/default/files/HelenMorgan_AHA2018Presentation.pdf (accessed June 29, 2019).
5. Jennifer Sinor, *The Extraordinary Work of Ordinary Writing: Annie Ray's Diary* (Iowa City: University of Iowa Press, 2002), 3.

6. *Culture Victoria*, Web site, https://cv.vic.gov.au/stories/immigrants-and-emigrants/many-roads-chinese-on-the-goldfields/cash-brown-full-interview/ (accessed November 22, 2019).

7. Communication from Robyn Ansell, Chinese Australian Family Historians of Victoria, 2018.

8. Sophie Couchman, ed., *Journeys into Chinese Australian Family History* (Melbourne: Chinese Australian Family Historians of Victoria Inc, 2019), 3.

9. Wayne Brown, "Henry Lamson (Lim Son) of Cheshunt, King Valley", in *Journeys into Chinese Australian Family History*, ed. Sophie Couchman (Melbourne: Chinese Australian Family Historians of Victoria Inc, 2019), 77–93.

10. Sally Keam, "Harm Goong and Leung Mang Yee", in *Journeys into Chinese Australian Family History*, ed. Sophie Couchman (Melbourne: Chinese Australian Family Historians of Victoria Inc, 2019), 21–37.

11. Kate Bagnall, "The murderer and the missionary: Gazettes and newspapers in Trove uncover Chinese-Australian history", *Trove blog* (Canberra: National Library of Australia, 2018), https://www.nla.gov.au/blogs/trove/2018/01/11/the-murderer-and-the-missionary (accessed June 29, 2019). Kate Bagnall, "Chin Sheng Geong and George Ah Len", *The Tiger's Mouth: Thoughts on the History and Heritage of Chinese Australia*, http://chineseaustralia.org/chin-sheng-geong/ (accessed May 24, 2019).

12. Stephen Nova, "The Artist of the River: The Unemployed Camps on the Torrens River, 1930-1938", *Trove blog* (Canberra: National Library of Australia, 2018), https://www.nla.gov.au/blogs/trove/2018/10/25/the-artist-of-the-river (accessed November 22, 2019).

13. "Doesn't Want to Leave River Bank Home," *News* (Adelaide, SA), December 14, 1937, https://trove.nla.gov.au/newspaper/article/131566126 (accessed November 22, 2019).

14. "Village of Forgotten Men," *The Mail* (Adelaide, SA), January 14, 1933, https://trove.nla.gov.au/newspaper/article/59387242 (accessed November 2, 2019); "Picturesque River Camp," *News* (Adelaide, SA), March 12, 1932, https://trove.nla.gov.au/newspaper/article/129324153 (accessed November 22, 2019); "They Live in Huts, Tents, and Humpies: River Dwellers Remain," *The Mail* (Adelaide, SA), https://trove.nla.gov.au/newspaper/article/55932479 (accessed November 22, 2019).

15. Data from Australian National Bibliographic Database at the National Library of Australia, 2017.

16. Data from Australian National Bibliographic Database.

17. The Office of Multicultural Affairs and University of Wollongong, *Different Agenda: Economic and Social Aspects of the Ethnic Press in Australia*,

Working Papers on Multiculturalism, no. 8 (Wollongong: Centre for Multicultural Studies, University of Wollongong, 1991), 84.

18. The Office of Multicultural Affairs and University of Wollongong, *Different Agenda*, 74.
19. *The Chinese Advertiser* (Ballarat, Vic.: 1856), https://trove.nla.gov.au/newspaper/title/706 (accessed June 24, 2019).
20. *The English and Chinese Advertiser* (Vic.: 1856–1858), https://nla.gov.au/nla.news-title685 (accessed June 24, 2019); Kate Bagnall, "Early Chinese newspapers: Trove presents a new perspective on Australian history," Trove blog (Canberra: National Library of Australia, 2015), https://www.nla.gov.au/blogs/trove/2015/02/19/early-chinese-newspapers (accessed June 24, 2019).
21. Communication from Ballarat Library, January 2013.
22. *Guang yi hua bao = The Chinese Australian Herald* (Sydney, NSW: 1894–1923), https://trove.nla.gov.au/newspaper/title/704 (accessed 24 June 2019). "Chinese language Australian newspapers," Chinese-Australian Historical Images in Australia, http://www.chia.chinesemuseum.com.au/biogs/CH00047b.htm (accessed June 24, 2019). *Chinese Times* (Melbourne, Vic.: 1902–1922), https://trove.nla.gov.au/newspaper/title/705 (accessed June 24, 2019).
23. *Chinese Republic News* (Sydney, NSW: 1914–1937), https://trove.nla.gov.au/newspaper/title/1186 (accessed June 24, 2019). "Chinese language Australian newspapers," Chinese-Australian Historical Images in Australia, http://www.chia.chinesemuseum.com.au/biogs/CH00047b.htm (accessed June 24, 2019). *Tung Wah News* (Sydney, NSW: 1898–1902), https://trove.nla.gov.au/newspaper/title/1185 (accessed 24 June 2019). "Chinese language Australian newspapers," Chinese-Australian Historical Images in Australia, http://www.chia.chinesemuseum.com.au/biogs/CH00047b.htm (accessed June 24, 2019). *Tung Wah Times* (Sydney, NSW: 1901–1936), https://trove.nla.gov.au/newspaper/title/1184 (accessed 24 June 2019).
24. Kate Bagnall, "Early Chinese newspapers".
25. Marianne Reimann, "The German Language Press", in *The Ethnic Press in Australia*, ed. Abe I. Wade Ata and Colin Ryan (Melbourne: Academia Press, 1989) 158.
26. *Suedaustralische Zeitung* (Adelaide, SA: 1850-1851), https://trove.nla.gov.au/newspaper/title/314 (accessed June 24, 2019). *Süd Australische Zeitung* (Tanunda and Adelaide, SA: 1860–1874), https://trove.nla.gov.au/newspaper/title/278 (accessed June 24, 2019). *Adelaider Deutsche Zeitung* (SA: 1851–1862), https://trove.nla.gov.au/newspaper/title/277 (accessed June 24, 2019). *Australische Zeitung* (Adelaide, SA: 1875–1916), https://trove.nla.gov.au/newspaper/title/1150 (accessed June 24, 2019).

27. R. Walker, "German-Language Press and People in South Australia, 1848–1900", *Journal of the Royal Australian Historical Society* 58, no. 2 (1973), 122.

28. Walker, "German-Language Press", 123.

29. "Good Neighbour Council", *Nasza droga* (Adelaide, SA: 1952–1954), December 24, 1952, p. 3. http://nla.gov.au/nla.news-article240227464 (accessed June 17, 2019).

30. Robert Pascoe, "The Italian Press in Australia", in *The Ethnic Press in Australia*, ed. Abe I. Wade Ata and Colin Ryan (Melbourne: Academia Press, 1989), 201. *Il Giornale Italiano* (Sydney, NSW: 1932–1940), https://trove.nla.gov.au/newspaper/title/279 (accessed June 24, 2019).

31. Pascoe, "The Italian Press in Australia".

32. Pascoe, "The Italian Press in Australia".

33. *Stampa Italiana = The Italian Press* (Perth, WA: 1931–1932), https://trove.nla.gov.au/newspaper/title/1380 (accessed June 24, 2019). *Eco Italiano* (Perth, WA: 1958–1959), https://trove.nla.gov.au/newspaper/title/1387 (accessed June 24, 2019). *Il Canguro = The Kangaroo* (Perth, WA: 1955–1957), https://trove.nla.gov.au/newspaper/title/1378 (accessed June 24, 2019). *La Rondine* (Perth, WA: 1969–1994), https://trove.nla.gov.au/newspaper/title/1388 (accessed June 24, 2019).

34. *Meie Kodu = Our Home* (Sydney, NSW: 1949–1956), https://trove.nla.gov.au/newspaper/title/280 (accessed June 24, 2019).

35. *Dutch Australian Weekly* (Sydney, NSW: 1951–1993), https://trove.nla.gov.au/newspaper/title/1044 (accessed June 24, 2019); *Dutch Weekly* (Sydney, NSW: 1993–2004), https://trove.nla.gov.au/newspaper/title/1045 (accessed June 24, 2019).

36. *Le Courrier Australien* (Sydney, NSW: 1892–2011), https://trove.nla.gov.au/newspaper/title/829 (accessed June 24, 2019).

37. Miriam Gilson and Jerzy Zubrzycki, *The Foreign-language Press in Australia 1848–1964* (Canberra: Australian National University Press, 1967), 17.

38. Mark Braham, "The Jewish Press in Australia," in *The Ethnic Press in Australia*, ed. Abe I. Wade Ata and Colin Ryan (Melbourne: Academia Press), 1989, 29; *The Hebrew Standard of Australasia* (Sydney, NSW: 1895–1953), https://trove.nla.gov.au/newspaper/title/488 (accessed 24 June 2019). *Trove: Jewish Herald* (Vic.: 1879–1920), https://trove.nla.gov.au/newspaper/title/712 (accessed June 24, 2019); *The Voice of Jacob. or, the Hebrews' Monthly Miscellany* (Sydney, NSW: 1842), https://trove.nla.gov.au/newspaper/title/1039 (accessed 24 June 2019).

39. *The Irish Exile and Freedom's Advocate* (Hobart Town, Tas.: 1850–1851), https://trove.nla.gov.au/newspaper/title/1244 (accessed 24 June 2019).

40. Dymphna Lonergan, "The Irish Exile," *Tinteán*, April 6, 2018, https://tintean.org.au/2018/04/06/the-irish-diaspora-in-australia-has-

played-a-significant-part-in-the-promotion-and-maintenance-of-irish-not-least-in-the-press-and-as-far-back-as-1850/.

41. *The Irish Harp and Farmers' Herald* (Adelaide, SA: 1869–1873), https://trove.nla.gov.au/newspaper/title/1148 (accessed 24 June 2019). State Library of South Australia, *SA Newspapers: Religious newspapers*, http://www.samemory.sa.gov.au/site/page.cfm?u=1478 (accessed 29 June 2019).

42. *Hellenic Echo* (Perth, WA: 1967–1968), https://trove.nla.gov.au/newspaper/title/1389 (accessed June 24, 2019). *The Voice of Freedom = Elefthera Phoni* (Perth, WA: 1956–1957), https://trove.nla.gov.au/newspaper/title/1381 (accessed 24 June 2019). *Vesnik* (Perth, WA: 1975–1994), https://trove.nla.gov.au/newspaper/title/1382 (accessed 24 June 2019). *Mediterranean Voice* (Perth, WA : 1971–1972), https://trove.nla.gov.au/newspaper/title/1390 (accessed 24 June 2019).

43. "EDITORIAL," *Mediterranean Voice* (Perth, WA: 1971–1972), December 1, 1971, http://nla.gov.au/nla.news-article249643487 (accessed June 17, 2019).

44. Marie-Louise Ayres, "'Singing for their supper': Trove, Australian newspapers, and the crowd", Paper presented at: ILFA WLIC 2013—Singapore, 2013. http://library.ifla.org/245/1/153-ayres-en.pdf (accessed November 21, 2019).

45. R. David Lankes, Joanne Silverstein and Scott Nicholson, "Participatory Networks: The Library As Conversation", *Information Technology and Libraries* 26, no. 4 (2007): 17–33, https://ejournals.bc.edu.

46. Karen Calhoun, *Exploring Digital Libraries: Foundations, Practice, Prospects* (Chicago: Neal-Schuman, an imprint of the American Library Association, 2014), 77, 140.

47. National Library of Australia, *Trove stats for environment: prod*, https://trove.nla.gov.au/system/stats (accessed June 29, 2019).

48. Tim Sherratt, "QueryPic: Exploring digitised newspapers from Australia & New Zealand", http://dhistory.org/querypic/ (accessed June 29, 2019).

49. Tim Sherratt, "Who belongs? Reading identity, ownership, and legitimacy", Invited presentation at: From text to data – new ways of reading—National Library of Sweden, 2019, https://timsherratt.org/blog/who-belongs/ (accessed May 20, 2019).

50. See, for example: The Prosecution Project, Web site, https://prosecution-project.griffith.edu.au/ (accessed June 29, 2019); and Katherine Bode, "To Be Continued: Discovering serialised fiction in Trove's digitised newspapers", *Trove blog* (Canberra: National Library of Australia, 2018), https://www.nla.gov.au/blogs/trove/2018/02/28/to-be-continued (accessed June 29, 2019).

BIBLIOGRAPHY

PRIMARY

1. ARCHIVES AND MANUSCRIPTS

FRYER LIBRARY, UNIVERSITY OF QUEENSLAND, BRISBANE

Zuzenko, Aleksandr. "Zakon klyka i dubiny" [The Law of the Fang and the Cudgel], no date. University of Queensland, Fryer Library, Poole-Fried Collection, 336, Box 8, Folder 10.

NATIONAL ARCHIVES AUSTRALIA, CANBERRA

Arov to Bolotnikoff, March 11, 1919, QF3408, National Archives of Australia (NAA): A6286 1/114.

Baucia, Cesare—Queensland investigation case file, NAA: BP242/1, Q25546.

Bolotnikoff to Zuzenko, March 6, 1919, QF3368, NAA: MP95/1/0.

Censor's Notes, Week ending May 29, 1918, QF1073, NAA: A6286 1/29.

Colless Norman Morris: SERN DEPOT: POB Brewarrina NSW: POE Broken Hill NSW: NOK S Colless Nellis Monar, NAA: B2455, COLLESS N M.

Cristofaro [or Christopher] ALBANESE and wife Rosalia, NAA: BP242/1, Q16961.

Galch[enko] to Zuzenko, Censor's notes. August 5, 1918, QF1540, NAA: A6286 1/50.

© The Author(s) 2020
C. Dewhirst, R. Scully (eds.), *The Transnational Voices of Australia's Migrant and Minority Press*, Palgrave Studies in the History of the Media,
https://doi.org/10.1007/978-3-030-43639-1

Gamanoff to Cherbakoff, March 2, 1919, MF2628, NAA: A6286 3/96.

Displaced Persons Publicity, NAA: B550, 1948/23/5454.

Immigration—'Tomorrow's Australia'—Part 1, NAA: CP815/1, 021.153 Part 1.

Immigration—'The New Australian' [newspaper for migrants], NAA: CP815/1, 021.188.

Immigration—'The New Australian' [newspaper for new migrants]—Part 3, NAA: CP815/1, 021.188 Part 3.

Immigration—'The New Australian'—Letters from readers—Part 1, NAA: CP815/1, 021.192 Part 1.

Immigration—'The New Australian' Letters from readers—Part 2, NAA: CP815/1, 021.192 Part 2.

Immigration—'The New Australian'—Letters from readers—Part 3, NAA: CP815/1, 021.192 Part 3.

Immigration—'The New Australian'—Letters from readers—Part 4, NAA: CP815/1, 021.192 Part 4.

Intelligence Report, 1st Military District, December 11, 1918, QF2538, NAA: A6286 1/86.

Kalinin, C. Censor's notes, January 10, 1919, QF2941, NAA: A6286 1/100.

[L'Italiano—Newspaper], 1940–1944, NAA: A373, 6230.

Matulichenko, Week ending November 27, 1918, QF2441, NAA: A6286 1/81.

"Nashi zadachi" [Our Tasks], 5. NAA: BP4/1 66/4/2165.

"O tom, kak my uchimsia samoupravleniiu i kontroliu" [How We are Learning Self-Management and Control]. February 1919, NAA: BP4/1, 66/4/2165.

"Peredovitsa" [Editorial], 2, NAA: BP4/1 66/4/2165.

PIETROBELLI, Guido [Italian—born 1894]—Queensland investigation case file, NAA: BP242/1, Q49369.

Publication—"The Good Neighbour", NAA: A445, 261/6/5.

Prisoner of War/Internee: Albanese, Cristofaro; Date of birth—06 November 1903; Nationality—Italian, NAA: NAA: MP1103/1, PWQ7298.

"Rus´ avstraliiskaia, iz zapisnoi knizhki 'trampera'" vii, NAA: BP4/1, 66/4/2165.

Short, Sgt. to Commissioner, December 26, 1918, NAA: BP4/1 66/4/1817.

Simonoff to Lagutin, July 18, 1918, QF1469, NAA: A6286 1/46.

Simonoff to Zaremba, September 10, 1918, QF1861, NAA: A6286 1/62.

Simonoff to Robertson, January 23, 1919, Censor's notes, QF2951, NAA: A6286 1/100.

Soviet of Souse to Gooseff, March 6, 1919, NAA: A6286 1/112.

Steward to Secretary, PM's Department, April 24, 1917. Suspected Persons—Russians, NAA: A1606 A35/1.

"REFERENCE COPY, "Jewish Unity Association," (1941–1949)," NAA: A6122, 155.

Tweed to Zuzenko, Censor's Notes, October 19, 1918, QF2274, NAA: A6286 1/76.

VACCARI, Gualtiero, NAA: A6126, 58.
Zuzenko to Simonoff, August 8, 1918, QF1701, NAA: A6286 1/58.
Zuzenko, week ended October 2, 1918, QF1963, NAA: A6286 1/66.
Zuzenko to Tyutin, September 29, 1918, QF2019, NAA: A6286 1/68.

NATIONAL LIBRARY OF AUSTRALIA

Brezniak, Hyam. Interview by Hazel de Berg, 29 April, 1975, Hazel de Berg collection, National Library of Australia.

QUEENSLAND STATE ARCHIVES, BRISBANE

Abaza to Macdonald, December 7, 1915. Queensland State Archives (QSA):
A/45329 ID317879.
Criminal Investigation Branch to Commissioner of Police, January 5, 1914a.
QSA: A/45328 ID318868.
Criminal Investigation Branch to Commissioner of Police, June 12, 1911. QSA:
14812 ID86529.
Criminal Investigation Branch to Commissioner of Police, January 5, 1914b.
QSA: A/45328 ID318868.
O'Hara, Sgt. to Commissioner, Queensland Police, February 12, 1916. QSA:
A/45329 ID317879.
Soosenko to Prime Minister of Queensland, January 2, 1918. QSA: ID 862638,
PRE/A578.

STATE LIBRARY OF NEW SOUTH WALES, SUZANNE RUTLAND COLLECTION, SYDNEY

Goldbloom, Sam. Interview by Suzanne Rutland, 12 April 1988, CY MLOH
437/135.

2. NEWSPAPERS AND PERIODICALS

All the Year Round
Adelaide Punch
Advertiser
Argus
Australian Jewish News
Australian Jewish Outlook
Ballarat Punch

Canberra Times
Chinese Republic News
Chinese Times
Commonwealth of Australia Gazette
Daily Standard
Design and Art Australia Online
Dutch Weekly
Ekho Avstralii
Echo-Opowiadania
Elefthera Phoni
El Español en Australia
El Expreso
Empire
Everyones
Forum
Geelong Advertiser and Intelligencer
Good Neighbour
Guang yi hua bao
Hellenic Echo
Huon Times
Izvestiia
Jewish Herald
Knowledge and Unity
Kurier Zachodni
La Crónica
La Rondine
Il Canguro
Il Globo
Il Canguro = The Kangaroo
L'Italo-Australiano
Jewish Currents
Jewish Life
Le Courrier Australien
L'Italiano
Maryborough Chronicle
Mediterranean Voice
Meie Kodu
Melbourne Punch
Nabat [The Tocsin]
Nasza droga
New South Wales Government Gazette
Noticias y Deportes

Observer
Press of the Polish Diaspora
Queensland Figaro and Punch
Rabochaia zhizn'
Stampa Italiana
Sydney Punch
Tasmanian Punch
The Age
The Bulletin
The Courier Mail
The English and Chinese Advertiser
The Hebrew Standard of Australasia
The Irish Harp and Farmers' Herald
The Mercury
The Sydney Gazette, And New South Wales Advertiser
The Sydney Morning Herald
The Sun
The Voice of Jacob. or, the Hebrews' Monthly Miscellany
The Zionist
Tung Wah News
Tung Wah Times
Tygodnik Katolicki
Tygodnik Polski
Vesnik
Vistazo
Western Argus
Wiadomości Polskie

Secondary

1. Books

Abarca, Luis. *Viaje por la juventud*. Santiago, Chile: Quimantú, 1972.
_____. *Las historias de un Blady Woggie*. Sydney, Australia; Santiago, Chile: Ediciones del Blady Woggie, 1992.
Anderson, Benedict. *Imagined Communities: Reflections on the Origin and Spread of Nationalism*. London: Verso, 1983.
Arendt, Hannah. *The Origins of Totalitarianism*. Orlando: Harcourt Books, [1951] 1976.
Artem (Sergeev, F.A.). *Stat'i, rechi, pis'ma* [Articles, Speeches and Letters]. Moscow: Izdatel'stvo politicheskoi literatury, 1983.

Artemov, Iurii. *Russkaia revoliutsiia v Avstralii i seti shpionazha* [The Russian Revolution in Australia and Espionage Networks]. St Petersburg: Aleteiia, 2017.

Aspinall, Clara. *Three Years in Melbourne*. London: L. Booth, 1862.

Ata, Abe (I.) Wade and Colin Ryan, ed., The Ethnic Press in Australia. Melbourne: Academia Press and Footprint Publications, 1989.

Australian Bureau of Statistics, Census of the Commonwealth of Australia, *Census Bulletin No. 15, Summary of the Commonwealth of Australia*. Canberra: L. F. Johnson, 1933.

Batnitzky, Leora. *How Judaism Became a Religion: An Introduction to Modern Jewish Thought*. Princeton, NJ: Princeton University Press, 2011.

Bekken, Jon. "Negotiating Class and Ethnicity: The Polish-Language Press in Chicago". *Polish American Studies* 57, no. 2 (2000): 5–29.

Bencomo, Anadeli. *Voces y voceros de la megalópolis: la crónica periodístico-literaria en México*. Madrid: Iberoamericana; Frankfurt Am Main: Vervuert, 2002.

Bevege, Margaret. *Behind Barbed Wire: Internment in Australia during World War II*. St Lucia, Qld: University of Queensland Press, 1993.

Biale, David. *Power and Powerlessness in Jewish History*. New York: Schocken Books, 1986.

Bielsa, Esperança. *The Latin American Urban Crónica: Between Literature and Mass Culture*. Lanham, MD: Lexington Books, 2006.

[Blanchard, Sidney]. *Mr Punch: His Origin and Career*. London: Jas. Wade, 1870.

Bonwick, James. *Early Struggles of the Australian Press*. London: Gotch & Gordon, 1890.

Borrie, W. D. *Italians and Germans in Australia: A Study of Assimilation*. Melbourne: F. W. Cheshire, 1954.

Bowling, Benjamin, and Coretta Phillips. *Racism, Crime and Justice*. Harlow, UK: Pearson Education, 2002.

Brake, Laurel, Aled Jones, and Lionel Madden, eds. *Investigating Victorian Journalism*. Basingstoke, Hampshire: Palgrave Macmillan, 1990.

Briggs, Asa. *Victorian Cities*. Berkeley: University of California Press, 1993.

Brown-May, Andrew, and Shurlee Swain, eds. *The Encyclopedia of Melbourne*. Port Melbourne: Cambridge University Press, 2005.

Buxton, G. L. "1870–90". In *A New History of Australia*, edited by Frank Crowley, 165–215. Melbourne: Heinemann, 1974.

Calhoun, Karen. *Exploring Digital Libraries: Foundations, Practice, Prospects*. Chicago: Neal-Schuman, an imprint of the American Library Association, 2014.

Chernenko, A. M. *Rossiiskaia revoliutsionnaia emigratsiia v Avstralii (1900–1917 gg.* [The Russian Revolutionary Emigration in Australia (1900–1917)]. Dnepropetrovsk: Dnepropetrovsk State University, 1978.

Choate, Mark I. *Emigrant Nation: The Making of Italy Abroad*. Cambridge, MA: Harvard University Press, 2008.

Cohen, Daniel G. *In War's Wake: Europe's Displaced Persons in the Postwar Order.* Oxford: Oxford University Press, 2012.

Corona, Ignacio and Beth E. Jörgensen. *The Contemporary Mexican Chronicle: Theoretical Perspectives on a Liminal Genre.* Albany, NY: State University of New York Press, 2002.

Costanza, Salvatore. *Socialismo, emigrazione e nazionalità tra Italia e Australia.* 2nd edn, revised. Trapani: Corrao, 1995.

Couchman, Sophie. ed. *Journeys into Chinese Australian Family History.* Melbourne: Chinese Australian Family Historians of Victoria Inc, 2019.

Coutts, Margaret. *Stepping Away from the Silos: Strategic Collaboration in Digitisation.* Cambridge, MA: Elsevier, 2017.

Craig, Clifford. *Mr Punch in Tasmania: Colonial Politics in Cartoons, 1866–1879.* Hobart: Blubber Head Press, 1980.

Cresciani, Gianfranco. *Fascism, Anti-Fascism and Italians in Australia, 1922–1945.* Canberra: Australian National University Press, 1980.

Dacy, Marianne. *Periodical Publications from the Australian Jewish Community: A Union List,* 5th edn. Sydney: University of Sydney, Archive of Australian Judaica, 2007.

Davies, Richard A. *Inventing Sam Slick: A Biography of Thomas Chandler Haliburton.* Toronto: University of Toronto Press, 2005.

Deacon, Desley, Penny Russell and Angela Woollacott, eds. *Transnational Ties: Australian Lives in the World.* Canberra: ANU E Press, 2008.

Egan, Linda. *Carlos Monsiváis: Culture and Chronicle in Contemporary Mexico.* Tucson, AZ: University of Arizona Press, 2001.

Elepov, B. S. and S. A. Paichadze. *Geopoliticheskii kharakter rasprostraneniia russkoi knigi: k postanovke voprosa* [The Geo-political Nature of the Dissemination of Russian Books: towards a framing of the question]. Novosibirsk: GPNTB SO RAN, 2001.

Evans, Raymond. "Agitation, Ceaseless Agitation." In *Russia and the Fifth Continent: Aspects of Russian-Australian Relations,* edited by McNair, John and Thomas Poole, 126–171. St Lucia, Qld: University of Queensland Press, 1992.

_____. *The Red Flag Riots: A Study of Intolerance.* St Lucia, Qld: University of Queensland Press, 1988.

Fabian, Suzane, ed. *Mr. Punch Down Under: A Social History of the Colony from 1856 to 1900 via Cartoons and Extracts from Melbourne Punch.* Richmond & Drouin: Greenhouse & Landmark, 1982.

Foucault, Michel. *The Archaeology of Knowledge,* trans. A. M. Sheridan Smith. London: Routledge, 1969.

Gabaccia, Donna. *Italy's Many Diasporas.* London: UCL Press, 2000.

García, Ignacio. *Operación Canguro: The Spanish Migration Scheme, 1958–1963.* Jamison Center, ACT: Spanish Heritage Foundation, 2002.

_____. *Concurso literario Club Español de Sydney 1969–1996*. Campbelltown, NSW: s.n., 1997a.

_____. *Spanish Fiction Writing in Australia*. Sydney: The author and University of Western Sydney Macarthur, 1997b.

Gawroński, Andrzej. *Mój punkt widzenia: Felietony australijskie*, ed. Bogumiła Żongołłowicz. Toruń: Uniwersytet Mikołaja Kopernika, 1999.

Gentile, Emilio. *La Grande Italia: The Myth of the Nation in the Twentieth Century*. George L. Mosse Series in Modern European Cultural and Intellectual History. Madison, WI: University of Wisconsin Press, 2009.

Georgiou, Myria. *Diaspora, Identity and the Media*. New Jersey: Hampton Press, 2006.

González, Aníbal. *Companion to Spanish American Modernismo*. Woodbridge: Tamesis, 2007.

_____. *La crónica modernista hispanoamericana*. Madrid: J. Porrúa Turanzas, 1983a.

Gilson, Miriam, Jerzy Zubrzycki. *The Foreign Language Press in Australia 1847–1964*. Canberra: Australian National University, 1967.

Goldstein, Eric L. *The Price of Whiteness: Jews, Race and American Identity*. Princeton: Princeton University Press, 2006.

Griffen-Foley, Bridget, ed. *A Companion to the Australian Media*. North Melbourne: Australian Scholarly Publishing, 2014.

Hage, Ghassan. *Alter-Politics: Critical Anthropology and the Radical Imagination*. Melbourne: Melbourne University Publishing, 2015.

Hallas, Duncan. *The Comintern*. London: Bookmarks, 1985.

Harder, Hans, and Barbara Mittler, eds. *Asian Punches: A Transcultural Affair*. Berlin & Heidelberg: Springer, 2013.

Hasluck, Paul. *The Government and the People, 1942–1945. Volume I*. Canberra: Australian War Memorial, 1970a.

Hasluck, Paul. *The Government and the People, 1942–1945. Volume II*. Canberra: Australian War Memorial, 1970b.

Hawkins, Darnell F. *Ethnicity, Race, and Crime: Perspectives across Time and Place*. Albany, NY: SUNY Press, 1995.

Holden, W. S. *Australia Goes to Press*. Detroit: Wayne State University, 1961.

Howitt, William. *Land, Labour, and Gold; or, Two Years in Victoria*. 2 Volumes. London: Brown, Green, and Longmans, 1855.

Hughes-D'Areth, Tony. *Paper Nation: The Story of the Picturesque Atlas of Australasia, 1886–1888*. Melbourne: Melbourne University Press, 2001.

Hunt, Tristram. *Ten Cities that Made an Empire*. London: Penguin, 2015.

Jacobson, Matthew Frye. *Special Sorrows: The Diasporic Imagination of Irish, Polish, and Jewish immigrants in the United States*. Cambridge: Harvard University Press, 1995.

Jörgensen, Beth E. *Documents in Crisis: Nonfiction Literatures in Twentieth-Century Mexico*. Albany: State University of New York Press, 2011.

Jupp, James. *From White Australia to Woomera: The Story of Australian Immigration.* Port Melbourne, Vic.: Cambridge University Press, 2007.

Kanellos, Nicolás. *Hispanic Immigrant Literature: El Sueño del Retorno.* Austin, TX: University of Texas Press, 2011.

Kath, Elizabeth, ed. *Australian-Latin American Relations: New Links in a Changing Global Landscape.* New York: Palgrave Macmillan, 2016.

Kennedy, James, W. A. Smith and A. F. Johnson. *Dictionary of Anonymous and Pseudonymous English Literature.* New and Enlarged Edition. Volume Four. Edinburgh & London: Oliver and Boyd, 1928.

Kerr, Joan. *Artists and Cartoonists in Black and White—the Most Public Art.* Sydney: S. H. Irvin, 1999.

King, Jonathan. *'Stop Laughing, This is Serious!' A Social History of Australia in Cartoons.* North Ryde: Cassell, 1980.

Kirkpatrick, Rod. *Sworn to No Master: A History of the Provincial Press in Queensland to 1930.* Toowoomba: Darling Downs Institute Press, 1984.

Kujawa, Joanna. *Migration, Belonging, Alienation: The narratives of Polish adventurers, artists and intellectuals in Australia.* Saarbrucken, Germany: VDM Verlag Dr. Muller, 2010.

Kunz, Egon. *Displaced Persons. Calwell's New Australians.* Sydney: Australian National University Press, 1988.

Lauret. Maria. *Wanderwords: Language Migration in American Literature.* New York & London: Bloomsbury Academic, 2014.

Lawson, Sylvia. *The Archibald Paradox: A Strange Case of Authorship.* Melbourne: Allen Lane, 1983.

Lenczarowicz, Jan. *Prasa i społeczność polska w Australii 1928–1980.* Kraków: Księgarnie Akademickie, 1994.

Levy, Hyman. *Jews and the National Question.* London: Hillway Publishing Company, 1958.

Lindesay, Vane. *The Inked-In Image: A Survey of Australian Comic Art.* Melbourne: Heinemann, 1970.

_____. *The Way We Were: Australian Popular Magazines, 1856–1969.* Melbourne: Oxford University Press, 1983b.

Lowenthal, Rudolf. *The Chinese Press in Australia.* Peking: [s.n.], 1937.

Lubbock, Basil. *The Colonial Clippers.* Glasgow: J. Brown & Son, 1921.

Lupo, Salvatore. *"Quando la mafia trovò l'America."* ["When the Mafia found America"]. Torino: Einaudi, 2008.

Lyons, Martin and John J. Arnold, ed. *A History of the Book in Australia 1891–1945: A National Culture in a Colonised Market.* St Lucia, Qld: The University of Queensland Press, 2001.

Macintyre, Stuart. *The Reds: The Communist Party of Australia from Origins to Illegality.* St Leonards, NSW: Allen & Unwin, 1998.

Macmahon Ball, W. ed., *Radio Press and World Affairs: Australia's Outlook*. Melbourne: Melbourne University Press, 1938.

Mahieux, Viviane. *Urban Chroniclers in Modern Latin America: The Shared Intimacy of Everyday Life*. Austin: University of Texas Press, 2011.

Mahood, Marguerite. *The Loaded Line: Australian Political Caricature, 1788–1901*. Melbourne: Melbourne University Press, 1973.

Marginson, Simon, Chris Nyland, Erlenawati Sawir, and Helen Forbes-Mewett. *International Student Security*. Cambridge: Cambridge University Press, 2010.

Martin, David. *My Strange Friend: An Autobiography*. Sydney: Pan Macmillan, 1991.

Mason, Robert. *The Spanish Anarchists in Northern Australia: Revolution in the Sugar Cane Fields*. Cardiff: University of Wales Press, 2018.

Massov, Alexander, Marina Pollard and Kevin Windle, ed. *A New Rival State? Australia in Tsarist Diplomatic Communications*. Canberra: ANU Press, 2018.

Mayer, Henry. *The Press in Australia*. Melbourne: Lansdowne Press, 1964.

McMinn, W. G. *Nationalism and Federalism in Australia*. Melbourne: Oxford University Press, 1994.

Medding, P.Y. *From Assimilation to Group Survival: A Political and Sociological Study of an Australian Jewish Community*. Melbourne, Canberra, Sydney: F.W. Cheshire, 1968.

Monsiváis, Carlos. *A ustedes les consta: antologia de la crónica en Mexico*. Mexico City: Ediciones Era, 1980.

Morley, David, and Kuan-Hsing Chen, eds. *Stuart Hall: Critical Dialogues in Cultural Studies*. Comedia. London: Routledge, 1996.

Morrison, Elizabeth. *Engines of Influence: Newspapers of Country Victoria, 1840–1890*. Carlton: Melbourne University Press, 2005.

Morrison, Gordon, and Anne Rowland, eds. *In Your Face! Cartoons about Politics and Society, 1760–2010*. Ballarat: Art Gallery of Ballarat, 2010.

Myers, David N. *Resisting History: Historicism and Its Discontents in German-Jewish Thought*. Princeton: Princeton University Press, 2003.

_____. *Re-Inventing the Jewish Past*. New York and Oxford: Oxford University Press, 1995a.

Nagle, John Flood. *Report of the Special Commission of Inquiry into the Police Investigation of the Death of Donald Bruce Mackay*. Sydney: Government Printer, 1987.

Noble, Gregory. *Lines in the Sand: The Cronulla Riots, Multiculturalism and National Belonging*. Sydney: Institute of Criminology Press, 2009.

Paoli, Letizia. *Mafia Brotherhoods: Organized Crime, Italian Style*. Oxford and New York: Oxford University Press, 2003.

Pascoe, Robert. "The Italian Press in Australia". In *The Ethnic Press in Australia*, edited by Abe I. Wade Ata and Colin Ryan, 201–206. Melbourne: Academia Press, 1989.

Peñaloza, Fernanda and Sarah Walsh, eds. *Mapping South-South Connections: Australia and Latin America*. Cham, Switzerland: Palgrave Macmillan, 2019.

Potter, Simon J. *News and the British World: The Emergence of an Imperial Press System, 1876–1922*. Oxford: Oxford University Press, 2003.

Price Charles A. *Southern Europeans in Australia*. Melbourne: Oxford University Press, 1963.

Ramos, Julio. *Divergent Modernities: Culture and Politics in Nineteenth-Century Latin America*, trans. John D. Blanco. Durham, NC: Duke University Press, 2001.

Raymond, Joad, ed. *News, Newspapers, and Society in Early Modern Britain*. London & Portland, OR: Frank Cass, 2002.

_____. *The Invention of the Newspaper*. Oxford: Clarendon Press, 1996.

Reimann, Marianne. "The German Language Press". In *The Ethnic Press in Australia*, edited be Abe I. Wade Ata and Colin Ryan, 158–169. Melbourne: Academia Press, 1989.

Reynolds, Andrew. *The Spanish American Crónica Modernista, Temporality, and Material Culture*. Lewisburg, PA: Bucknell University Press, 2012.

Riall, Lucy. *Garibaldi: Invention of a Hero*. New Haven, CT: Yale University Press, 2007.

Ricatti, Francesco. *Italians in Australia: History, Memory, Identity*. Palgrave Studies in Migration History. Basingstoke, Hampshire: Palgrave Macmillan, 2018.

Rothberg, Michael. *Multidirectional Memory: Remembering the Holocaust in the Age of Decolonization*. Stanford, CA: Stanford University Press, 2009.

Rothfield, Norman. *Many Paths to Peace*. Fairfield, Vic.: Yarraford Publications, 1997.

Rotker, Susana. *La invención de la crónica*. Buenos Aires: Ediciones Letra Buena, 1992.

Rovner, Adam. *In the Shadow of Zion: Promised Lands before Israel*. New York: New York University Press, 2014.

Rutland, Suzanne. *Edge of the Diaspora: Two Centuries of Jewish Settlement in Australia*. Rose Bay, NSW: Brandl & Schlesinger, 1997.

_____. *Pages of History: A Century of the Australian Jewish Press*. Darlinghurst, NSW: Australian Jewish Press, 1995b.

Russell, John, Rod Kirkpatrick and Victor Isaacs (compilers). *Australian Newspaper History: A Bibliography*. 2nd edn, Andergrove, Qld: Australian Newspaper History Group, 2009.

Samuels, Maurice. *The Right to Difference: French Universalism and the Jews.* Chicago and London: The University of Chicago Press, 2016.

Sceusa, Francesco. *Hail Australia! Morituri Te Salutant!* Sydney: Jarrett & Co., 1888. https://nla.gov.au/nla.obj-570166992.

Schneider, Miriam Magdalena. *The 'Sailor Prince' in the Age of Empire: Creating a Monarchical Brand in Nineteenth-Century Europe*. Basingstoke, Hampshire: Palgrave Macmillan, 2017.

Science and Art Department of the Committee of Council on Education. *The Cruise of His Royal Highness the Duke of Edinburgh—Catalogue*. London: George E. Eyre & William Spottiswoode, 1872.

Scully, Richard. *Eminent Victorian Cartoonists—Volume I: The Founders*. London: The Political Cartoon Society, 2018.

Scully, Richard, and Marian Quartly, eds. *Drawing the Line: Using Cartoons as Historical Evidence*. Clayton: Monash University ePress, 2009.

Shannon, Mary L. *Dickens, Reynolds, and Mayhew on Wellington Street: The Print Culture of a Victorian Street*. Farnham: Surrey, 2016.

Shattock, Joanne, ed. *Journalism and the Periodical Press in Nineteenth-Century Britain*. Cambridge: Cambridge University Press, 2017.

Shell, Marc, ed. *American Babel: Literatures of the United States from Abnaki to Zuni*. Cambridge: Harvard University Press, 2002.

Sinor, Jennifer. *The Extraordinary Work of Ordinary Writing: Annie Ray's Diary*. Iowa City: University of Iowa Press, 2002.

Smith, Anthony. *The Newspaper: An International History*. London: Thames and Hudson, 1979.

Sori, Ercole. *L'emigrazine italiana dall'Unità alla seconda guerra mondiale*. [Italian Emigration from Unity to the Second World War]. Bologna: Il Mulino, 1979.

Spielmann, M. H. *The History of "Punch"*. London: Cassell & Co., 1895.

Staub, Michael E. *Torn at the Roots: The Crisis of Jewish Liberalism in Postwar America*. New York: Columbia University Press, 2002.

The Office of Multicultural Affairs and University of Wollongong, *Different Agenda: Economic and Social Aspects of the Ethnic Press in Australia*. Working Papers on Multiculturalism, no. 8. Wollongong: Centre for Multicultural Studies, University of Wollongong, 1991.

U. S. Department of Commerce. *Fifteenth Census of the United States: 1930. Population. Special Report of Foreign-Born White Families by Country of Birth by Head, Volume VI [Supplement]*. Washington: United States Government Printing Office, 1933.

White, Richard. *Inventing Australia: Images and Identity 1688–1980*. Sydney: Allen & Unwin, 1981.

Volkogonov, Dmitrii. *Lenin: A new biography*, trans. Harold Shukman. New York: Free Press, 1994.

Windle, Kevin. *Undesirable: Captain Zuzenko and the Workers of Australia and the World*. Melbourne: Australian Scholarly Publishing, 2012.

Wolfe, Patrick. *Traces of History: Elementary Structures of Race*. London and New York: Verso, 2016.

Wong, Aliza S. *Race and the Nation in Liberal Italy, 1861–1911: Meridionalism, Empire, and Diaspora*. Italian and Italian American Studies. New York: Palgrave Macmillan, 2006.

Wyman, Mark. *DPs Europe's Displaced Persons, 1945–1951*. London: Cornell University Press, 1998.

Zangheri, Renato. *Storia del socialism italiano. Dalla rivoluzione francese ad Andrea Costs, [Volume] 1*. Torino: Giulio Einaudi Editore, 1993.

2. Articles and Chapters

Abbé, Derek van. "The Interests of the South Australian German Language Press in the Nineteenth Century." *Journal of the Historical Society of Australia and New Zealand* 8, no. 31 (November, 1958): 319–321.

Agutter, Karen. "Fated to Be Orphans: The Consequences of Australia's Post-War Resettlement Policy on Refugee Children." *Children Australia* 41, no. 3 (2016): 224–31.

———. "Displaced Persons and the 'Continuum of Mobility' in the South Australian Hostel System." In *On the Wing: Mobility Before and After Emigration to Australia*, edited by Margrette A Kleinig, and Eric Richards, 136–52. Spit Junction, NSW: Anchor Books Australia, 2013.

———. "Her Majesty's Newest Subjects: Official Attempts to Assimilate Non-English Speaking Migrants in Post-War Australia." *History Australia* 16, no. 3 (2019): 480–95.

Agutter, Karen, and Catherine Kevin. "'The 'Unwanteds' and 'Non-Compliants': 'Unsupported Mothers' as 'Failures' and Agents in Australia's Migrant Holding Centres." *The History of the Family* 22, no. 4 (2017): 554–74.

Alcorso, Caroline. "Early Italian Migration and the Construction of European Australia 1788–1939". In *Australia's Italians: Culture and Community in a Changing Society*, edited by Stephen Castles, Caroline Alcorso, Gaetano Rando, and Ellie Vasta, 1–17. North Sydney: Allen & Unwin, 1992.

Allatson, Paul, "Foreword". In *Killer Crónicas: Bilingual Memories*, edited by Susana Chávez-Silverman, ix-xiii. Albany: State University of New York Press, 2011.

Altman, Vivien. "'The Spark in the Ash'." *Australian Jewish Historical Society Journal* 23, part 1 (November 2016): 79–92.

Baggio, Fabio, and Matteo Sanfilippo. "L'emigrazione italiana in Australia." *Studi Emigrazione/Migration Studies* 48, no. 183 (2011): 477–99.

Balint, Ruth. "Industry and Sunshine." *History Australia* 11, no. 1 (2014): 432–45.

Balint, Ruth, and Zora Simic. "Histories of Migrants and Refugees in Australia." *Australian Historical Studies* 49, no. 3 (2018): 378–409.

Ballantyne, Tony. "Mobility, empire, colonization." *History Australia* 11, no. 2 (2014): 7–37.

Banti, Alberto Mario. "Deep Images in Nineteenth-Century Nationalist Narrative". *Historein* 8 (2012): 54–62.

Bazhanov, Boris. "Pobeg iz nochi" [Flight from the Night]. *Kontinent* 8 (1976): 253–303.

Benjamin, David J. "The Case for the Racial Group." *The Australian Jewish Outlook* 1, no. 8 (1947).

Bennetts, Stephen. "'Undesirable Italians': Prolegomena for a History of the Calabrian 'Ndrangheta in Australia." *Modern Italy* 21, no. 1 (2016): 83–99.

Bersani, Bianca E. "An Examination of First and Second Generation Immigrant Offending Trajectories." *Justice Quarterly* 31, no. 2 (2014): 315–43.

Besemeres, Mary. "Evoking a Displaced Homeland: The 'Poetic Memoir' of Andrzej Chciuk". *Transnational Literature* vol. 10 no. 1 (2017). http://fhrc.flinders.edu.au/transnational/home.html

Betts, Katharine. "Boat People and Public Opinion in Australia." *People and Place* 9, no. 4 (2001): 34.

Blanco, José Joaquin, Vincente Leñero, and Juan Villoro. "Questioning the Chronicle". In *The Contemporary Mexican Chronicle: Theoretical Perspectives on the Liminal Genre*, edited by Ignacio Corona and Beth E. Jörgensen, 61–68. Albany: State University of New York Press, 2002.

Bonilla-Silva, Eduardo. "Rethinking Racism: Towards a Structural Interpretation." *American Sociological Review* 62, no. 3 (1997): 465–480.

Bozdag, Cigdem, Andreas Hepp, and Laura Suna. "Diasporic Media as the 'Focus' of Communicative Networking Among Migrants." In *Mediating Cultural Diversity in a Globalized Public Space*, edited by Isabelle Rigoni, Eugenie Saitta, 96–115. London: Palgrave Macmillan, 2012.

Braham, Mark. "The Jewish Press in Australia." In *The Ethnic Press in Australia*, edited by Abe I. Wade Ata and Colin Ryan, 25–38. Melbourne: Academia Press, 1989.

Brown, David. "Fascism within the pre World War II Italian population of Queensland: a study of community processes and interaction." *Queensland History Journal* 93 (2017): 55–74.

———. ""Gathered around the Sign of the Littorio": The Italo-Abyssinia Conflict and Its Impact on Italian Fascism in Queensland, 1935–1939." *Spunti e Ricerche*, Special issue "150 Years of Italians in Queensland", edited by Catherine Dewhirst, Claire Kennedy and Francesco Ricatti, 24 ([2009] 2011): 57–59.

Brown, Wayne. "Henry Lamson (Lim Son) of Cheshunt, King Valley." In *Journeys into Chinese Australian Family History*, edited by Sophie Couchman, 77–93. Melbourne: Chinese Australian Family Historians of Victoria Inc, 2019.

Buxton, G. L. "1870–90". In *A New History of Australia*, edited by Frank Crowley, 165–215. Melbourne: Heinemann, 1974b.

Byrnes, J. V. "Howe, George (1769–1821)." *Australian Dictionary of Biography*. Canberra: National Centre of Biography, 1966. http://adb.anu.edu.au/biography/howe-george-1600/text2851.

Cannistraro, Philip V. and Gianfranco Rosoli. "Fascist Emigration Policy in the 1920: An Interpretive Framework." *The International Migration Review* 13, no. 4 (1979): 686–687.

Cecilia, Tito. "Gli italiani in Australia, 1788–1940: una cronistoria". In *Italoaustraliani. La popolazione di origine italiana in Australia*, edited by Stephen Castles, Caroline Alcorso, Gaetano Rando, and Ellie Vasta, 33–49. Torino: Fondazione Giovanni Agnelli, 1992.

Colic-Peisker, Val, Maša Mikola, and Karien Dekker. "A Multicultural Nation and Its (Muslim) Other? Political Leadership and Media Reporting in the Wake of the 'Sydney Siege'." *Journal of Intercultural Studies* 37, no. 4 (2016): 373–89.

Collins, Jock, and Carol Reid. "Minority Youth, Crime, Conflict, and Belonging in Australia." *Journal of International Migration and Integration/Revue de l'integration et de la migration internationale* 10, no. 4 (2009): 377–91.

Conzen, Kathleen Neils, David A. Gerber, Ewa Morawska, George E. Pozzetta and Rudolph J. Vecoli. "The Invention of Ethnicity: A Perspective from the U.S.A." *Journal of American Ethnic History* 12, no. 1 (Fall, 1992): 3–41.

Cresciani, Gianfranco. "'Socialismo per La Generazione Presente': Rifugiati Politici Italiani e Movimento Socialista Australiano" ['Socialism for the Present Generation': Italian Political Refugees and the Australian Socialist Movement]. *Italian Historical Society Journal* 20, no. 2012 (2012): 25–49.

———. "The Italians in Sydney". *Sydney Journal* 1, no. 1 (March 2008).

———. "The Bogey of the Italian Fifth Column." In *Italians in Australia: Historical and Social Perspectives*, ed. Michael Arrighi and Gaetano Rando, 67–83. Wollongong, NSW: Department of Modern Languages, University of Wollongong, Dante Alighieri Society, 1993.

———."Sceusa, Francesco (1851–1919)". In *Australian Dictionary of Biography*. Canberra: National Centre of Biography, Australian National University, 1988. http://adb.anu.edu.au/biography/sceusa-francesco-8351.

Cunneen, Chris. "Steward, Sir George Charles Thomas (1865–1920)", *Australian Dictionary of Biography* (Canberra: National Centre of Biography, Australian National University, 1990) http://adb.anu.edu.au/biography/steward-sir-george-charles-thomas-8657 (accessed November 20, 2019).

Curthoys, Ann. "Volatility of Racism in Australia." In *Hate Speech and Freedom of Speech in Australia*, edited by Katharine Gelber and Adrienne Stone, 20–33. Annandale, NSW: The Federation Press, 2007.

———. "Disputing National Histories: Some Recent Australian Debates". *Transforming Cultures EJournal* 1, no. 1 (March, 2006): 6–18.

———. "Liberalism and Exclusionism: A Prehistory of the White Australia Policy". In *Legacies of White Australia: Race, Culture and Nation*, edited by Laksiri

Jayasuriya, Jan Gothard, and David Walker, 8–32. Crawley: University of Western Australia Press, 2003.

Dellios, Alexandra. "Displaced Persons, Family Separation and the Work Contract in Postwar Australia," *Journal of Australian Studies* 40, no. 4 (2016): 418–32.

Dewhirst, Catherine. "Colonising Italians: Italian Imperialism and Agricultural 'Colonies' in Australia, 1881–1914." *Journal of Imperial and Commonwealth History* 44, no. 1 (2016): 23–47.

———. "The Anglo-Italian Treaty. Australia's Imperial Obligations to Italian Migrants, 1883–1940". In *Italy and Australia: An Asymmetrical Relationship*, edited by Gianfranco Cresciani and Bruno Mascitelli, 81–113. Ballarat, Vic.: Connor Court Publishing, 2014.

———. "The 'Southern Question' in Australia: The 1925 Royal Commission's Racialisation of Southern Italians." *Queensland History Journal* 22, no. 4 (2014): 321–325.

———. "Collaborating on whiteness: representing Italian in early white Australia." *Journal of Australian Studies* 31, no. 2 (2008): 38–40.

Divine, Donna Robinson. "Exiled in the Homeland." *Shofar: An Interdisciplinary Journal of Jewish Studies* 21, no. 2 (2003): 66–81.

Dowling, Peter A. "Grosse, Frederick (1828–1894)." *Australian Dictionary of Biography*. Canberra: National Centre of Biography, Australian National University (2005). http://adb.anu.edu.au/biography/grosse-frederick-12955/text23415.

Edgar, Suzanne. "Scott, Eugene Montagu (Monty) (1835–1909)." *Australian Dictionary of Biography*. Canberra: National Centre of Biography, Australian National University (1976). http://adb.anu.edu.au/biography/scott-eugene-montagu-monty-4547/text7453.

Fitzgerald, Jennifer, K. Amber Curtis, and Catherine L. Corliss. "Anxious Publics: Worries About Crime and Immigration." *Comparative Political Studies* 45, no. 4 (2012): 477–506.

Foucault, Michel. "On the Archaeology of the Sciences: Response to the Epistemology Circle". In *Aesthetics, Method, and Epistemology, Volume 2*, edited by James D. Faubion, 297–333. New York: New Press, 1998.

Gabaccia, Donna. "L'Italia fuori d'Italia". In *Storia d'Italia. Annali 24. Migrazioni*, edited by Paola Corti and Matteo Sanfilippo, 225–48. Torino: Einaudi, 2009.

Galbally, Ann E. "Campbell, Oswald Rose (1820–1887)." *Australian Dictionary of Biography*. Canberra: National Centre of Biography, Australian National University (1969). http://adb.anu.edu.au/biography/campbell-oswald-rose-3157/text4717.

Gale, Peter. "The Refugee Crisis and Fear: Populist Politics and Media Discourse." *Journal of Sociology* 40, no. 4 (2004): 321–40.

García, Ignacio. "La Crónica: Mirroring a Community in the Making". In *Some Historical Ties between Australia and the Spanish World*, edited by Ignacio García, 120–144. Newtown, NSW: Sociedad Cultural Española, 1988.

Gilliam Jr, Franklin D, Shanto Iyengar, Adam Simon, and Oliver Wright. "Crime in Black and White: The Violent, Scary World of Local News." *Harvard International Journal of Press/Politics* 1, no. 3 (1996): 6–23.

Grassi, Fabio. "Un socialista tra l'Italia e l'Australia". *Affari Sociali Internazionali* 1, no. 1 (March, 1973): 101–14.

Irving, T. H. "1850–70". In *A New History of Australia*, edited by Frank Crowley, 124–64. Melbourne: Heinemann, 1974.

Gromyko, Andrei. "Palestine at UNO: Extracts from the Speech Made by Mr. Andrei Gromyko at the General Assembly of UNO on May 14th." *New Life* 1, no. 5 (1947).

Hagan, John, Ron Levi, and Ronit Dinovitzer. "The Symbolic Violence of the Crime-Immigration Nexus: Migrant Mythologies in the Americas." *Criminology & Public Policy* 7, no. 1 (2008): 95–112.

Hall, Dianne. "'Now him White Man': Images of the Irish in Colonial Australia." *History Australia* 11, no. 2 (2014): 167–195.

Hall, Stuart. "The Work of Representation". In *Representation: Cultural Representations and Signifying Practices*, 13–69. London: Sage, 1997.

_____. "Gramsci's Relevance for the Study of Race and Ethnicity". In *Stuart Hall: Critical Dialogues in Cultural Studies*, edited by David Morley and Kuan-Hsing Chen, 411–440. London and New York: Routledge, 1996b.

_____. "Gramsci's Relevance for the Study of Race. "Encoding, Decoding". In *Culture, Media, Language: Working Papers in Cultural Studies, 1972–79*, edited by Stuart Hall, Dorothy Hobson, Andrew Lowe, and Paul Willis, 128–38. London: Hutchinson, 1980.

Harper, Katherine. "Ashton, George Rossi (1857)". *Australian dictionary of biography*. Canberra: National Centre of Biography, Australian National University (1979). http://adb.anu.edu.au/biography/ashton-george-rossi-5654/text8461.

Harris, Casey T. and Jeff Gruenewald. "News media trends in the framing of immigration and crime, 1990–2013". *Social Problems* 67, (2020): 452–470.

Harzig, Christiane and Dirk Hoerder. "Transnationalism and the Age of Mass Migration, 1882–1920." In *Transnational Identities and Practices in Canada*, edited by Vic Satzewich and Lloyd Wond, 35–51. Vancouver & Toronto, UBC Press, 2006.

Hobsbawm, Eric. "Introduction: Inventing Traditions." In *The Invention of Tradition*, edited by Eric Hobsbawm and Terence Ranger, 1–14. Cambridge: Cambridge University Press, 2000.

Hoffman, Louise. "A Review of the Jewish Press in Western Australia." *Journal of The Royal Western Australian Historical Society* 8, no. part 2 (1978).

Hoffman, Matthew B., and Henry F. Srebrnik. "Introduction." In *A Vanished Ideology*, edited by Matthew B. Hoffman and Henry F. Srebrnik, 135–158. Albany: State University of New York Press, 2016.

Hofman, Iwona. "Kroniki emigracyjne paryskiej *Kultury*, Rekonesans badawczy" [Emigration's chronicles of the *Culture*. A study of the problem]. *Annales Universitatis Mariae Curie-Skłodowska, Lublin—Polonia* 9 (2002): 87–99.

Hollinsworth, David. ""My Island Home": Riot and Resistance in Media Representations of Aboriginality." *Social Alternatives* 24, no. 1 (2005): 16–21.

Hugh, Chisholm, ed. "Feuilleton". *Encyclopædia Britannica* 10 (11th edn.). Cambridge: Cambridge University Press, 1911.

Husband, Charles. "Media and the Public Sphere in Multi-Ethnic Societies." In *Ethnic Minorities and the Media*, edited by Simon Cottle, 199–214. Buckingham: Open University Press, 2000.

Jacklin, Michael. "Latin American Diasporic Writing in the Australian Migrant Magazine *Tabaré*." In *Mapping South-South Connections: Australia and Latin America*, edited by Fernanda Peñazola and Sarah Walsh, 173–196. Basingstoke, Hampshire: Palgrave Macmillan, 2019.

_____. "Translated Lives in Australian Crónicas." In *Bearing Across: Translating Literary Narratives of Migration*, edited by Arvi Sepp and Philippe Humble, 27–36. Trier: Wissenschaftlicher Verlag Trier, 2016.

_____. "Desde Australia para todo el mundo hispano": Australia's Spanish-Language Magazines and Latin American/Australian Writing." *Antipodes* 24, no. 2, Special Issue 'Australia and Latin America' (December, 2010): 177–186.

Johansson, Clare, and Simone Battiston. "Ethnic Print Media in Australia: Il Globo in the 1980s." *Media History* 20, no. 4 (2014): 416–30.

Kaiser, Max. ""A new and modern golden age of Jewish culture": shaping the cultural politics of transnational Jewish antifascism." *Journal of Modern Jewish Studies* 17, no. 3 (2018): 287–303.

Kakakios, Michael and John van der Velden. "Migrant Communities and Class Politics: The Greek Communities in Australia." In *Ethnicity, Class and Gender in Australia*, edited by Gill Bottomley and Marie De Lepervanche, 144–163. Sydney: Allen and Unwin, 1984.

Kaladelfos, Andy and Mark Finnane. "Immigration and criminality: Australia's post-war inquiries." *Australian Journal of Politics and History* 64. (2018): 48–64.

Kałuski, Marian. "Prasa Polska w Australii 1928–1988." *Studia polonijne*, 13 (1989): 221–235.

Karim, H. Karim. "Mapping the Diasporic Mediascape." In *The Media of Diaspora*, edited by Karim H. Karim, 1–18. London: Routledge, 2003.

Kaul, Chandrika. "An imperial village: communications, media, and globalization in India." In *International Communication and Global News Networks:*

Historical Perspectives, edited by Peter Putnis, Chandrika Kaul, and Jürgen Wilke, 83–98. New York: Hampton Press, 2011.

Khanduri, Ritu Gairola. "*Punch* in India: Another History of Colonial Politics?" In *Asian Punches: A Transcultural Affair*, edited by Hans Harder and Barbara Mittler, 165–184. Berlin & Heidelberg: Springer, 2013.

Kusher, M. "The Jewish Cultural Conference: Critical Comments." *Australian Jewish Forum* 8, no. 71 (1948).

Lake, Marilyn. "Race and Gender in Australia". In *Gendered Nations: Nationalisms and Gender Order in the Nineteenth Century*, edited by Ida Blom, Karen Hagemann and Catherine Hall, 159–76. Oxford: Berg, 2000.

Lee, Matthew T., and Ramiro Martinez. "Immigration Reduces Crime: An Emerging Scholarly Consensus." *Immigration, Crime and Justice* 13, (2009): 3–16.

Leiva, Adrian, and David A. Bright. "The usual suspects": Media representation of ethnicity in organised crime." *Trends in Organized Crime* 18, no. 4 (2015): 311–325.

Lenczarowicz, Jan. "*Wiadomości Polskie* w Sydney." *Kwartalnik Historii Prasy Polskiej* 31, no. 2 (1992): 25–45.

Levy, Hyman. "A Letter to Jewish Intellectuals." *Unity: A Magazine of Jewish Affairs* 1, no. 3 (1948).

_____. "What Is a Nation?" *Unity: A Magazine of Jewish Affairs* 1, no. 2 (1948).

Lonergan, Dymphna. "The Irish Exile." *Tinteán*, April 6, 2018. https://tintean. org.au/2018/04/06/the-irish-diaspora-in-australia-has-played-a-significant-part-in-the-promotion-and-maintenance-of-irish-not-least-in-the-press-and-as-far-back-as-1850/.

Mahood, Marguerite. "Bradley, Luther (1853–1917)." *Australian Dictionary of Biography*, Canberra: National Centre of Biography, Australian National University (1979). http://adb.anu.edu.au/biography/bradley-luther-5333/text9015.

_____. "Carrington, Francis Thomas Dean (Tom) (1843–1918)." *Australian Dictionary of Biography*. Canberra: National Centre of Biography, Australian National University (1969a). http://adb.anu.edu.au/biography/carrington-francis-thomas-dean-tom-3170/text4725.

_____. "Melbourne *Punch* and its Early Artists." *The La Trobe Journal* 4 (October, 1969b): 65–81.

Mark, Ber. "Voice of the Oppressed: World Congress of Intellectuals in Wroclaw, Poland, August, 1948." *Unity: A Magazine of Jewish Affairs* 1, no. 6 (1949).

Markowski, Stefan, Katarzyna Kwapisz Williams. "Australian Polonia: A Diaspora on the Wane?" *Central and Eastern European Migration Review* 2, no. 1 (2013): 13–36.

Masel, Phillip. "The Case for the Religious Group." *The Australian Jewish Outlook* 1, no. 8 (1947).

Mason, Robert. "Australian Multiculturalism: Revisiting Australia's Political Heritage and the Migrant Presence." *History Compass* 8, no. 8 (2010): 817–827.

McCallum, Kerry, and Kate Holland. "Indigenous and Multicultural Discourses in Australian News Media Reporting." *Australian Journalism Review* 32, no. 2 (2010): 5–18.

Mears, Daniel P. "Immigration and Crime: What's the Connection." *Federal Sentencing Reporter* 14 (2001): 284.

Mendes, Philip. "The Australian Left's Support for the Creation of the State of Israel, 1947–48." *Labour History* 97 (2009): 137–148.

Miller, Moses. "Zionism and the State of Israel : 1." *Jewish Life* 3, no. 7 (1949).

Monsiváis, Carlos. "On the Chronicle in Mexico." In *The Contemporary Mexican Chronicle: Theoretical Perspectives on the Liminal Genre*, edited by Ignacio Corona and Beth E. Jörgensen, 25–35. Albany: State University of New York Press, 2002.

Nasielski, Adam. "Australia." *Kultura* 4, no. 295 (1972): 124–130.

_____. "Początek końca." *Kultura* 5 no. 320 (1974): 102–108.

Nolan, David, Karen Farquharson, Violeta Politoff, and Timothy Marjoribanks. "Mediated multiculturalism: Newspaper representations of Sudanese migrants in Australia." *Journal of Intercultural studies* 32, no. 6 (2011): 655–671.

Ousey, Graham C., and Charis E. Kubrin. "Exploring the Connection between Immigration and Violent Crime Rates in US Cities, 1980–2000." *Social Problems* 56, no. 3 (2009): 447–73.

Perera, Suvendrini. "Whiteness and Its Discontents: Notes on Politics, Gender, Sex and Food in the Year of Hanson." *Journal of Intercultural Studies* 20, no. 2 (1999): 183–198.

_____. "Introduction: Fatal (Con)Junctions." In *Asian & Pacific Inscriptions: Identities, Ethnicities, Nationalities*, edited by Suvendrini Perera, 1–12. Bundoora, Vic.: Meridian, 1995c.

Poynting, Scott. "Ethnicising Criminality and Criminalising Ethnicity." In *The Other Sydney: Communities, Identities and Inequalities in Western Sydney*, edited by Jock Collins and Scott Poynting, 63–105. Melbourne: Common Ground, 2000.

Pugliese, Joseph. "Migrant Heritage in an Indigenous Context: For a Decolonising Migrant Historiography". *Journal of Intercultural Studies* 23, no. 1 (2002a): 5–18.

———. "Race as Category Crisis: Whiteness and the Topical Assignation of Race." *Social Semiotics* 12, no. 2 (2002b): 149–168.

Putnis, Peter. "Telegraphy, Mass Media, and Mobilization: Australians in Sudan, 1885". In *International Communication and Global News Networks: Historical Perspectives*, edited by Peter Putnis, Chandrika Kaul, and Jürgen Wilke, ed., 119–142. New York: Hampton Press, 2011.

Ratzaby, Shalom. "The Polemic About the "Negation of the Diaspora" in the 1930 and Its Roots." *Journal of Israeli History* 16, no. 1 (1995): 19–38.

Raz-Krakotzkin, Amnon. "Exile Within Sovereignty: Toward a Critique of the 'Negation of Exile' in Israeli Culture." *Theory and Criticism*, 4 and 5 (1993): 23–56, 113–132.

Rea, Christopher G. "'He'll Roast All Subjects That May Need the Roasting': Puck and Mr Punch in Nineteenth-Century China." In *Asian Punches: A Transcultural Affair*, edited by Hans Harder and Barbara Mittler, 389–422. Berlin & Heidelberg: Springer, 2013.

Riall, Lucy. "Martyr Cults in Nineteenth-Century Italy." *The Journal of Modern History* 82, no. 2 (2010): 255–287.

Roberts, Tom D. C. "Herald and Weekly Times." In *A Companion to the Australian Media*, edited by Bridget Griffen-Foley, 203–205. North Melbourne: Australian Scholarly Publishing, 2014.

Rubinstein, W.D. "The Revolution of 1942–1944." *Australian Jewish Historical Society Journal* 11, part 1 (1990): 142–153.

Rutland, Suzanne. "Creating Intellectual and Cultural Challenges: The Bridge." In *Feast and Fasts: Festschrift in Honour of Alan David Crown*, edited by Marianne Dacy, Jennifer Dowling and Suzanne Faigan, 323–347. Sydney: Mandelbaum, 2005.

Saunders, Kay. ""Discovering" the Subversive and Saboteur: The Disjuncture between official records of internment policy and practice and the remembered experiences of internees in Australia in the Second World War." *Oral History Association of Australia Journal* 13 (1991): 1–11.

Savchenko, Aleksandr. "Pervye russkie gazety v Avstralii" [The First Russian Newspapers in Australia]. *Avstraliada* 15 (1998): 12–13.

Savchenko, A. I. "Bol´sheviki i rossiiskaia trudovaia emigratsiia v Avstralii 1907–1917 gg." [The Bolsheviks and the Russian Labour Community in Australia 1907–1917]. In *Nauchnaia konferentsiia po izucheniiu Avstralii i Okeanii, 19-aia: tezisy dokladov* [Nineteenth Scholarly Conference on Australia and Oceania: Abstracts]. Moscow: Nauka, 1988, 155–62.

Scully, Richard. "Britain in the *Melbourne Punch*." *Visual Culture in Britain* 20, no. 2 (2019): 152–171.

Scully, Richard and Marian Quartly. "Using Caroons as Historical Evidence." In *Drawing the Line: Using Cartoons as Historical Evidence*, edited by Richard Scully and Marian Quartly, 01.1–01.13. Melbourne: Monash University ePress, 2009b.

Sergi, Anna. "The Evolution of the Australian 'Ndrangheta. An Historical Perspective." *Australian & New Zealand Journal of Criminology* 48, no. 2 (2015): 155–74.

Shannon, Mary L. "Colonial Networks and the Periodical Marketplace." In *Journalism and the Periodical Press in Nineteenth-Century Britain*, edited by Joanne Shattock, 203–223. Cambridge: Cambridge University Press, 2017.

Simini, Ezio Maria. "Un Operaio Agli Antipodi: Pietro Munari, Italiano in Australia." *Altreitalie*, no. 14 (1996): 52–70.

Simon, Rita J., and Keri W. Sikich. "Public Attitudes toward Immigrants and Immigration Policies across Seven Nations." *International Migration Review* 41, no. 4 (2007): 956–62.

Sinclair, Clive. "The Kimberley Fantasy." *Wasafiri* 24, no. 1 (2009): 33–43.

Smolicz, Jerzy. "Personal Cultural Systems in a Plural Society." *The Polish Sociological Bulletin* 50, no. 2 (1980): 21–34.

Spagnolo, Pierluigi. "L'ascesa della'Ndrangheta in Australia." *Altreitalie* 40 (2010).

Spenkuch, Jörg L. "Understanding the Impact of Immigration on Crime." *American Law and Economics Review* 16, no. 1 (2013): 177–219.

Stalin, Joseph. "Marxism and the National Question." In *Marxism and the National and Colonial Question*. Moscow: Co-operative Publishing Society of Foreign Workers in the U.S.S.R., 1935, 3–53.

Stuart, Lurline. "*Melbourne Punch*." In *The Encyclopedia of Melbourne*, edited by Andrew Brown-May and Shurlee Swain, 468. Port Melbourne: Cambridge University Press, 2005.

Struer-Tranberg, T. M., and J. M. Innes. "Media Influence on Host Society Responsibility in the Integration of Immigrants." *Journal of Psychological Sciences* 3, no. 1 (2017): 50–68.

Tavan, Gwenda. "'Good Neighbours': Community Organisations, Migrant Assimilation and Australian Society and Culture, 1950–1961." *Australian Historical Studies* 27, no. 109 (1997): 77–89.

Teo, Hsu-Ming. "Multiculturalism and the Problem of Multicultural Histories: An Overview of Ethnic Historiography." In *Cultural History in Australia*, edited by H. Teo and R. White, 142–155. Sydney: Allen and Unwin 2003.

Tipping, Marjorie J. "Chevalier, Nicholas (1828–1902)." *Australian Dictionary of Biography*, National Centre of Biography, Australian National University (1969). http://adb.anu.edu.au/biography/chevalier-nicholas-3200/text4807.

Tonry, Michael. "Ethnicity, Crime, and Immigration." *Crime and Justice* 21 (1997): 1–29.

Walker, R. "German-Language Press and People in South Australia, 1848–1900." *Journal of the Royal Australian Historical Society* 58, no. 2 (1973): 121–140.

Webby, Elizabeth. "Images of Europe in Two Nineteenth-Century Australian Illustrated Magazines." *Victorian Periodicals Review* 37, no. 4 (2004): 10–24.

Vanni Accarigi, Ilaria. "The Transcultural Edge." *Portal: Journal of Multidisciplinary International Studies* 13, no. 1 (2016): 1–8.

Vasta, Ellie. "Italian Migrant Women". In *Australia's Italians: Culture and Community in a Changing Society*, edited by Stephen Castles, Caroline Alcorso, Gaetano Rando, and Ellie Vasta, 140–54. North Sydney: Allen & Unwin, 1992.

Vecoli, Rudolph J. "The Italian Immigrant Press and the Construction of Social Reality, 1850–1920." In *Print Culture in a Diverse America*, edited by James Philip Danky and Wayne A. Wiegand, 17–33. Urbana and Chicago, IL: University of Illinois Press, 1998.

Vidal, Bel. "The First Australian". In *Culture Is…: Australian Stories across Cultures*, edited by Anne-Marie Smith, 1–13. Kent Town, SA: Wakefield Press, 2008.

Weiss, Daniel H. "A Nation without Borders?: Modern European Emancipation as Negation of Galut." *Shofar: An Interdisciplinary Journal of Jewish Studies* 34, no. 4 (2016): 71–97.

Williams, Katarzyna Kwapisz. "Between Utopia and Autobiography: Migrant Narratives in Australia". In *Migrant Nation: Australian Culture, Society and Identity*, edited by Paul Longley Arthur, 177–199. London & New York: Anthem Press, 2018.

Windle, Joel. "The Racialisation of African Youth in Australia." *Social Identities* 14, no. 5 (2008): 553–66.

Windle, Kevin. "*Listok Gruppy rossiiskih rabochikh*: a 1918 Brisbane Russian Newspaper." *Australian Slavonic and East European Studies* 32 (2018): 52–78.

———. "An Anarchist's Farewell." *Australian Slavonic and East European Studies* 30 (2016a): 87–112.

———. "Pervyi konsul Sovetskoi Rossii v Avstralii P. F. Simonov i ego druz´ia i nedrugi." [The First Soviet Russian Consul in Australia: P. F. Simonov, his friends and foes]. *Klio* 114, no. 3 (2016b): 176–188.

———. "'Trotskii's Consul': Peter Simonoff's account of his years as Soviet representative in Australia (1918–1921)." *Slavonic and East European Review* 93 (2015): 493–524.

———. "Hades or Eden? Herman Bykoff's *Russian Australia*." *Australian Slavonic and East European Studies* 26 (2012): 1–25.

———. "'A Crude Orgy of Drunken Violence': A Russian Account of the Brisbane Red Flag Riots of 1919." *Labour History* 99 (2010): 163–178.

———. "Murder at Mt Cuthbert: A Russian Revolutionary Describes Queensland Life in 1915–1919." *AUMLA* 110 (2008): 53–71.

———. "*Nabat* and its Editors." *Australian Slavonic and East European Studies* 21 (2007): 143–164.

———. "'Unmajestic Bombast': The Brisbane Union of Russian Workers as Shown in a 1919 Play." *Australian Slavonic and East European Studies* 19 (2005): 29–51.

Wortley, Scot. "Introduction. The Immigration-Crime Connection: Competing Theoretical Perspectives." *Journal of International Migration and Integration/ Revue de l'integration et de la migration internationale* 10, no. 4 (2009): 349–358.

———. "Misrepresentation or Reality? The Depiction of Race and Crime in the Toronto Print Media." In *Marginality & condemnation: An introduction to critical criminology*, edited by Bernard Schissel and Carolyn Brooks, 55–82. Halifax, NS: Fernwood Publishing, 2002

Yin, Hang. "Chinese-Language Cyberspace, Homeland Media and Ethnic Media: A Contested Space for Being Chinese." *New Media and Society* 17, no. 4 (2013): 556–572.

Yan, Shu-chuan. "'Kangaroo Politics, Kangaroo Ideas, and Kangaroo Society': The Early Years of *Melbourne Punch* in Colonial Australia." *Victorian Periodicals Review* 52, no. 1 (2019): 80–102.

Zusman, Nate. ""Unity" a Magazine of Jewish Affairs." *Australian Jewish Historical Society Journal* 9, part 5 (1983): 341–355.

3. Theses

Curtis, Louise Ann. "Red Criminals: Censorship, surveillance and suppression of the radical Russian community in Brisbane during World War I." Doctor of Philosophy thesis. Griffith University, 2010.

Di Paolo, Louis Vincent. "Las Historias de un Blady Woggie: Stories of South American Migration to Australia." Masters thesis. Macquarie University, 2014.

Johansson, Clare. "The editorial commentary of the Italian-language newspaper *Il Globo* from 1979 to 1989: A critical analysis." Honours dissertation. Swinburne University of Technology, 2011.

Kaiser, Max. "Between Nationalism and Assimilation: Jewish Antifascism in Australia in the Late 1940s and Early 1950s." Doctor of Philosophy thesis. University of Melbourne, 2019.

Rechter, David. "Beyond the Pale: Jewish Communism in Melbourne." Masters thesis, University of Melbourne, 1986.

Seaton, Catherine. "Of Cats and Wogs: "Translating" the Migrant Experience through 20th Century *Crónicas* in Spanish-Language Newspapers in Australia." Doctor of Philosophy thesis, University of Wollongong, 2018.

4. Websites

Aly, Waleed. "Curse of Australia's silent pervasive racism: The polite racism of the educated middle class is much worse than ugly tirades that go viral on YouTube", *The Sydney Morning Herald*, April 5, 2013, https://www.smh.com.au/opinion/curse-of-australias-silent-pervasive-racism-20130404-2h9i1.html (accessed November 6, 2019).

Australian Bureau of Statistics 2018. "3412.0—Migration, Australia, 2017–18.", https://www.abs.gov.au/ausstats/abs@.nsf/mf/3412.0/ (accessed June 25, 2019).

Australian Bureau of Statistics 2017. "Census reveals a fast changing, culturally diverse nation, Australian Bureau of Statistics." https://www.abs.gov.au/ausstats/abs@.nsf/lookup/Media%20Release3 (accessed June 25, 2019).

Ayres, Marie-Louise. "Digging deep in Trove: Success, challenge and uncertainty." National Library of Australia, 2012. https://www.nla.gov.au/our-publications/staff-papers/digging-deep-in-trove-success-challenge-and-uncertainty (accessed November 22, 2019).

Ayres, Marie-Louise. "'Singing for their supper': *Trove*, Australian newspapers, and the crowd." Paper presented at: ILFA WLIC 2013—Singapore, 2013. http://library.ifla.org/245/1/153-ayres-en.pdf (accessed November 21, 2019).

Bagnall, Kate. "Chin Sheng Geong and George Ah Len." *The Tiger's Mouth: Thoughts on the History and Heritage of Chinese Australia*, Web site, http://chineseaustralia.org/chin-sheng-geong/ (accessed 24 May, 2019).

Bagnall, Kate. "Early Chinese newspapers: Trove presents a new perspective on Australian history." *Trove blog*, National Library of Australia, 2015. https://www.nla.gov.au/blogs/trove/2015/02/19/early-chinese-newspapers (accessed June 24, 2019).

Bagnall, Kate. "The murderer and the missionary: Gazettes and newspapers in Trove uncover Chinese-Australian history." *Trove blog*, National Library of Australia, 2018. https://www.nla.gov.au/blogs/trove/2018/01/11/the-murderer-and-the-missionary (accessed June 29, 2019).

Berthon, Hilary and Wong, Wan. "Facing the future of Australian newspapers." Paper presented at: ILFA WLIC 2013—Singapore, 2013. http://library.ifla.org/234/1/153-berthon-en.pdf (accessed November 22, 2019).

Bode, Katherine. "To Be Continued: Discovering serialised fiction in Trove's digitised newspapers." *Trove blog*, National Library of Australia, 2018. https://www.nla.gov.au/blogs/trove/2018/02/28/to-be-continued (accessed June 29, 2019).

Budarick, John. "Why the media are to blame for racialising Melbourne's 'African gang' problem." *The Conversation*, 2018, https://theconversation.com/why-the-media-are-to-blame-for-racialising-melbournes-african-gang-problem-100761 (accessed June 25, 2019).

Carr, Barry and John Minns, eds. *Australia and Latin America: Challenges and Opportunities in the New Millennium*. Canberra, ACT: Australian National University Press, 2014.

"Cruel, and no deterrent: why Australia's policy on asylum seekers must change." *The Conversation*http://theconversation.com/cruel-and-no-deterrent-why-australias-policy-on-asylum-seekers-must-change-117969 (accessed January 3, 2020).

Evans, Raymond. *Loyalty and Disloyalty: Social Conflict on the Queensland Homefront, 1914–18.* Sydney: Allen & Unwin, 1987.

Gerardo Papalia, "The Italian "Fifth Column" in Australia: Fascist Propaganda, and Internment." *Australian Journal of Politics and History* 66, no. 2 (2020): 214-231.

Howard, Katherine. "International Comparators: How does Australia compare internationally?: A research report contributing to the Digital Access to Collections initiative." *GLAM Peak Report.* http://www.digitalcollections.org.au/sites/default/files/GLAM-Peak-International-comparators-research-report.pdf (accessed November 21, 2019).

Institute for Professional Editors. Resources for Editors. http://iped-editors.org/Resources_for_editors.aspx (accessed November 28, 2019).

Lauret, Maria. Wanderwords: *Language Migration in American Literature.* New York & London: Bloomsbury Academic, 2014.

Morgan, Helen. "Discovering history at scale through Trove: The Australian Women's Register." Paper presented at: Australian Historical Association Annual Conference, 2018. https://help.nla.gov.au/sites/default/files/HelenMorgan_AHA2018Presentation.pdf (accessed June 29, 2019).

Nova, Stephen. "The Artist of the River: The Unemployed Camps on the Torrens River, 1930–1938." *Trove blog,* National Library of Australia, 2018. https://www.nla.gov.au/blogs/trove/2018/10/25/the-artist-of-the-river (accessed November 22, 2019).

Rucker, Laurent. *Moscow's Surprise: The Soviet-Israeli Alliance of 1947–1949.* Cold War International History project, Woodrow Wilson International Center for Scholars, 2005. https://www.wilsoncenter.org/sites/default/files/CWIHP_WP_461.pdf (accessed 20 October 2017).

Schirru, Riccardo and Laura Egan. "The Italian community in Australia bids fare-well to Nino Randazzo." *Il Globo,* July 16, 2019. https://ilglobo.com.au/news/44189/the-italian-community-in-australia-bids-farewell-to-nino-ran-dazzo/ (accessed November 20, 2019).

Scully, Richard. "A Comic Empire: The Global Expansion of Punch as a Model Publication, 1841–1936." *International Journal of Comic Art* 15, no. 2 (2013): 6–35.

Sherratt, Tim. "Who belongs? Reading identity, ownership, and legitimacy". Invited presentation at: From text to data—new ways of reading—National Library of Sweden, 2019.https://timsherratt.org/blog/who-belongs/ (accessed May 20, 2019).

State Library of South Australia. SA Newspapers : Religious newspapers. http://www.samemory.sa.gov.au/site/page.cfm?u=1478 (accessed June 29, 2019).

Sydney Anglicans, "The Unforgettable Fire: Burning Memories from Barney's," https://sydneyanglicans.net/blogs/insight/the_unforgetable_fire_burning_memories_from_barneys, May 12, 2006 (accessed February 4, 2019).

World Jewish Congress, Papers from the World Jewish Congress Second Plenary Assembly, 1948, http://www.bjpa.org/Publications/details.cfm?PublicationID=22287 (accessed 21 June 2017).

Index[1]

---

[1] Note: Page numbers followed by 'n' refer to notes.

© The Author(s) 2020
C. Dewhirst, R. Scully (eds.), *The Transnational Voices of Australia's Migrant and Minority Press*, Palgrave Studies in the History of the Media,
https://doi.org/10.1007/978-3-030-43639-1

Printed by Printforce, the Netherlands